Parables
Poetry
and Prayers

ADENA H. PAGET

Suite 300 - 990 Fort St
Victoria, BC, V8V 3K2
Canada

www.friesenpress.com

First Edition — 2016

Front cover photograph taken by Bob Paget

ISBN
978-1-4602-8585-5 (Hardcover)
978-1-4602-8586-2 (Paperback)
978-1-4602-8587-9 (eBook)

1. RELIGION, CHRISTIAN LIFE, DEVOTIONAL

Distributed to the trade by The Ingram Book Company

"*Parables, Poerty, and Prayers* comes right from Adena's heart to the reader. This devotional book is filled with wisdom, stories, insight and especially warmth. The daily readings are like that early morning coffee or that afternoon hot cup of tea. It warms you as you hold it and then sets you on your way renewed and centred."

— *Keith Schnell, former colleague from Board of Education, Calgary*

Introduction

Fear not, for I am with you. Be not afraid for I am your God. I will strengthen you and I will help you. I will uphold you with my glorious right hand.

I have learned the word of God, the Bible, is like a road map for the journey of life. It is not only relevant but a source of instruction for daily living.

When my husband and I drive through a new city or area, I usually do the navigating while he does the driving. My independent personality does not easily conform to using a map. I am more of an "It's in that direction" type person. He, on the other hand, is a very organized and need-to-know guy. He would never drive into a strange area without first looking at a map to familiarize himself with where he is and where he is going. I have learned His way is much better, and we actually arrive at our destination easily at the designated time without the frustration of getting lost.

These days he uses the GPS and I am still the adventuresome candidate and leave the technology in the glove compartment unless it becomes an absolute necessity.

Our journey in life has been planned for us by our Creator and He has also provided a map to help us on our pilgrimage. Our destination is Heaven and in my personal travels, I have found the Bible has directions for all the dilemmas that can occur on the road to the ultimate destination.

As I spend time in the God-inspired Word, I gain wisdom and direction for my journey. Often the road is rough and those are the times when I need to be near Jesus. When my longing becomes strong I spend time in His Word, in communion and meditation with Him. He draws me close to His side where I feel comforted and protected under the shelter of His mighty hand.

In this book you'll find some insights that have been helpful in my life and some truths that the Holy Spirit has brought to my mind, interspersed with parables that God used to teach me valuable lessons in everyday life. I have included some of my journal writings, a few of my own stories, and some stories from my daughter, Robyn, and her husband, Randy Movold. I hope you benefit from the words on the pages of ***Parables, Poetry, and Prayers*** – *A Daily Devotional Book.*

Adena H. Paget †

WEEK 1

Monday

choosing the narrow road

But the Lord waits for you to come to Him so He can show you love and compassion. For the Lord is a faithful God. Blessed are those who wait for Him to help them.

Isaiah 30:18

There was a time in my life when I wandered away from God. I chose the wide road that ultimately leads to destruction. Because of the choices I made, I allowed the gap between Jesus and me to grow very wide.

My lifestyle led to disinterest in my job until one day, my supervisor told me my services were no longer needed. Devastated, angry, and somewhat depressed, I immediately began a pity party for myself thinking I had been unjustly treated. I didn't understand my poor performance was because of my loss of interest.

Several months later, I was prompted to complete my education, which led to a new career of teaching for the Calgary Board of Education. I spent many rewarding years teaching school and meeting wonderful children and colleagues. During this time, I also renewed my relationship with Jesus.

While I had been experimenting with worldly pleasures, God was patiently waiting for me to return to Him. It wasn't God who moved away from me, it was my move that caused the gap. He had compassion for me in my rebellious state and it was His love that enabled me to return and ask forgiveness.

My relationship with Christ is the most important thing in my life and I am so thankful He is a faithful God who waits for us to come to Him.

If you are out of fellowship with God, looking for satisfaction in worldly pleasures, you can be sure it is leading to a dead end, but He is waiting for you to ask forgiveness. It does not matter what you've done or how long you have been waiting. It only takes desire, the act of asking Him to help you and forgive you, and waiting on him to receive his infinite love and compassion.

Prayer for today

Father, thank you for being a forgiving God, who never gives up on us. Forgive me for all the times I have not heard your still, small voice but instead have gone my own way. I know I can be argumentative and stubborn at times and yet you have the patience and willingness to forgive me and wait for me to hear you. I want to stay close to you, Lord, and remain under the shelter of your hand.

In Jesus's name. Amen.

Tuesday

a great hero

You alone are the Lord. You made the skies and the Heavens and all the stars. You made the earth and the seas and everything in them. You preserve them all, and the angels of Heaven worship you.

Nehemiah 9:6

Nehemiah was a determined man of God with a passion to rebuild the walls of Jerusalem and give glory and acknowledgement to God's marvellous works.

He was the cup-bearer to King Artaxerxes of Persia. After spending much time in prayer and fasting, Nehemiah was convinced to return to Jerusalem to rebuild the walls. After receiving permission from the king, he proceeded to go and supervise the reconstruction of the walls. In a very short time the task was completed and dedicated to the glory of God.

Nehemiah is a great hero of the Bible. He displays passion, obedience, diligence, determination, wisdom, and inspiration. He does what he feels God wants him to do.

Could we be more like Nehemiah? Could we take on a task that looks impossible, but trust God to give us the tools and power to perform to the end?

With God all things are possible and we are able to accomplish what He calls us to do.

Prayer for today

Heavenly Father, I know you are God of all and you can enable me to complete what you put before me. Even if I don't see a way out, I know you already have it planned. Help me see you in this problem.

In Jesus's name. Amen.

Wednesday
the benefits of adversity

Though the Lord gave you adversity for food and affliction for drink, He will still be with you to teach you.

Isaiah 30:20.

Aren't you glad that God is faithful? Perhaps you have been disappointed or hurt by someone. Putting your trust in another person can result in disappointment. There is one who will never let you down, who is always faithful and knows exactly what is best for you. This is Jesus Christ, who promises to stay close to us, even closer than a brother.

This scripture is a wonderful promise because it tells us if we are in a state of adversity, the Lord is with us and He is faithful. He does not say we are exempt from tragedy and despair, but He will be with us through it all. Not only will He be with us and respond to our cries, He will use these experiences to teach us and help us become spiritually mature, bringing us closer to him, to His wounded side. This is where we can truly feel close to Jesus because He knows better than anyone the wounds of affliction and despair and every hurt known to us. He lived on this earth and experienced every hurt that we can imagine and then He suffered for all our sins on the cross.

"Many people owe the grandeur of their lives to their tremendous afflictions."

C. Spurgeon

It supports the idea that our lives are shallow and meaningless if we never experience adversity or affliction. So, my friend, if you are in a state of bereavement or feeling abandoned, ask God what He wants you to learn by allowing you to go through this low time in your life. He will respond in His time and then you will experience such a wondrous feeling of accomplishment and purpose.

Prayer for today

Thank you for walking with me through the deep waters in my life. Many times you needed to carry me because I could not manage to stay afloat without you. Help me to look to you when life's burdens are heavy and to keep my focus on you. With your help, Lord, I can learn from my adversities and not waste time feeling sorry for myself. Help me to learn what I need to learn and I will give you the honour and glory for you are a great and mighty God.

In Jesus's name. Amen.

Thursday

learning to listen

You will hear a voice say, "This is the way, turn around and walk here."

Isaiah 30: 21

This promise assures us, when we find ourselves at a crossroads and we don't know which way to turn, God will direct us.

Through the years, when I have been in turmoil or confused by indecision, I realized my eyes and ears were turned inward, towards myself. This caused my perception of the problems to loom larger than they really were. In ourselves we are seldom capable of bringing resolve to an issue.

God says we will hear Him tell us which way to go. It is not always an audible voice because many times the answer is found in His Word. It is our responsibility to turn our focus toward Him and be sensitive to His direction. He promises to speak to us and guide us in the path He wants us to follow but we need to stop and listen and tune in to His voice and then proceed.

Prayer for today

Dear Lord: I am so thankful that you are with me to solve my problems and help me see the answers. I pray for an increase in faith so I can trust you implicitly and learn to lean on you. Help me to keep looking to you and not to perceive my problems as unsolvable. I know all things are possible with you, Lord.

In Jesus's name. Amen.

Friday

filling the void

> *Then you will destroy all your silver idols and gold images. You will throw them out like filthy rags, "Ugh." you will say to them, "Be gone."*
>
> Isaiah 30:22

What silver idols or gold images are in your life? Money, cars, houses, fashions? Are you escalating status symbols above your relationship with Jesus Christ? Are you willing to release everything that brings recognition or status in this life and only dwell on your relationship with Jesus? It's a serious question – I am not sure I could answer it confidently.

We are a greedy society in North America, the land of plenty. Not many of us really know what it is like to be hungry. We are spoiled and find it difficult to allow God to test our faith. Today's society is accustomed to plentiful supplies and bountiful provisions, and yet there still exists a void that we search to fill. We look for new thrills and excitement to satiate that empty place in our hearts. We fill our homes with modern conveniences and physical comforts, and still there is a hole in our souls that we long to fill.

Only Jesus can fill that void. He can fill that space with peace that passes all understanding and unspeakable joy. In Him, unconditional love is found. He accepts us as we are through grace.

Some time ago I was asked to accompany a group of high school students on a visit to Mexico. While we were there, we visited the Oaxacan Indians, who are poverty-stricken people. We also became acquainted with other Mexican people who are very poor, and yet the thing that was most evident was the difference in their demeanours. The ones who knew God had contented dispositions. The ones who did not know Jesus had a hopelessness about them that really spoke to my heart, and yet the social and financial status was the same in both cases. This visual difference spoke a thousand words to our young people and confirmed their faith in God.

Today, my friend, I encourage you to look to the Lord and embrace the life that brings real fulfillment and fills the void in our materialistic world. Material things bring instant happiness but are short-lived and soon the enjoyment wears thin, whereas the abundant life with Jesus brings a deep peace, joy unspeakable, and unconditional love that never fails or comes to an end.

Prayer for today

Precious Lord, I am thankful that you are a God that provides joy even in hopeless situations. Forgive me for clinging to material things and associating them with happiness. I know they only bring temporary happiness, but you, Oh Lord, are always with me and provide the deep peace that brings true contentment. Even when sad times are upon me, you promise to walk with me through the valleys and take me to the other side where the promise awaits. Help me to keep my eyes on you.

In Jesus's name. Amen.

A Weekend Read

smooth stones

A parable from the beach

I sat on the shore writing in my journal. It was my second visit to French Beach. The first visit had filled me with awe as I watched the awesome power and beauty of the waves crashing against the rocky shoreline. I returned, wanting to share the magic of this wondrous place with my best friend, my husband.

French Beach is not a white, sandy beach like most resorts, rather, it is a shoreline carpeted with thousands of stones, driftwood, and huge logs that have been swept onto the beach by gigantic waves and storms of biblical proportions. Other ocean debris is also present, abandoned by the elements of the fierce weather patterns. To say it is a rustic beach is an understatement.

As I sat in wonder enjoying this magnificent view, I noticed how perfectly smooth most of the stones on the beach were. It was intriguing, almost hypnotic to sit and listen to the regulated sounds of the stones being swept back and forth as they collided with each other. As the waves ebbed and flowed, I was reminded of the fierceness of a rainstorm beating against a window, and yet it brought a calmness to my being.

I thought of how blessed I was to be able to enjoy this magnificent part of creation. As I started to collect a few of the glossiest stones, I reflected on how perfectly round and smooth they were, and then I discovered why. For all of their existence, the water had washed over them, wearing away the rough edges as they were swept back and forth, colliding with each other and into the driftwood and other obstacles that were in the way.

While I was enjoying this experience and listening to the melody, it was as if the stones were joyfully permitting this tumbling action. To me it sounded like a cadence of beautiful music. I knew it would have taken days, weeks, and even years of sanding, scraping, and polishing to make a beautiful creation like that.

The sun's reflection on the perfectly rounded stones was indescribable. They shone like gold and silver and all the colors were visible; greens, blues, pinks, and shades of gray and coal black. As I picked up a few and cradled them in my hands I was amazed at the peaceful and calm emotion I felt. The touch reminded me of smooth silk and decadence.

As I looked off to the side, I noticed there were other stones that had escaped the impact of the moving water. They were rough with sharp edges and unattractive debris adhering to the sides. I felt almost sympathetic towards the stones that were just left to lie without being disturbed because they were not beautiful like the ones being tossed around in the tempest and turmoil of the waves.

Is the same thing true about us? Without the pain of crashing into obstacles, we remain unfinished, with rough edges; misshapen and even unattractive. A life that has never experienced rough waters is often shallow and incomplete and does not truly reflect the love and acceptance of Jesus Christ, the forgiver and healer of every hurt and affliction.

Then I thought, wouldn't it be a good thing if we were a little more like those stones and allowed the Lord to refine us and remove the ugly bumps and notches that interfere with the beauty our Creator intended for us to display. Not necessarily an outward difference but an inner beauty, reflected to those around us.

I realized by letting the Holy Spirit wash over us, we could become as perfect as the stones on the beach. You see, the stones didn't resist but just allowed the water to wash over them and that's what God wants to do for us if we let Him. He wants to wash us and fill us with the Living water that only He can supply.

We need the lessons of the tempest; the turmoil of the waves, and the turbulence of the water to smooth and refine us to be the beautiful creation that God can use to reflect His love. It is not always easy to let God have His way but I pray that I will remember the lesson I learned in the analogy from the stones on French Beach. Maybe, in some small way, you will realize that letting God have His way in your life is the secret to becoming a more beautiful creation.

And now God is building you, as living stones, into His spiritual temple.

1st Peter 2:5

WEEK 2

Monday

harvest and blessing

> *Then the Lord will bless you with rain at planting time. There will be wonderful harvests and plenty of pastureland for your cattle.*
>
> Isaiah 30:23.

Harvest is a time of gathering; of reaping what we've sown. In the New Testament, harvest is a metaphor for the gathering-in of the redeemed saints at the end of that age. In the Old Testament the harvest was a very significant event because the Israelites had a strictly agricultural society.

There were three harvests each year.

1. Barley (Ruth 1:22)
2. Wheat (Gen.30:14)
3. Fruits of trees or vines in September or October

An abundant harvest was the greatest blessing because their lives depended on the harvest for the year. Rain therefore denoted a rich blessing from the Lord (Duet.28:12). When the rains didn't come at the right time, it would lead to a year of hardship and hunger (N.I.V. dictionary).

Our lives are not complete without the blessing of the Lord. Is there a famine in your life? We need to be asking, "What have I harvested for the Lord?" His desire is to lavish us with blessings but we often make the wrong choices and reject Him, in which case, it is impossible for us to receive His blessings. With Him we are blessed and fully alive. Without Him there is a void and an absence of blessing…a famine.

This morning, let's ask, "What can I do for you today, Lord?" Then, when you sense His leading, go forth and do His work. You will reap an abundant harvest for him and in turn be blessed beyond measure.

Prayer for today

Father, I praise you and thank you for who you are and I am so thankful to be your child. Let me never take your love for granted but continue to praise you at all times. I ask you to make me a blessing to someone today to bring honour and glory to your name. Help me to keep my eyes on you so that I can be a part of the harvest. I need your blessings and long for a closeness with you.

In Jesus's name. Amen.

Tuesday

words with meaning

The oxen and donkeys that till the ground will eat good grain, its chaff having been blown away by the wind.

Isaiah 30:24

Chaff, partly dust and dirt and the inedible coat of the grain, means dry hay, fit for burning. It is often used as a metaphor for worthless or Godless men.

God cares about all creation; He remembers all animals here. Chaff provides only empty calories, like eating potato chips (but not as tasty). If donkeys and oxen ate chaff, it would have weakened them.

People are promised much more than they can even conceive. We are all included in this promise; even the children of God who have come to Him with repentant hearts to have their sins forgiven.

This is a good analogy to help us remember that speaking meaningless words is like empty calories; they fill the time but for no purpose and often damage the recipient and ourselves. It is better to keep quiet than to speak empty words.

Too much talk leads to sin. Be sensible and keep your mouth shut.

Proverbs 10:19

A truly wise person uses few words....

Proverbs 17:27

These verses clearly caution us to control our speech.

Prayer for today

Help me to say only what you want me to say, today, Lord. Solomon said it is more difficult to control the tongue than a ship, so Lord, I ask for wisdom and the ability to think before I speak. Let my words be more than chaff, help me to utter meaningful words that will be a blessing to you and others.

In Jesus's name. Amen.

Wednesday
living water

...there will be streams of water flowing down every mountain and hill.

Isaiah 30: 25.

In Canada, we have not experienced a lack of water, but water is becoming a premium in other countries. I visited Mexico a short time ago and carried my own water because the water there is contaminated. Many residents have to buy water in order to survive.

This promise that we read in Isaiah must be very precious for those who are thirsty for physical water, but what about the thirst for peace, joy, and fulfillment? These days many are searching for inner peace and spiritual fulfillment. Perhaps they are looking in the wrong direction. It cannot be found in psychics, New Age philosophy, crystals, self-help books, or horoscopes.

In the Bible, water refers to the Holy Spirit and when we desire and seek to be full, He fills us so full it bubbles over or down every mountain and hill. If you are thirsting today, ask the Lord to fill you with His water that quenches forever, so you need never thirst again.

These streams of water can only be found in Jesus Christ, who is sometimes referred to as living water. What a glorious gift, to have the water of the Holy Spirit flowing down and around you. This is the blessing of living water when we walk in the steps that He desires for us.

Prayer for today

Lord, I desire to be filled with your Holy Spirit, help me to welcome all that you have for me. I want to be so full that I won't be able to contain all you give. My heart yearns for your presence to come and fill me to overflowing. I want to know you more and love you more and praise you more. Give me a thirst for you that will never be satiated until it bubbles over. I love you Lord.

In Jesus's name. Amen.

Thursday
sweet reconciliation

Look. The Lord is coming from far away, burning with anger, surrounded by a thick rising smoke. His lips are filled with fury. His words consume like fire.

His anger pours out like a flood on His enemies, sweeping them all away. He will sift out the proud nations. He will bridle them and lead them off to their destruction.

But the people of God will sing a song of joy, like the songs at the Holy Festivals. You will be filled with joy, as when a flutist leads a group of pilgrims to Jerusalem – to the Rock of Israel.

Isaiah 30:27 - 29

There is such an evident contrast between the Children of God and the stubborn- hearted enemies of the Lord. We can clearly see that God is a jealous God and will show no mercy to His enemies on the day of reconciliation. The promise He makes to His children at the other end of the spectrum is filled with light, joy, understanding, and forgiveness.

Have you ever disciplined your children after they misbehaved or had a temper tantrum, displaying defiance? Have you ever had a heated argument with your spouse? Do you remember the reconciliation time? The sweetness of making up and the joy you felt after the thing was over? Oh such sweetness. Often, after making up, relationships are better than they were before.

When we stray from our Heavenly Father we experience the emptiness and disappointment it brings, but when we come to Him in repentance, asking forgiveness He fills us with a new joy that knows no guilt or condemnation. He waits patiently to embrace and forgive us. It is easy to let unforgiven sin come between the sweet relationship of Jesus and you.

My friend, ask the Lord to forgive any sin that has not been dealt with in your life. God promises to remove your sin as far as the east is from the west and remember it no more. What a sweet joy He desires to implant in you.

Prayer for today

Dear Lord, thank you for your sweet joy and peace. You are an awesome God and have the power to forgive and remove all sin from me. I ask you today, draw me closer and keep me from straying from you.

In Jesus's name. Amen.

Friday

God is so good

How we praise God, the Father of our Lord Jesus Christ, who has blessed us with every spiritual blessing in the Heavenly realms because we belong to God.

Ephesians 1:3

Have you ever asked yourself, "Why is God so good to me?" Even though we experience adversities in life, we are assured of the tremendous love of God always shining through any circumstances. As we allow the illumination, our troubles diminish. I encourage you to dwell on the blessings and allow the love of God to overshadow your troubles.

Sometimes I find myself in an emotional state with a lump in my throat when I think of how very much God must love me to bestow such blessings of peace and joy in the midst of my afflictions. The gifts are overwhelming and are much sweeter and more vivid than any hardships in life.

When I slip into a phase of self-pity and concentrate on my troubles, the day gets dark and difficult to bear. Then I remind myself how much God loves me and how numerous my blessings are.

We know the adversities we suffer are there because God loves us and cares enough to invest the time to teach us new things in order to bring us closer to Him and find His sweet peace once again. I encourage you to spend time thinking about how special you are to Him. Soon the day will change into a brighter and blessed time where it becomes easy to praise Him.

Prayer for today

Heavenly Father, I am so thankful that you are my personal Father as well as my Heavenly Father because I can bring all my troubles to you, and I know you will understand. I know your hand is upon me to protect me and keep me safe. Help me to keep my thoughts on you and your blessings to me.

In Jesus's name. Amen.

Weekend Read
tragedy

Our son, Drew was killed in a single car accident October 1998. He was learning how to be a Christian dad to his two children after inviting Jesus into his life previously. It was a devastating time for our family and the days were very dark. As a mother I felt the loss greatly even though the Lord sustained me.

One day, after having endured a rain-drenched week with tears and sadness, I cried out to Jesus to help me see the world as a joyous place once again. As I was driving west, a beautiful, vivid rainbow appeared before me. God had answered my prayer and I knew his promise of hope was real.

He also gave me these words, which I have sung many times as an encouragement for others who may be feeling depressed. I began to realize as I turned my eyes on Jesus and not on myself, life could be filled with the joy of the Lord even though I had suffered a great loss.

There's A Rainbow in the Sky

Yesterday, was full of clouds and rain,
Yesterday, my mind was on my pain,
Then I looked on by, and I saw His lovely face,
And now there's a rainbow in the sky.

There's a rainbow in the sky,
All the clouds just slipped away,
There's a rainbow in the sky,
And the night has turned to day.
There's a rainbow in the sky,
When our eyes are lifted up,

Adena H. Paget †

There's a rainbow in the sky,
And His sunshine fills us up.

Yesterday, I was taking all the blame,
Yesterday, I was filled with guilt and shame,
Then Jesus came and He took away the pain,
And now there's a rainbow in my heart.

There's a rainbow in my heart,
Since the "Son" came shining through.
Jesus came and took the pain,
And He made me new again.
There's a rainbow in my heart,
For He takes away my sin,
There's a rainbow in my heart,
If I keep my eyes on Him.

For He takes away the sadness,
And He fills my heart with gladness,
And now there's a rainbow in the sky.

WEEK 3

Monday

adoption

Before we were even born, or before He made the world, God loved us and chose us in Christ to be holy and without fault in His eyes. His unchanging plan has always been to adopt us into His own family by bringing us to Himself through Jesus Christ. And this gave Him great pleasure.

Ephesians 1:4 – 5

In 1970 my husband and I had the privilege of choosing our youngest daughter. Our home was a refuge for babies who were on the list to be adopted. We had the blessing of caring for newborn babies until an adoptive home was found.

A special little girl was in our home for eighteen months before she was eligible for adoption. After this length of time our love formed a strong bond, and we could not bear the thought of letting her go. Instead of allowing Social Services to place her with another family, we applied to legally adopt her.

It was a very exciting day when she actually became ours. Our daughter is very special to us and has given us blessings our other four children could not. She has brought another dimension into our family because her genetic makeup is different from her siblings. She has also grown to be a beautiful, bright, and confident young woman and holds a very special place in our hearts.

I liken this experience to my adoption into the Kingdom of God. It makes me feel very special and privileged to be a child of God and know He has adopted me into his family. What a blessing to know He chose me.

After many years of ignoring my Heavenly Father, I made the decision to return to Him. Through grace I was welcomed into God's family with open arms. He is my Father just as my husband is our daughter's father.

Our daughter also had a choice, when she came of age, to reject us or to embrace us. She was always aware of her special placement. I am so thankful she also made the choice to continue to be an integral member of this family.

Adena H. Paget †

When we adopted our daughter, we weren't required to sacrifice anything in order for her to be legally ours. Her birth mother had done all the hard work and we enjoyed the benefits and blessings of her "labour."

The same holds true in the family of God. God allowed His Son to give up His own life so you and I can be accepted into the family of God. God loves us so much, He gave his only son to become the ultimate sacrifice for us so we could be accepted as God's child by simply accepting this truth.

I can't imagine giving up any of my children for others to enjoy, but our daughter's biological mother actually gave up her little girl so we could love her and enjoy her. I will be eternally grateful to her for her sacrifice just as I am to our glorious Father in Heaven who has adopted me into His family so I can reap the wondrous blessings which He gives to me daily.

Prayer for today

I am so thankful for the love you have for me, Lord, and for the privilege of having Shona in our family. Thank you for being willing to adopt me as your own child. Thank you for sacrificing your only Son for my salvation. Help me to bring praise and glory to your name in all that I do, and may my life be a blessing to you, Father.

In Jesus's name. Amen.

Tuesday

benefits

Furthermore, because of Christ, we have received an inheritance from God, for He chose us from the beginning and all things happen just as He decided long ago.

Ephesians 1:11

When my husband and I come to the end of our lives here on earth, our adopted daughter will receive the exact same share of what we leave as our other children, and that is how God considers us.

We truly are legal heirs because we receive an inheritance from God. Not because of our good deeds or efforts, but because God chose us long ago and He made it possible for us to become His legal heirs.

All of our children will receive what is rightfully theirs as well, not because they have been good to us or have done favours for us, but because we love them all equally no matter what happens in our relationship. They are legally our children and each one of them is entitled to an equal portion. (Whatever may be left over.)

In order to help me understand my relationship with my Heavenly Father, I often compare it to the relationships we have here on earth and it helps me understand the deep love my Heavenly Father has for me and you.

Prayer for today

Father, thank you for your grace, for it is by grace, we are saved through faith and it is only by your grace that I have been forgiven and adopted into the family of God. There is nothing I can do to earn or buy a place in Heaven. I am not deserving of your mercy and favour but by the sacrifice of your precious Son, I can be your child and my inheritance includes a home in Heaven. Thank you, Lord for choosing me to be your child.

In Jesus's name. Amen.

Wednesday
counting your blessings

> *And now you also have heard the truth, the Good News that God saves you, and when you believed in Christ, He identified you as his own by giving you the Holy Spirit, whom He promised long ago. 14) The Spirit is God's guarantee that He will give us everything He promised and that He has purchased us to be his own people. This is just one more reason to praise our glorious God.*
>
> Ephesians 1:13

This is what Paul conveys to us about the love our Father gives, a promise and truth about God's love for us.

It isn't always easy to praise God, especially in the midst of a storm, but in obedience we need to do it anyway. Usually the clouds lift and the sadness slips away when we lift our eyes to God and start to praise Him. If your day isn't going great I encourage you to start being thankful for the good things and soon the difficulties will shrink and actually become blessings.

As my life becomes less cluttered, I have more time to be thankful for the blessings I used to take for granted, like sunshine, plentiful water, a home, a family, hot water to shower with, a loving husband, good health, and the list goes on and on.

Rosemary Clooney used to sing, "When I'm worried and I can't sleep, I count my blessings instead of sheep..." I encourage you to remember your blessings and experience the joy it beings.

Prayer for today

Heavenly Father, my days aren't always what I consider good, but I thank you for being with me all the time. Help me to keep my eyes on you and not on my troubles. I am so glad you love me and always do what's best for me. I love you, Lord and long to be close to you.

In Jesus's name. Amen.

Thursday

boldness

The wicked run away when no one is chasing them,
but the Godly are bold as lions.

Proverbs 28:1

If you have ever watched a *National Geographic* documentary or have been so fortunate as to enjoy a visit to an African wildlife area, you may have had an opportunity to watch a lion attack. It is, first of all, cautious as it sneaks up to the victim, and then it pounces, tenaciously, without mercy – the only goal is to fight until the victory is won. Throughout scripture the lion is used as a symbol of might.

That is exactly how bold Christians are allowed to be. The model is in Jesus who is called The Lion of Judah. Lions were far more widespread in biblical times than the present day, reaching as far as Greece, as well as Asia Minor, Iran, Iraq, Syria, and Turkey. Lions are also associated with God's protection and with God's judgment (Judges 14:6, 1 Samuel 17:34-37).

We have nothing to hide or fear when we are walking in the light of our God. As long as we are sheltered under His hand, no harm can befall us because we will be safe and able to be bold as a lion. We, as Christians, can claim this verse to give us confidence and keep us from fear.

At the same time we are reminded that the devil prowls around like a roaring lion, seeking whom he may devour (1Peter 5:8). He waits for us to drift away from under the shelter of the mighty hand of God, and only then does he have the power to devour. The answer is simple, isn't it? Stay sheltered and protected under the hand of God.

Prayer for today

I am so thankful for the shelter of your mighty hand upon me, Lord. I pray, today, that you will give me a new boldness for you, Lord Jesus. I pray that I will be equipped to know what to say at the right time. May the power of your Holy Spirit give me the actions and words that help to bring someone to your precious side, Jesus, so that your promise can be embraced by a hurting soul. In return for your love and sacrifice for me, help me to be able to show your love and forgiveness each day.

In Jesus's name. Amen.

Friday

nip it in the bud

People who wink at wrong cause trouble,
but a bold reproof promotes peace.

Proverbs 10:10

Does this verse conjure up visions of our tolerant and permissive society today? We are being conditioned to be politically correct and therefore, we often become hesitant to stand up for Godly foundations and biblical teachings.

Parents are afraid to discipline their children and when they do, it seems as if the consequences are often inappropriate or non-existent. Our judicial system falls into the same category. Prisoners are given leniency and treated like victims instead of perpetrators. Prison facilities are often more luxurious and better equipped than private homes. Many people are afraid to stand up for their democratic rights for fear of being accused of being intolerant.

The Bible says we are allowed to be bold and in fact, Solomon says, "A bold reproof promotes peace." This always proves to be true.

As a young mother, I often looked the other way when my children did something wrong, if it wasn't too serious. But I discovered if I didn't put a stop to the misbehaviour early, the deed became more severe as time progressed. Soon the situation escalated to injury or something would get broken and then… I would lose my cool and reprimand more severely then was necessary. Things would have been much easier if I had disciplined early, and I could have saved myself much stress and anguish. It took me a long time to learn not to turn the other way or to wink at the wrong that was being done, but I learned through experience to deal with the situation as quickly as possible. As a teacher, I dealt with a situation as soon as I detected it. Whether the issue was behavioural or academic, the sooner I could act and resolve it the easier my job was. By my acting early and appropriately, the child learned not to repeat the problem and the classroom became a better learning environment for all concerned.

Prayer for today

Heavenly Father, thank you for your Word, your "blueprint" for my life. Help me to adhere to the teachings that bring honour to your Holy name. May I have the capability to speak up for what is righteous and true and not be ashamed or timid about your Word.

In Jesus's name. Amen.

Weekend Read

the dream

diamonds in the dust

One night I dreamed I was walking along a dusty path beside a barbed wire fence. The dirt was worthless, windblown, and thirsting for moisture, not good for growing. It appeared to be useless dust with a generous mixture of small rocks and stones.

As I walked along, I scuffed the useless dirt with the toe of my shoe and saw something bright and shiny. I kicked away the dirt and there, to my amazement, I saw two beautiful little diamond rings. As I stood and admired this treasure, I realized how often I had skimmed over treasures that were not evident at first glance, precious treasures in my classroom.

Many times, as a teacher, I spent less time than I could have with a student I thought was not capable of becoming a scholar or capable of completing the curriculum. I suspect I was often ignorant of realizing the potential of these treasures.

I believe God was showing me that if we take the time to look underneath the surface, we will find what is really important and what really counts and that's what He sees in us.

It is not our outward accomplishments He desires, but the true beauty of a heart that is uncontaminated, pure, and innocent. Sometimes we need to take the time to look closer at those God puts in our path, until we can see past the exterior shell, to the heart.

Prayer for today.

Please forgive me, Lord for being hasty with some you have put in my path. I know I often judge others by first appearances. Help me to see that person as you see them. Help me to see beneath the surface to the very heart of the person and learn to love them like you do, Jesus. I realize there is good in everyone but Lord, sometimes I have trouble seeing it. Give me a heart that's filled with love and understanding,

In Jesus's name. Amen.

WEEK 4

Monday

loving and accepting others

Don't be selfish; don't try to impress others. Be humble, thinking of others as better than yourselves. Don't look out only for your own interests, but take an interest in others too.

Philippians 2:3-4

Wow. This instruction from Paul seems like a difficult one to be obedient to, doesn't it? We often meet people who are not easy to like or respect or even to be with but God's Word, the Bible, tells us to think of others as better than ourselves. Could this be meant for everyone we know or meet?

Most of us want others to like us, to respect us, to listen to us, and look up to us.

How many times have I thought: I know more, I am smarter or dressed better than someone else, or other prideful things that often creep in and overtake my thoughts? Paul simply tells us to think of others as better than ourselves. If I ask Jesus to help me see others as He sees them, it becomes easier to be obedient to this instruction from Paul.

It is not wrong to be confident, but our confidence needs to lie in our relationship with God and the leading of the Holy Spirit, not in ourselves. I think I am guilty of relying on myself when I meet others or spend time with friends. Are you?

Prayer for today

Today, Lord Jesus, help me see people from your viewpoint. Help me to look beyond their outer appearance and look towards the heart. I pray for someone to come into my path today that I might encourage and bring hope by speaking about your forgiveness and promises. Thank you, Jesus, for seeing beyond my faults to my needs (as Dottie Rambo said in her song) Help me not to miss the "diamonds in the dust" but to be patient with all those that come into my life.

In Jesus's name. Amen.

Tuesday

speaking up for Jesus

...proclaiming the Kingdom of God with all boldness and teaching about the Lord Jesus Christ. And no one tried to stop Him."

Acts 28:31.

If we have read about any of Paul's life and ministry, we know he boldly declared who Jesus Christ was without fear of retaliation. Many times he was thrown into prison and severely punished but he pushed on despite adversity.

Here Paul models boldness after he was sent to Rome to be tried. He rented a place to live and used it to proclaim the Kingdom of God with boldness and to teach about Jesus. He was given the freedom to do this for several reasons; one was that he was a respected Roman citizen and deserved to be heard, but also the Holy Spirit was upon him to enable him to use this time to proclaim the truth.

My prayer is that I might take a lesson from Paul and have the boldness to proclaim Jesus Christ as the Son of God who waits to take our sins away and free us from the bondage of a fearful life. I encourage that to be your prayer today as well.

Prayer for today

Come, Holy Spirit, I need you. Come sweet Spirit, I pray. Come in thy strength and thy power, come in thine own gentle way." Come and equip me to be a soldier for Jesus and have a new boldness as Paul did. Keep me in the Holy Word so that I may study to be approved by God in order to proclaim truth and justice.

In Jesus's name. Amen.

Wednesday
confidence with wisdom

Since this new covenant gives us such confidence, we can be very bold.

11 Corinthians 3:12

I believe we are all gifted in unique ways. I have issues with standing on a street corner preaching to the masses. When God prompts me to do this, perhaps it will be the right time and place. This seems to be where Paul was when he preached on the streets. Isn't it wonderful that our

Creator knows our shortcomings and fears and still loves and understands us?

Even if we have confidence in these areas, we still need to exercise wisdom, which is gained by prayer. When we are in perfect alignment with God's plan, as Paul was, we will know the right time to be bold for Christ.

Perhaps, even today, God may put someone in your path who needs to be reminded or reassured Jesus loves him or her, is willing to forgive them and promises eternal life with Him forever. Or perhaps there is someone in your life who needs an encouraging word or a gesture that says someone cares.

For me, it is easier to show love by baking muffins, or giving someone a card of encouragement or flowers, or some type of similar gesture, which is also an act of Christ's love. Often by beginning in this way, it leads to an opportunity to talk about our relationship with Jesus Christ. Showing you care in this manner is never a waste of time and this can also be a bold step of faith.

Prayer for today

Heavenly Father, Thank you for giving us your Word full of examples that we can learn from. Help me to be more like Paul and grasp every opportunity to speak up for you.

In Jesus's name. Amen.

Adena H. Paget †

Thursday

a living testimony

For I live in eager expectation and hope that I will never do anything that causes me shame, but that I will always be bold for Christ, as I have been in the past and that my life will always honour Christ whether I live or die.

Philippians 1:20

Paul tells us our boldness for Christ is not embarrassing or the cause of shame but rather, **not** to be bold for Christ would cause shame. To speak out in defense and in truth keeps Paul from experiencing shame. In other words, Paul is saying, honouring Christ by being bold for Him while we are alive will be remembered after we die.

In a university class, I was encouraged to write down what I would like to have as my epitaph. It did not take me long to know exactly what the gist of the thing would be. The exact wording was not that important, but I knew I wanted to be known as a Child of God who put Christ first in my life.

At my teaching retirement party, our caretaker, who retired with me, stood up to say some parting words to and about me. The comment that was most precious was that I was a testimony for Christ. It meant more to me than all the other nice things that were said about me that evening or ever.

What would you like on your epitaph?

Prayer for today

Heavenly Father, let me be an example for you and not be embarrassed to speak out for you. Let my epitaph read that I was a soldier for you, oh Lord.

In Jesus's name. Amen.

Friday

privileged

> *So let us come boldly to the throne of our gracious God. There we will receive his mercy and we will find grace to help us when we need it.*
>
> Hebrews 4:16

In Old Testament times, only the high priest was allowed into the Holy of Holies and now, since Jesus sacrificed his life for us for the forgiveness of our sins, the curtain that divided that holy place from the masses, was split, exposing the sacred place to everyone. There are no exceptions, no restrictions.

All are invited to boldly enter into the most Holy Place (Hebrews 10:19). What a wonderful privilege this is… imagine…you and I are allowed to enter the Holy of Holies where before only one privileged, appointed, anointed priest was allowed to go.

We can all have a personal relationship with God because of what Jesus did for us on the cross. He offers grace for our freedom from the past. Hallelujah.

What a Saviour.

Adena H. Paget †

Prayer for today

I am so full of thanksgiving today because you, Lord, have made it possible for me to come to the throne of grace easily and often. Thank you for the ultimate sacrifice of your precious Son. Now I can come before you, Lord, anytime without reservations and know that you love me and wait for me to spend time talking to you. I am so privileged to be your child and know that my sins are forgiven. Praise be unto you, Blessed Redeemer.

In Jesus's name. Amen.

Weekend Thought

bold confidence

Dear friends, if our conscience is clear,
we can come to God with bold confidence.

John 3:21

I encourage you, friend, to pray
for a special portion of boldness,
so that more and more
people can come to know Christ by seeing
the love of Christ in you.

Remember we are the hands that God uses.
We are the lips that bring
encouragement and comfort.

We are the ears that listen
to the discouraged and bereaved.

God is asking you today to display
His wondrous love to someone.

WEEK 5

Monday
is the Bible relevant?

Help, O Lord, for the Godly are fast disappearing.
The faithful have vanished from the earth.

Psalm 12:1

Even though this psalm was written more than two thousand years ago, it seems more relevant today than ever before.

To meet someone new and discover he or she is a Christian is indeed a precious blessing. Is it becoming a rare experience?

Several years ago when I was enrolled in a secular university, where the absence of Christianity is increasingly evident, I met another mature student who I was drawn to. We spent free time chatting. After some time, we became coffee friends, which led to the realization we shared the same beliefs. I felt so immensely blessed because I believe God orchestrated this meeting. We were comfortable sharing passages from the Bible and experienced an amazing connection at once. We are still friends and I treasure the memory of that semester.

There are those who say the Bible is old fashioned and out-dated. I suspect they are the ones who have not read enough of the Bible to realize what it really says.

I would challenge anyone who thinks the Bible has lost touch with this world, to do a little reading and studying. If we just take the time to prayerfully read God's word, we discover passages that speak to us no matter what age or circumstance we are in. If you have difficulty finding specific answers, I encourage you to purchase a Bible commentary to help you. There are many good ones available.

Prayer for today

Thank you, Lord, for the numerous blessings that you provide each day. You are such a merciful and generous God. I am so grateful for your Word and the people who have spent time interpreting it so I am able to understand it. Thank you for loving me and providing the way to know that we have the promise of spending eternity with you and our loved ones who have gone before us. Thank you for placing people in my path that know you and love you. I am so thankful for Christian friends. Help me not to take them for granted.

In Jesus's name. Amen

Tuesday

teaching values

Neighbours lie to each other,
speaking with flattering lips and insincere hearts.

Psalm 12:2

Questions to ponder – Have you ever been lied to? Are lying lips more common in today's culture or am I just becoming more aware of it? Can we trust the media to report true events and stories or do we suspect the truth is being stretched? Do truth and commitment go hand in hand? When someone says, "I am committed," is he or she speaking truth?

I have noticed there seems to be less evidence of commitment from people in many areas of life. Jobs are often not valued, relationships lack respect, children are left to fend for themselves, and respect for elders is a thing of the past. I find commitment and truth lacking in the world around me more and more.

We need to gain wisdom and understanding of today's culture from learning what God's Word says about the issues that face us. In many instances people need to know unconditional love and understanding and feel accepted for who they are. In other situations, children need to be parented and taught the values that are necessary to live successfully in the world.

I encourage you to return to biblical principles and teach them to your children and grandchildren. A meaningful way to do this is by living daily as you ought.

God does not expect us to be holy and righteous on our own strength. He provides the wisdom and strength we need if we take the time to know Him and learn to trust and rely on Him to give us the direction and wisdom necessary in today's world.

Adena H. Paget

†

Prayer for today

Precious Lord, help me to always speak truth, never needing to stretch it into something else to enhance it or make it more sensational. I want to be an example for the teachings of Jesus Christ and be a credible witness for you. Help me to be aware at all times that I am a spokesperson for you, oh Lord. Thank you for your truths and your Word that teach me what I need to know.

In Jesus's name. Amen.

Wednesday
seeking truth

May the Lord bring their flattery to an end
and silence their proud tongues.

Psalm 12:3

Thank God, we know that one day the deception will end. We know this is true because one day Jesus will return to bring us unto himself and to our Heavenly home where there are no lying lips or deceit and so shall we ever be with the Lord. Amen.

They say, "We will lie to our hearts' content.
Our lips are our own – who can stop us?"

Psalm 12:4

Satan is using his evil servants to spread deceitfulness. People, in general, are searching for fulfillment but many are not willing to seek truth. Jesus says, "If you will seek me, I will be found by you," and "Study to show yourself approved unto God, a workman that doesn't need to be ashamed."

If we seek the truth, it will lead us to the inspired word of God. There have been countless men and women who have set out to disclaim the truth of the Bible only to discover the deception they lived under was shattered and the truth was revealed as they studied and researched. Today, many are looking for a quick fix and accept spoofs that sound inviting and provide a quick answer. The result is either disappointment or giving up the quest and settling for existence in the dark. There is a strong emphasis on the culture today to do what feels good at the time, often without regard for the consequences.

Although God created human beings with freedom to choose, we are not our own. We have been bought at a high cost; the sacrifice of Jesus, God's own Son, and we have a responsibility to search for the path our Maker designed for us to travel on. Be encouraged to seek the Lord while He may be found, and start traveling on the road that leads to the peace and joy that is waiting for you to embrace.

Prayer for today

Precious Lord, thank you for giving us your inspired word to help us understand and know what truth is. May my words be a blessing to you and others. Help me stay on the path that you chose for me.

In Jesus's name. Amen.

Adena H. Paget †

Thursday
God's timing

The Lord replies, I have seen violence done to the helpless,
and I have heard the groans of the poor.
Now I will rise up to rescue them as they
have longed for me to do.

Psalm 12:5

Often we may think, "God has not heard my prayer." Mostly it's because we have a narrow perspective and expect our prayers to be answered in the way we see the answer. This way of thinking is rather lofty because we are, in fact, elevating ourselves to the same level as God when we think this way.

God's timing is not ours and our timing is not God's. His timing is perfect – ours is flawed.

The story of Lazarus is a vivid example of this. Mary expressed her concern at the arrival of Jesus after Lazarus had died. She thought Jesus could have healed him if He had arrived before the death. Jesus was very aware of his timing and commanded Lazarus to come out of the grave. The illustration foreshadows the resurrection of Jesus at a later time.

Jesus rescues at the exact perfect moment. He sees the violence and the injustice and He answers at the right time.

When our prayers are not answered as we think they should be, we forget that our view is narrow, but God sees the panoramic view of our lives and knows exactly what we need and when we need it.

Prayer for today

Father, may my desires and aspirations be in perfect alignment with your will for me. You always hear my prayer and you see my suffering and anguish and you will rise up and answer at the right time, because you say you will.

In Jesus's name. Amen.

Friday

comfort of assurance

The Lord's promises are pure
like silver refined in a furnace purified seven times over.

Psalm 12:6

God's promises are compared to the purest silver with no unwanted substances – the pure truth. As my Christian walk continues, it becomes increasingly clear to me that his promises are true. In the book of Hebrews it says God will never leave us or forsake us.

When our son was killed, the peace of the Lord was upon me in a way that is difficult to explain. Our son was thirty-seven years old with two small children. He was the free-spirited son who was a delight and joy to be around; the son who had invited Jesus into his heart several months before his death.

Many of our friends thought I was a rock because I did not mourn the way the world mourns, but it wasn't me who was the rock – it was Christ, the solid Rock on which I stood, and it was God in His spirit, who gave me the peace and ability to carry on in spite of the tragic loss.

> He is our comfort when we don't know how we will be able to cope.

Adena H. Paget †

He is our strength when we have none of our own.
He is our joy when things look bleak and despairing.
How wonderful to know his promises are real.

Prayer for today

Father, I thank you for your promises that are like pure silver. I know you are a great God who keeps His promises and I have learned never to doubt you. I know that you cannot lie because you are Very God. Thank you for being my strength when I am too weak to stand and for being the solid Rock that I can always depend on. Help me to continue to rely on you and give all my cares to you.

In Jesus's name. Amen.

A Weekend Read

my dad's promise

When my dad made a promise, he always kept it. It was part of who he was and what he stood for. His word was a commitment that was never broken.

Can you remember promising something that you couldn't follow up on or making a promise that you did not keep? Have you ever stopped to think what a difference it really makes?

When I was about eleven years old, my dad told me about a fellow he worked with who had a motor scooter he wanted to sell, and Dad wondered if I would like it. Would I? Being the tomboy type of kid I was, of course I wanted it.

I guess the circumstances warranted my being somewhat spoiled. My mother had died the day before my eleventh birthday and my dad, in his grief and empathy towards me, thought it would be okay to spoil me just a little. So from time to time, I received gifts like this motor scooter.

Well, I waited and waited, it seemed like months, for Dad to bring home this much-anticipated machine. At first, of course, I continually bugged him about it and became quite bratty and demanding about his promise. I guess, my dad realized that he was actually contributing to my change of attitude and soon told me I would not be getting the motor scooter. Well. I became quite indignant and started to sulk and pout. Dad didn't say much but as time passed, I knew I had blown it. I was not getting my scooter. I'm sure I accused him of being a lot of things he wasn't but he never budged.

One day, he initiated a serious talk with me. He told me how I had let him down by acting spoiled and insensitive to his generosity. He also told me how difficult it was for him to be alone and how he needed my understanding to help him through these lonely days. He told me it was a rough road for all of us and it was impossible to bring my mom back, and we had to trust the Lord to bring us through this terrible trial.

I can never remember feeling such remorse and shame as I did at that time. We prayed together and I remember asking to be forgiven for my selfish attitude.

I knew I was forgiven; not only by my earthly father but I knew my Heavenly Father also had forgiven me. I think it was the disappointment I brought to him that affected me most and the fact that I had hurt him by only thinking of myself. The behaviour I displayed was unusual for me and I suppose I could justify it because of the circumstances, but in reality, it was against my personality and downright selfish.

Several weeks later while playing in our front yard, I heard the sound of a small, motored machine putt-putting into our driveway and there was my dad looking ridiculous riding on this little machine which was built for eleven-year-olds. What a guy.

I enjoyed many rides around the neighbourhood on this quaint little machine, which always seemed to need spark plugs or pistons or oil or gas. After several months, I realized it was more trouble than it was worth so I sold it.

The lesson I learned has remained with me, and I often think about our Heavenly Father and the promises that are in his Holy Book. He knows exactly when to grant our requests and when and how to answer our prayers. Even though they are not always what we want or exactly what we ask for, there is no question that He keeps his promises to us. He is such a faithful God, unchanging and ageless and true to every one of the promises. What an awesome Saviour we serve.

WEEK 6

Monday

God knows best

Therefore, Lord, we know you will protect the oppressed, preserving them from this lying generation.

Psalm 12:7

Sometimes it is difficult to see God's protection. There is much oppression and sadness in the world. It is only by faith we can confidently say that God is in control, even though it is not evident to our eyes. Sometimes we think there is little we can do to alleviate the suffering in this world, but we know one thing – God hears our prayers and answers them in his time. Our job is to learn to trust and allow God to do his work.

Even though the wicked strut about, and evil is praised throughout the land.

Psalm 12:8

Even though we may not see the evidence of God's protection, we know He is sovereign. When we see the wickedness and evil flourishing in the world, we cling to the knowledge that He has everything under control. Sometimes He allows the deceitfulness to continue in this day and age, but we also know one day there will be an end to suffering, tears, hardships, and sickness.

One day, when Jesus returns to gather us into his arms of love and purity and truth and safety, then the lies will end and truth will prevail. If you've read the book, you know how it ends.

This encouragement keeps us on the narrow path that leads to safety for when we stand before him and He says to us, "Well done good and faithful servant, welcome home." It will be worth it.

Prayer for today

Lord, Thank you for being with me every step of my way. Help me to walk on the path that you have for me and under the shelter of your hand. Lord, as I grow in my spiritual walk with you, keep me from becoming judgmental or self-righteous and keep me from evil. I thank you, Lord for being a God of compassion who takes care of the oppressed and one day everyone will receive his or her "just" rewards. Thank you that you are the one keeping score and we don't need to do that. Help me to cling to the promises in your Word.

In Jesus's name. Amen.

Tuesday

endurance – character – hope

We can rejoice too, when we run into problems and trials, for we know that they help us develop endurance.

And endurance develops strength of character, and character strengthens our confident hope of salvation.

And this hope will not lead to disappointment. For we know how dearly God loves us because He has given us the Holy Spirit to fill our hearts with his love.

Romans 5: 3-5.

Have you heard about the brook? If it wasn't for the rocks, the brook would be silent. It is the sound of the brook gliding over the rocks that enhances its beauty.

The trials we experience also enhance our beauty. The rocks along the way help us to mature and grow into the beautiful creations God intended us to become. Our beauty is not always evident until we encounter the interruptions and unexpected bumps that are caused by the rocks in the stream of life.

In the city of Ephesus there are many ancient structures that have been excavated through years of precise and painstaking efforts. It is amazing how carefully and meticulously archaeologists brush the years of grit and soil and other build-up off the treasured artefacts that have been unearthed. It takes long hours of careful scraping and cleaning to actually realize what has been found.

Our true beauty is often hidden by years of debris and that's when our Creator needs to allow a good cleaning to be able to display the hidden treasure that lies underneath. Sometimes this unpleasant experience enables us to fulfill our God- given purpose successfully.

Prayer for today

Dear Lord, I thank you and praise you for being a faithful God who always walks beside me. Even though I often feel like I am in the midst of unsolvable trials, I know you are there. I also know, dear Lord that I need much refining and when I look back on my life, I can see that the trials I endured, were necessary to get rid of years of collecting debris. I know the refining process helped my spiritual growth and brought me closer to your side. Help me to keep treading on and looking to you for strength as I live in the wonderful peace that your presence provides.

In Jesus's name. Amen

Wednesday

handling problems

We can rejoice too, when we run into problems and trials, for we know that they help us develop endurance.

Romans 5:3

No one is exempt from problems. Everyone experiences trials. It is what we do with the problem that is important.

Paul tells us to rejoice in the midst of our problems. In us this is hardly possible, but in the midst of a trial we draw near to God and seek his face. When we do this, we begin to feel his presence and then we can begin to rejoice in the middle of the trial. When we realize how great our need for God is we draw close to him and He draws close to us. When we abide close to him in his presence, we experience deep joy and peace.

Adena H. Paget

†

How then, does this result in endurance? It is in God's timing that the answer comes, not in our own timing. In God's timing our eyes are opened and we see the solution. In God's timing the trial ends and the problem is resolved. We are asked to wait and endure throughout the trial until the answer arrives. This is how we learn to wait on the Lord and endure.

Prayer for today:

Dear Lord, I know no one is exempt from facing trials in this earthly life and I know that they are necessary for me to learn what you are trying to teach me. My prayer is that you would grant me wisdom to know what you want me to learn. I am thankful for the valuable lessons I have learned by the experiences you have allowed to happen in my life, and even though some have been difficult, I know they have brought me closer to you. Help me to continue to allow you to be in control of my life and "wait" on you who always knows what is best for me.

In Jesus's name. Amen.

Thursday

developing character

And endurance develops strength of character in us, and character strengthens our confident hope of salvation.

Romans 5:4

What is the benefit of endurance? It is considered to be a valued quality because the result of endurance leads to strength of character.

It seems to me, when I meet someone who displays strength of character, they have usually experienced trials and problems. As life enfolds, with its trials and tests, we realize that the result is the birth of wisdom, which leads to strength of character.

I have met many who have endured a great amount of sadness in their lives. Sometimes it seems as if there are more hardships dealt to one particular person or family while others seem to escape trials or hardships. We don't know why this is, but God's word tells us problems lead to endurance and endurance develops character. Character ultimately leads to a glorious future with Jesus Christ and a confident hope of salvation.

I have met several people in my time who display strong character. I would trust them with my secrets, my money, my life, and my family because strong character tells much about someone. Strong character is a virtue that we all need to strive for.

Prayer for today

Thank you Lord for going through trials in life with me. Thank you for allowing me to experience problems and walking beside me to help me through them. Help me to give thanks in everything and to learn endurance through the trials. I know there is a reason for everything that happens in my life. Let me be a candidate that develops character by experience.

In Jesus's name. Amen.

Friday

showing love

And this hope will not disappoint us. For we know how dearly God loves us because He has given us the Holy Spirit to fill our hearts with love."

Romans 5:5.

We need to be thankful that God invests time in us and teaches us the things we are willing to learn. Developing strength of character leads us to the hope of salvation that will never disappoint us.

It is through the power of the Holy Spirit we are assured of his presence. And it is the presence of the Holy Spirit that gives us the love that enables us to love others. If we can't demonstrate God's love we are not in the right place with him.

If we are not in the right place for God to be able to use us, He will help us grow to that level by teaching us what we need to learn. Through this we receive endurance to love those God puts in our path.

To demonstrate God's love isn't always easy and we cannot do it on our own but with the power of the Holy Spirit, which God gives us, we can show His love.

The Holy Spirit enables us to reflect the love and joy and peace of the saving grace of Jesus to others. It is through love that our lives can bring others to the knowledge of Jesus Christ so they too can have this confidence.

Prayer for Today

He*avenly Father, thank you for providing the Holy Spirit, the Comforter, to bring peace and fullness to my being. Help me to be open to the leading and guiding of the Holy Spirit and to be sensitive to what you are saying* *to me through the Spirit. Let me have ears to hear and love in my heart for others.*

In Jesus's name. Amen.

A Weekend Thought

Strength of character – *Standing for truth or convictions. Moral, just, kind, honest. Integrity and fairness.*

Paul also says that character strengthens our confident expectation of salvation.

As my years increase, so does my longing to be with Jesus. There is not a shred of doubt in me that Heaven is my final destination. I have more confidence in that truth now than I did when I was younger. Perhaps, through the years, a strengthening of character has developed and still is.

When I was a youth I had doubts about my salvation because of the absence of faith. This was also evident in the way I lived my life, often making unwise choices, which resulted in consequences that were unpleasant.

Even though I accepted the Lord at a very young age and knew the truth, I chose to wander and go my own way for some time. When I rededicated my life to Jesus, it was the beginning of wisdom for me.

Even though I made numerous bad choices during that rebellious time, remembering them enables me to understand others who may be in the same place and inhibits me from criticizing or judging them.

As I learn to walk the path that is chosen for me by God, I am gaining confidence and with it comes endurance and strengthening of character. I am thankful God, in His love and compassion, invested time in me to teach me and grant me the wisdom to make the right choices.

Adena H. Paget †

He is waiting for you as well. If you have been making choices that have not benefitted you, perhaps it is time to change direction. With Jesus as your friend and teacher, all things are possible. It takes a willing heart to accept Jesus as your personal Saviour and make a conscious decision to follow the path that God planned for you. Although this action does not promise a life of ease and comfort, He will always be with you to help you through whatever you encounter.

WEEK 7

Monday

mercy

Receiving God's promise is not up to us. We can't get it by choosing it or working hard for it. God will show mercy to anyone He chooses.

Romans 9:16.

How many of us work long hours and frustrating days, hold positions on committees, and are always busy trying to win God's love? There is nothing wrong with being diligent but it will not assure mercy or promises from God.

Paul says we cannot make it happen. This verse confirms that God is ultimately in control and there is nothing we can do to make God love us more and there is nothing we can do to make God love us less. God's mercy is freely given. All we need to do is accept it with repentance. God will not reject anyone who comes to him asking for forgiveness.

When we receive the gift of salvation we gain a desire to do what is right. God provides the Holy Spirit to give us the power and wisdom to do what is right. All we need to do is let him have control in our lives.

I spent many years unwilling to let God control my life. I made hasty decisions without consulting him and most of them were detrimental to me as a person.

I did the running-around thing trying to win my way into the Kingdom and I tried to do good so everyone would think that I was a good Christian. Guess what? God didn't love me more because I was trying to be the kind of person I thought I should be.

In all fairness, I should confess that I was doing all these good things to benefit myself, to make me feel better and to impress other people. My motives were wrong and all my deeds were for nought. God loved me just as I was, without me trying to impress him or others. It is not our works He wants but our whole selves.

Prayer for today

Heavenly Father, thank you for loving me just the way I am, in all my imperfection and selfishness and human frailty. I know you are my salvation and you only; there is nothing I can do to earn it. You did it all on the cross. Help me, Lord, to relinquish my stubborn nature and totally allow you to control my life and guide me along the path you have prepared for me.

In Jesus's name. Amen.

Adena H. Paget †

Tuesday

by God's grace

Salvation is not a reward for the good things we have done, so none of us can boast about it.

Ephesians 2:9

It doesn't matter how hard you try to win God's favour, it will never be enough to enter into eternity with him. We don't have to work for salvation at all. He has already paid the entire price, and all we have to do is accept him and come to him through the grace of Jesus Christ.

Stop running around worrying and trying to earn a place in Heaven, just be willing to allow God to forgive you and save you. He saves us because He is a merciful God and it is only by His grace that we can be saved. We cannot take credit for our assurance of eternal life with Jesus.

Can you imagine what Heaven would be like if we had to earn our place there? I fear there would be bragging and boasting and some would feel like they deserved to be on a higher level than others.

Instead, none really deserve to be redeemed, we are all sinners, but the wonderful news is that Christ died for our sins and made atonement for us. He is the ultimate sacrifice and so our freedom from death is a free gift because God loves us just the way He created us.

My friend, take comfort in the fact that God loves you, Christ died for you, and you can know the wondrous love of the Father and all the good things that He has prepared for you here and for eternity...and all you have to do is accept Him.

Prayer for today

Dear Lord Jesus, you have made it easy for me to know you and I am thankful that you love me. I also know that as I grow in my spiritual walk with you, my desire is to be more Christ-like and in order to do that, I want to do things that will bless you. So in my feebleness, I desire to do good things for you and I pray as I take action to please you that my faith will increase, thereby showing others that you are a God of love and forgiveness. Help me to be active for you, Lord.

In Jesus's name. Amen.

Wednesday
predestination or not

For the scriptures say that God told Pharaoh, "I have appointed you for the very purpose of displaying my power in you, and so that my fame might spread throughout the earth." So you see, God shows mercy to some just because He wants to, and He chooses to make some people refuse to listen.

Romans 9:17 & 18.

This scripture tells us why God created Pharaoh; Pharaoh, who was instrumental in having Jesus crucified. I find this verse fascinating and a good illustration to seeing God's sovereignty.

I have learned the timing of accepting Christ needs to be God's, not ours. If it is not the right time for a particular person to accept a relationship with God, all the talking will not accomplish our wish.

Even though we have a desire to do God's will and bring unbelievers to Jesus, many times our desires are not met. We know God is not willing that any should perish, and yet in Pharaoh's case it says the Pharaoh was created for one purpose. It seems to corroborate the idea of predestination, or the belief that God establishes who goes to Heaven and who doesn't.

Humanity was created in the image of God and was meant to acknowledge and consult the Creator on all things. Instead, human beings have claimed their destiny as a man-made responsibility, making all decisions without consulting God. As a result, many bad things are happening to people and everyone asks, "How can a loving God allow these things to happen?"

Despite the choices of humans, we are still created in God's image and therefore we know He loves us. We know He created us with free will to choose God or not. When we choose to follow him, we have the comfort of knowing He is always and ultimately in control.

Prayer for today

Thank-you, Lord for being in control and lavishing your love on me. You are an unchanging God and I know I can always depend on you. I want to return your love, Lord, so I ask you to guide me and look to you for direction. Help me to be patient with others as you are patient with me. I love you, Lord.

In Jesus's name. Amen.

Thursday

contentment

Who are we, mere human beings, to criticize God? Can we as creations of God say, "Why have you made me like this?" When a potter makes containers, he makes some for valuables and others for garbage.

God has every right to exercise His judgment
and His power but He also

has the right to be patient with those who are
the objects of His judgment and are fit only for
destruction. He also has the right to pour out the
riches of His glory upon the objects of His mercy.

Romans 9: 20- 23

We have a tendency to put God in a box. We all have our own idea of what God is like. Some think God plays with us like a puppeteer while others think God doesn't really care about all of our problems. This verse tells us we are not in a position to question God. As I read more of His word, the message becomes clear that He is my creator and I am in awe of His greatness.

We are not in a position to judge anyone else because God will do that and we are not in a position to complain about our existence or who we are because He created us.

We are not always content with our situation, but if we are in God's will then it is up to him to place us where He needs us. Our unhappiness and grumbling and complaining are not conducive to His plan. Every time we accept our assignment with gratitude and thanksgiving, praising him for walking with us, no matter our circumstances, He hears and blesses us.

Life becomes an amazing adventure when we realize who is really in control. When we learn to revere God and rely on Him every minute of every day, we can face any situation with the assurance that God's mercy is being poured out upon us.

Prayer for today

Thank you, Lord for your mercy and grace, poured out upon me this day. Help me to be content in any circumstance and refrain from complaining.

Adena H. Paget †

Thank you for who I am and help me to be a vessel that can be used by you. I want to be available for your use, Lord. Help me to turn my experiences into opportunity to bring glory to your Holy name.

In Jesus's name. Amen.

Friday
transformation

Don't copy the behaviour and customs of this world, but let God transform

you into a new person by changing the way you think. Then you will know what God wants you to do, and you will know how good and pleasing and perfect His will really is.

Romans 12:2

It sounds as if Paul is recommending total submission to God here, doesn't it?

We are a rebellious people and as such, we have a strong desire to follow our own path, but we read here that we should let God transform us into new people and actually change the way we think. This is totally adverse to what the world is teaching today.

In our society we are told to follow our own dreams, claim our rights, be ourselves, and not to let anyone tell us what to do. It is considered a weakness to be submissive in any area of life. We have preached this to such an extent that it has affected common sense and manners.

Many of our young people think it not cool to display good manners. The element of respect seems to be diminishing in some of our youth.

Tolerance is the valued idea today and despite the mess our world is in, there is an evident absence of God and Biblical values taught in our homes and schools.

It is when we are in the perfect will of God that we find how truly wonderful and pleasing and perfect His love is to us.

While God is ultimately in control, our job is to align our own will with His. Seek to do His will, spend time with him, communicate with him, know him, listen for His voice, search His word and meditate upon it, learn to live the way He intended for you to live.

Prayer for today

Heavenly Father, my prayer today is that you will continue to reform me to what you want me to be. Let me be pliable so that you can work with me. Let me be useful to you, Lord.

In Jesus's name. Amen.

A Weekend Read

contentment

My husband and I have spent the last several winters in a variety of RVs. After we retired, it seemed a good thing for us to try and escape the cold and snowy Alberta winters.

Considering the fluctuation of our Canadian dollar, Victoria, BC seemed like a great alternative. I have to admit I was a bit dubious about living in confined quarters for six months. I spent time in prayer asking God if this was really what He wanted me to do. It seemed as if there was no alternative, so in September 1999 we set out to experience our first adventure in 200 sq. feet of space.

You need to know I am the type of person who requires my own space and alone time and my husband is even more so inclined. Needless to say, we both had concerns but we were ready for an adventure. The worst thing that could happen was maybe we would come home sooner than spring…

By God's grace, for that's what it was, we had a fabulous winter. We became better friends and we thoroughly enjoyed each other's company. We also learned much. We found some of the things that used to seem important really weren't, and we learned to be more giving with alone-time and understanding each other.

We learned to accept each other's shortcomings and realized we each needed to make some changes within ourselves. My husband became a great cook and also cleans from time to time. (Mind you, it only takes about seven minutes to clean a small motor home.) I learned how to dump the tanks and to drive this machine.

My most important lesson was to become less controlling, more submissive, and realize that it is really God who controls my life. I also discovered, as long as I allow God to control my life, it goes pretty smoothly, and when I run ahead or lag behind, things get rough. I learned to be more laid back and not sweat the small stuff, (as someone eloquently said, often…).

I learned my husband is becoming a very patient and loving partner and we fall in love with each other again and again.

Even though our beliefs are very different, it is possible to thoroughly enjoy each other in confined quarters.

The second winter was even better than the first. Now, after seventeen winters, we are accomplished RVers and looking forward to our next winter. Our living quarters have increased over the years from a small, C-class motor home to a thirty-five foot fifth wheel with three push-outs, so we actually have a door to divide two rooms, though it doesn't seem necessary anymore.

I'm not sure if it comes with age or experience, but I know I am a better person when I stop trying to control every situation and really allow God to control my life.

I have often asked the question, "Why did you create me this way, Lord, if it's going to take the rest of my life to strive to be what you really want me to be?"

As I allow my will to become His, I am more at peace and I daily experience new wonders and many blessings that I know I often missed before.

I wonder how I can convey this message to young people today? If only we could realize how perfect God's will is for us and learn to accept it while we are younger, we would not waste so much time searching and floundering.

Scripture to contemplate today

Yet true Godliness with contentment is itself great wealth.
After all, we brought nothing with us when we came into the world, and we can't take anything with us when we leave it.
So if we have enough food and clothing let us be content.

1 Timothy 6:6-8

WEEK 8

Monday
being positive

Be glad for all God is planning for you.
Be patient in trouble, and always be prayerful.

Romans 12:12

This is easier said than done, right? We know this is impossible to do without the help of the Holy Spirit. I remember a lady at a church I went to for several years who seemed to always be thankful… for everything. Actually it became quite exasperating at times. I remember thinking,

"I wonder what she's really like?"

One Sunday, it had been raining for about two solid weeks and everyone was complaining about the weather. I just happened to make a comment about the dreary weather and she came back with,

"Yes, isn't it wonderful? When God waters my garden, He waters everything. When I water it I miss spots all the time."

One day I stopped competing with her and saw her for the positive person she really was. I prayed and asked the Lord to help me see with new eyes. Little by little, I started to appreciate the things around me. I heard people complaining about the weather and the government, and the price of gas and inflation, but I kept on asking the Lord to help me see the positive.

I realized lately, I am becoming the person that everyone gets exasperated with because I have trouble seeing the negative side of things around me.

That's not to say we shouldn't be realistic about life, but to see things as Jesus might see them is a gift. Ask the Lord to help you be a more positive person this week.

Prayer for today

Heavenly Father, I am not a very patient person naturally, but since I have allowed you to work in me, I feel like we might be making progress. Thank you for helping me become a more positive person.

In Jesus's name. Amen.

Tuesday

be who you were created to be

In a wealthy home some utensils are made of gold and silver, and some are made of wood and clay. The expensive utensils are used for special occasions, and the cheap ones are for everyday use.

2 Timothy 2:20

In my years as a teacher, I came to know many students and each one was unique in appearance and personality. I taught several sets of twins in my classroom at different times and even identical twins had different traits. Although it took longer to notice the differences, it confirmed how creative God really is.

The Bible compares us to clay vessels and I believe this verse confirms our diversity. Uniqueness is truly a gift to celebrate and we are to be thankful for who we are created to be. It is a hindrance and an insult to God, The Creator, to wish we were someone else.

We also need to accept others as they are and not judge them, look down on them, or ignore them because they are not like us.

Everyone can be a utensil used by God to do His work on earth.

The prayer for today:

Oh Lord, keep me pure so I can honour you by becoming what you created me to be. Help me to strive to be like pure gold and silver but also to be content with who I am. Help me to remain like new clay and allow you to mould me into being someone who can be useful to you and I will give you all the glory and honour and praise.

In Jesus's name. Amen.

Wednesday
creativity

He is the potter and He is certainly greater than you. You are only the jar He makes. Should the thing that was created say to the one who made it, "He didn't make us"? Does a jar ever say, "The potter who made me is stupid"?

Isaiah 29:16.

God is the potter that created you and as Creator, He also planned your life to benefit you in ways that are amazing.

I was enrolled in an art class that had quite an extensive clay component several years ago. I have never excelled in artistic creativity, but as I started to work the cool moist clay with my fingers, I began to feel almost successful at moulding creations that actually resembled familiar shapes.

I remember making mugs, small trinket dishes, and other creations that I thought were quite acceptable for a novice student. Even though my creations would never win any prizes, I never experienced anyone telling me that I did a lousy job or that I was stupid.

We are like clay jars, created by the Master Artist, God, to be used by him for whatever purpose He sees fit. We need to be willing to allow God to use us in the capacity for which we were created.

One way to assure we are doing God's work is to know him, and to know him we need to be familiar with His Word, the Bible, and to be in constant communication with him, through prayer, so we can easily recognize His voice and directions.

Prayer for today

Father, thank you for my life and the way you created me. Help me to be all that I can be without complaining or envying others. I know you love me just the way I am but Lord, I want to be ALL that I can be, and only with your help is this possible. I am so glad you are a faithful God and you are willing to teach me and wait for me to become what you desire for me.

In Jesus's name. Amen.

Thursday

staying pliable

Destruction is certain for those who argue with their Creator. Does a clay pot ever argue with its maker? Does the clay dispute with the one who made it, saying, "Stop, You are doing it wrong." Does the pot exclaim," How clumsy can you be?"

Isaiah 45:9

And yet, Lord, you are our Father. We are the clay, and you are the potter. We are all formed by your hand.

Isaiah 64:8.

It is imperative that we become supple as new clay, so the Lord can use us for His purpose.

When I was transferred to a new school, my initial goal was to impress my principal and colleagues with my expertise. I just wasn't sure how. As I was rearranging my new classroom, I found two large boxes of new clay that appeared to be unopened. "Aha." I thought, "I will teach my students to complete an awesome clay project and integrate it into the mandatory Greek unit for Social Studies." I knew there was a kiln in working order – I had it made.

The day before the project, I took out my secret treasure. As I started to unwrap it, I detected a stale, mildew odour coming from the box and then I realized the plastic wrap had holes in it that had let in too much dry air. As I attempted to shape it, I realized it was out-dated, dried out and unusable. I proceeded to throw it away and racked my brain to think of another project. So much for impressing my new staff.

I learned a valuable lesson that day. Be prepared, think ahead, and don't do anything just to show off. I also learned clay needs to be supple and moldable in order to be able to do anything with it. I use this experience as a metaphor to remind me God needs me to be supple and mouldable in order for him to be able to use me.

New clay is uncontaminated and pliable, but clay that has been stored incorrectly is not usable. It is our responsibility to make sure we are usable vessels for God and part of that responsibility is ensuring that we protect ourselves from becoming stale and dried out.

Prayer for today

Father, thank you for having patience with me and loving me through a time of rebellion. Thank you for your grace and forgiveness. Help me, Lord, to remain close to you, abiding in your perfect love and staying pliable and ready for your use.

In Jesus's name. Amen.

Friday

being useful for God to use

If you keep yourself pure, you will be a utensil God can use for His purpose. Your life will be clean and you will be ready for the Master to use you for every good work."

2 Timothy 2:21

After my disastrous episode of finding the old clay unusable, the next year I ordered new clay so I could complete my plans. I remembered working the cool, moist clay with my fingers when I had been enrolled in art class and I wanted my students to have the same hands-on opportunity.

Many times a treasured piece of artistic structure created by the students, fell and broke, and I thought how indicative of our lives this was. We are so fragile and easily broken in our weak human state, but if we manage to hold on to our faith, we also know that the Mighty Potter can mend us if we remain pliable. And the end result of allowing him to fix us will strengthen our walk with God.

The most breakages occurred in the kiln, where the heat was intense, but the firing process is an important step because it gives the object strength. Then it is glazed and baked again. When the first coat of glaze is applied, it looks dull and the colors are usually quite mundane and drab, but after the firing and removal from the kiln, the object is completely reformed in appearance. It is smooth like satin, the brilliant colors are bright and shiny, and it is much stronger than before. The firing has transformed it into a thing of beauty and strengthened it to be useful as well. It takes the entire process to make it lovely and useful.

Are you experiencing a firing process today? Are you being tested in the coals of learning? Remember, when the Potter moulds you, He does it because He loves you and wants you to be beautiful and useful. He transforms you into a new creature that will be fully alive and then the Master himself will use you because you will be the vessel that He can use.

Prayer for today

Oh Lord, I know I have a great deal to learn and I want to be supple and ready to do what you want me to do. When I go through the fire help me remember that you are with me and you will not give me more than I can bear. I know I am special in your sight and you love me. Lord, I love you and thank you for the time you are investing in me to make me more beautiful.

In Jesus's name. Amen.

A Weekend Story

the potter

A metaphorical story depicting how the Master Artist can restore broken lives.

Many years ago, before you or I were born, there lived a man by the name of Jedadia. Jedadia was a gifted and great artisan, who created the finest pottery in all the land. Many of the inhabitants of the land possessed some of the beautiful pieces created by Jedadia and proudly displayed them in their homes.

One day Jedadia decided to create something very special for the love of his life. He thought and planned and finally had the masterpiece in his head. He spent many hours in his studio kneading, sculpting, trimming, and shaping the finest piece of pottery that had ever been created. Then the glaze was lovingly mixed to just the right shade and finally it was time for the firing.

After many weeks, he finally asked Annabelle, his wife, to come and see what he had been working on.

As he unveiled his creation, Annabelle was breathless. In front of her was the most beautiful vase she had ever laid eyes on. It seemed to her a work of perfection.

The lines were sleek and smooth and the color was something extraordinary; it seemed to shine like gold. It stood as a slender reed, rounded at its base for balance and strength.

She knew this would be a masterpiece and thought it would bring an excellent price. Jedadia then presented the work of art to her and said, “It’s for you, my dear.”

Annabelle was overwhelmed and fell in love with him all over again. She had always admired his work, but this was a magnificent creation and he was actually giving it to her. She felt blessed beyond measure. She carefully put it in a place of honour in their home. Every day Annabelle carefully and meticulously took the vase from its place to admire it and shine it.

As time passed, hard times befell upon Jedadia and Annabelle. There was a great famine in the land that affected everyone. Money became scarce and people stopped buying anything that wasn't absolutely necessary. As a result, Jedadia and Annabelle suffered greatly. In order to survive they had to sell their belongings. Annabelle tucked away the precious vase and refused to part with it for as long as she could.

Times and famine continued to worsen and finally everything saleable had been sold. The reality was they knew they would starve if something couldn't be done.

Annabelle knew it was time to sell her precious gift. It gave them enough money to survive for quite a while.

Several years passed and things became a little easier. The rains came and crops started producing. The people were once again spending and enjoying their lives. Jedadia's pottery became a valuable commodity once again and things were looking up.

One day Annabelle asked Jedadia to recreate the beautiful gift he had once made for her. He moulded many beautiful and masterful pieces but he could never recreate the perfect, unique piece he had so carefully sculpted many years ago.

Now in another part of the land, the vase sat in a dusty corner of an abandoned house. Throughout its travels it had been nicked, scuffed, forgotten, and left to its fate.

One day a traveler searching for valuables came upon this abandoned dwelling. As he wandered around, he spotted the unique masterpiece.

He could not believe this find. You see, he had a keen eye for quality and immediately recognized the value of this wonder. He carefully wrapped it in his cloak and carried it to his secret place where he set upon himself to clean and restore it.

He polished and rubbed it to restore the lustre and sleekness, however, he soon grew weary and discouraged. Finally, he decided to sell it to a traveling collector for a pittance of its worth.

As it happened, this collector had a wife who collected vases. He immediately decided to present the vase as a gift to his wife. He could see the intrinsic value because he had been gifted with a keen eye.

Upon receiving the vase the wife, who did not have an eye for quality, laughed at his gift and threw it back at him whereupon it shattered into several pieces. Instead of throwing it away, the collector picked up the pieces and carefully wrapped them in a cloth and placed the package under the seat of his wagon.

One day as the collector entered a small village, he was impressed by the beautiful water jugs the women were filling at the town well. He had never seen such magnificent pottery and he inquired about it. He was told that this village was very blessed to have an expert potter who provided the village people with containers. The collector asked directions to the potter's home and promptly made his way to the artisan's place.

As he approached Jedadia's dwelling, he was met by the potter's wife. She introduced herself as Annabelle and took him to meet her husband. The collector and Jedadia had much in common and spent a lengthy time in conversation. After a while the collector mentioned the vase he had hidden in his wagon. Annabelle and Jedadia couldn't believe their eyes when they saw the man's treasure, for they recognized it immediately.

Jedadia started to put the pieces back together carefully and perfectly. As his masterful loving hands began to reassemble the creation, a wonderful thing happened. The vase took on a new beauty. The sleek lines and shape were recreated, but where the cracks of the broken pieces had been lovingly melded, there seemed to appear new color and depth that added another dimension that had never before been evident. A new indescribable beauty.

In wonderment, the collector and Annabelle watched like wide-eyed children as the transformation of the broken pieces took shape. After many hours of tedious and careful mending and melding, before them sat a magnificent masterpiece that was a one-of-a-kind creation. Even more beautiful than before.

The collector felt proud and humble at the same time. To think that he, a humble collector had been privileged to be a part of this wondrous creation was more than he could ever have hoped for. He was thrilled to have returned the piece to its rightful owner for he knew it was in the master's hand where it belonged.

As for Annabelle and Jedadia, they never again parted with this priceless treasure and lovingly cared for it always.

WEEK 9

Monday
forgiveness

Dear friends, never avenge yourselves. Leave that to God. For it is written, "I will take vengeance; I will repay those who deserve it," says the Lord.

Romans 12:19

When others hurt us, it is our human nature to retaliate, and we justify it by telling ourselves we feel better because we saw justice done. This process seems to conflict with God's word. He says we should treat our enemies with love.

We hear of horrendous crimes being committed daily and the victims are angry and cry for justice to be administered. While we know it is imperative to uphold the law of the land and punish these criminals, there seems to be a great cry for vengeance.

Even though we believe in justice, we also need to find it in our hearts to forgive. This is not always possible on our own, but with God, all things are possible, even to forgive our enemies.

Prayer for today

Thank you, Lord, for this day. Thank you for your inspired Word. Thank you that you are a God of justice as well as a God of love, and in time our enemies will receive justice without our help or hindrance. Lord, my desire is to let you control every situation in my life and I pray that you will grant me the wisdom to wait for your guidance in everything, even when someone does me wrong.

In Jesus's name. Amen.

Tuesday

loving others

Continue to love each other with true Christian love.

Hebrews 13:1

We know some people are easier to love than others.

Many times, I have made excuses and argued with God saying, "Lord, how do you expect me to love *that* person?"

I have discovered it can only be accomplished with the help of the Holy Spirit. It *is* possible to love with a Christ-like love. We don't always like everyone and we are not expected to agree with everyone, but we can, with Christ, love everyone.

The definition from The New Living Translation Bible:

love: The ultimate expression of God's loyalty, purity, and mercy extended toward His people – to be reflected in human relationships of brotherly concern, marital fidelity, and adoration of God.

There are many scriptures about love. The greatest commandment tells us to love the Lord our God with all our hearts and with all our minds and all our souls and to love all mankind. In 1Peter 4:8 we are told, "*Love* covers a multitude of sins."

We are commanded to love, even though God knows we cannot always do that by ourselves. He is ready and willing to send the Comforter, the Holy Spirit, to help us accomplish what we cannot do on our own and He knows us better than we know ourselves.

The closer we walk with God, the easier it becomes for us to show His unconditional love.

Prayer for today

Thank you for your unconditional love for me, Lord. You know better than anyone my shortcomings and trespasses, and you know how many times I have failed in truly showing love for others. Father, I come to you with a big request today, Please help me to love others with a love like Jesus. Help me to dwell on the good things and not even see the negative side of others. Only with you is this possible, Lord.

In Jesus's name. Amen.

Wednesday
entertaining angels

Don't forget to show hospitality to strangers, for some who have done this have entertained angels without realizing it.

Hebrews 13:2

This does not tell us to invite our best friends to our home for lunch or coffee, and it does not say to ask your husband's colleagues or boss over for dinner, and we are not asked to invite our family for a weekend.

It actually tells us to show hospitality to strangers. I admit, I am negligent in this area. I love to entertain our friends and family, but I rarely invite new people to my home.

When I was a little girl, we lived in northern Saskatchewan on a rather primitive homestead. We rarely had strangers drop in because everyone was familiar with all the neighbours in a remote community.

One day, a tramp with ragged clothes and a handkerchief tied around a pole with a few cherished belongings knocked at our kitchen door. My mother asked him to come inside and rest while she cooked him some food, and she placed it before him. He ate every morsel without hesitation. She also sent a substantial amount of food with him when he left. In those days in northern Saskatchewan, this was a long, laborious task. The wood had to be brought in, a good fire was needed in the cookstove, and preparing food was different than it is for me. No freezers or fridges or electricity or running water. As I watched with curiosity, my mom was joyful and hospitable as she did all the preparing and serving.

This memory is extremely vivid for me and a wonderful example of what it means to show hospitality to strangers. As I remember, only my mom and I were at home without any means of communication to the neighbours, but she did not think about any dangers – her goal was to show hospitality to this stranger. I believe we were entertaining an angel that day without realizing it.

Adena H. Paget †

My prayer Lord

Help me improve in this area and be able to show hospitality to strangers. Give me the wisdom and discernment to know when the right time is for me to obey this request. Bless me Lord as I strive to do your will.

In Jesus's name. Amen.

Thursday

suffering for Christ

Don't forget about those in prison. Suffer with them as though you were there yourself. Share the sorrow of those being mistreated, as though you feel their own pain in your own bodies.

Hebrews 13:3

Throughout the world there are many suffering for their faith in Christ. Every day we read of Christians in different countries; in China, in the Middle East, in India, and numerous smaller countries and areas we are not even aware of, suffering because of their faith in Jesus Christ.

There is more persecution now than ever before in our world. I know I am guilty of repressing this fact, pretending that it isn't really taking place. I make excuses and think it doesn't affect me because it's far away and removed from my world.

Paul says we should share in their sorrow. He tells us to empathize with them, put ourselves in their place, feel their pain and torture. I tell myself I could not endure the pain that many are experiencing today and so I continue to behave in a cowardly way and deny that it's even happening.

We often say, "I can only pray," but don't we realize prayer is the most important thing for us to do when we feel a burden.

Prayer is the basis and foundation for living a Christian life and being in touch with God's will. People who suffer for Jesus Christ need our prayers desperately. Even though we may not know anyone in a foreign place, praying for ministers of the gospel is always a requirement.

Prayer for today

Lord, help me to empathize with Christians who are suffering at the hands of the devil's workers, the hate mongers who are under the influence of the deceiver. Help me to spend time in prayer for those who have given everything to spread your word to people less fortunate. Give me a burden for the ones who are under the influence of the evil one. Help me to lift them in prayer so they may know the love that Christ offers. Help me to remember the Christians around the world, to value the work they are doing and let them know they are being remembered in prayer.

In Jesus's name. Amen.

Friday

honouring your spouse

Give honour to marriage and remain faithful to one another in marriage.

Hebrews 13:4

What a wonderful institution God ordained when He gave us the gift of marriage. There is a special blessing to being yoked to a loving and kind spouse.

I married at a very young age many years ago. After all these years, we have had many valleys and peaks in our lives. Our beliefs are much different and when I realized that it was not my job to save my husband and let God deal with him, I discovered our marriage escalated to another level, which brought more joy and contentment. After my nagging and preaching to my husband, God impressed upon me my job was to love him and let God do the rest.

Even though my husband does not yet share my faith; God has given me new insight and a deeper appreciation and love for him and our marriage.

Despite our differences, God has blessed us without measure and each day I learn to trust Him more for our happiness and contentment.

God wants to bless your marriage today. If you are harbouring hurts He will make it possible for you to forgive. None of us have ideal spouses because no one is perfect, but with prayer and submission to God our marriages can be restored and healing can begin.

I encourage you to take the first step in giving the negative to God and in praying for wisdom and strength so the perfect will of God can be displayed in your life.

Prayer for today

Dear Lord, help me today to be the kind of spouse you want me to be. Help me to be forgiving and understanding of the mate you have blessed me with. I want to be in your complete and total will and only through your strength can I accomplish this. Walk with me today and guide my steps and my words so they may be the words you want me to speak, and I ask you to give my spouse the wisdom to understand me better.

In Jesus's name. Amen.

A Weekend Read

getting my attention

Although I was raised in a Christian home with parents who loved the Lord, there was a time in my life when I turned my back on everything I had been taught.

As a teenager, Biblical teaching seemed irrelevant to me and I decided Christian living was no fun. I started dating non-Christian boys and when I turned sixteen, I discovered I was pregnant.

I am so thankful that even though I was not walking with the Lord, He was still with me and even though I had committed a sin, God made something good out of my mistake.

We were married six weeks later and were blessed with a beautiful baby boy about seven months after that. We were just children, barely sixteen and eighteen, and had very little knowledge about adulthood, never mind parenting. I am so thankful that my young husband has always been a responsible man and stuck by me despite my youth and ignorance. The difference in our beliefs didn't seem to be an issue for several years and we were pretty content in our situation.

The next four years were very busy – we were blessed with another three babies before I was twenty years old; three boys and finally a little baby girl. I didn't have time to think about my spiritual demise because I mostly spent my time washing diapers, making formula, and trying to keep our basement suite decent.

My husband had a steady job and always brought home his entire pay-cheque. Although times were tough, God blessed us with providing our needs from day to day.

When our first-born son reached his fifth birthday, he developed a case of chronic nephritis, which became serious…so serious that the doctor informed us not to expect him to survive past the age of nine. We were devastated and I realized I needed God in my life to help me deal with this insurmountable obstacle.

Adena H. Paget †

I started taking my little ones to church on Sunday mornings, but if you can imagine sitting in a church service with four youngsters, trying to keep them quiet and listening, you have some inkling of what I was experiencing. Soon this became such an onerous chore that I gave it up. I decided my life was just fine the way it was and I really didn't have time for a relationship with Christ.

Our son's condition worsened and after a few years the doctors had exhausted all their treatments for him. My husband was busy with work and climbing the corporate ladder. The other children demanded attention as well and I was becoming frustrated.

After a time of us worrying and taking care of so many demands, our paediatrician called to tell us of a new drug on the market. He said there were nine children across the country on it, and it seemed to be working for this condition. We agreed to participate in testing this drug. After several months, we began to see improvements in our son and after a year, we realized the new drug was a successful treatment.

I slowly came to the realization of how very much God must love me to spare my son and make it possible for him to live in a healthy body. It was several years later that I recommitted my life to Christ, but the experience of watching a transformation like this, from very little hope to complete recovery, was an eye-opening experience to help me see what a loving God we serve.

I am so thankful that God knew exactly how to get my attention and helped me realize who He really is, and how great and how wide and how deep His love for me (and you) really is.

Years later, our son was married to our wonderful daughter-in-law, and they have three healthy children and a beautiful grand-daughter. Their children were raised knowing God and His love.

Prayer for today

Oh Lord, I am so thankful that you always know exactly what we need. Thank you for all the wonderful miracles and blessings in my life. Help me to trust you, even when it seems things are going badly, for I know you are with me. Thank you for all the praying friends and relatives that have carried me in times of trouble. Most of all, Lord, thank you for your mercy and grace each day of my life.

In Jesus's name. Amen.

WEEK 10

Monday

getting our priorities in order

Stay away from the love of money, be satisfied with what you have. For God has said, "I will never fail you. I will never forsake you."

Hebrews 13:5

We are not reprimanded for having money or wealth or possessions, but we are told not to love it.

Often, the possession of material wealth leads to a skewed value system. When the goal of earning profits becomes the main focus of our lives, our priorities become fuzzy and our spiritual lives suffer. Many wealthy people have put God on the back burner and spent all their energies on their material profits.

In order to understand and strive toward exerting our energies in the right direction, we need to have our priorities in order. I believe this is how God meant them to be. It has been my thermostat for keeping my life prioritized.

1. God – *Thou shalt have no other Gods before me.*
2. Spouse – *This explains why a man leaves his father and mother and is joined to his wife and the two are made one.*
3. Children and Family – *Children are a heritage from the Lord*
4. Career – *Be a workman who does not need to be ashamed. Work with enthusiasm as though you were working for the Lord rather than for people.*
5. Church – *And let us not neglect our meeting together as some people do, but encourage and warn each other especially now that the day of His coming is drawing near."*

God promises to never leave us or forsake us, therefore, if we put God first, it gives Him opportunity to bless us abundantly, which is His desire.

Prayer for today

Dear Lord, make me what you want me to be and show me how to put my priorities in perspective so that you are first in my life. Don't let anything or anyone hinder my relationship with you because you are my strength and without you, nothing is worth anything. Help me to submit to you in all areas of my life and to trust you for everything.

In Jesus's name. Amen.

Tuesday

God is our helper

That is why we say with confidence, the Lord is my helper so I will not be afraid. What can mere mortals do to me?

Hebrews 13: 6

When I watch a movie or TV show with a superhero as the star, no matter how hopeless the situation seems, I know the hero can and will rescue the victim. All kinds of gimmicks are used and always our hero comes through. In James Bond movies, the hero 007, always becomes the victor. At times the villain has a plethora of tricks in his bag, but the hero can always go one better in order to make his escape and capture the villain.

All classic literature or lasting literature uses this strategy. In order for the story to be considered a classic or a time-honoured tale, the hero escapes and captures the antagonist. Often the hero also achieves the ultimate goal like saving the world from disaster, or getting the girl or the gold or some other valued treasure.

The model for these stories is found in the Bible. David and Goliath, Daniel in the Lion's Den, Joseph and his achievement of victory over the seemingly insurmountable circumstances, Ruth, Esther, and many others are heroes of the Bible.

What gimmicks were used by these heroes to win their battles? The gimmicks were absent; it was the unshakeable faith in a God Almighty that enabled them to win victories. They lived their faith, even under duress and persecution, and in every instance the Creator delivered them. Their superhero was the Mighty God. They never lost their faith.

By faith these people overthrew kingdoms, ruled with justice, and received what God had promised them. They shut the mouths of lions, quenched the flames of fire, and escaped death by the edge of the sword. Their weakness was turned to strength. They became strong and put whole armies to flight.

Hebrews 11:33-34

It was the faith in God's promises that carried them through victoriously, not to escape trials and battles, but to go "through" the fire and emerge as refined gold.

Our superhero is much more than a superhero who relies on manmade gimmicks to escape or win the reward. He is the very God, the Creator of life. Just think, we have His promise in His Word, the Bible.

The ultimate answer is found in our verse today. When God is on our side, nothing can harm us. Be encouraged today that God is watching over you.

Prayer for today

Heavenly Father, I am so thankful that you are a God of power and promise. What can harm me if you are on my side? Help me to have unshakeable faith in you.

In Jesus's name. Amen.

Wednesday
overcoming confusion

The ungodly are hopelessly confused. Their closed minds are full of darkness; they are far away from the life of God because they have shut their minds and hardened their hearts against him. They don't care anymore about right or wrong, and they have given themselves over to immoral ways. Their lives are filled with all kinds of impurity and greed.

Ephesians 4:17-19

Our society seems to reflect portions of today's scripture verse. It becomes increasingly difficult to distinguish between right and wrong. We allow the demarcation line to become vague when we depend on ourselves and leave God out.

The longer we stay in this state of sinfulness, the less we care about doing the right thing. This often results in confusion and this is not from God. God is not a God of confusion – that is evident from creation, because our natural world is orderly and logical.

It is through the conviction of the Holy Spirit, we recognize sin and He gives us the desire to repent and ask Christ to forgive us. We become new persons, righteous and holy in the sight of God.

We cannot become holy by ourselves but only through the shed blood of Jesus Christ, the perfect sacrifice. After we accept His forgiveness, the Holy Spirit enters into our lives and enables us to distinguish the light from the darkness, thereby giving us wisdom to make right choices in our walk with God.

So you see, we don't have to remain in a state of confusion. Through the acceptance of Jesus into our lives, and by studying the word of God, we recognize sin and become ambassadors for truth.

Prayer for today

Heavenly Father, thank you for being an orderly God. Thank you for giving us a blueprint to help us live the way we should each day. We are not even aware of the intricate and perfect synchronization of your marvellous works and yet the weaknesses of human beings continue to interrupt your beautiful handiwork by trying to gain control and alter your perfection in the name of greed and immorality. Help me to reverence you.

In Jesus's name. Amen.

Adena H. Paget †

Thursday

overcoming anger

Don't sin by letting anger gain control over you.
Don't let the sun go down while you are still angry,
for anger gives a mighty foothold to the devil.

Ephesians 4:26-27

As a teacher in a large public-school system, I observed many young people who found it difficult to control their anger. This is also evident by the rages we see and hear about; like road rage, parking rage, shopping rage, and even standing in line rage.

This inability to control emotions is becoming increasingly evident and our children are seeing adults modeling this behaviour. I'm not advocating suppression, I realize it is healthy not to fear the evidence of emotions, however, there is no honour in displaying anger that is out of control. Criminal acts are being performed and justified in the name of anger because of the acceptance of temper-tantrum and many other wrong behaviours. It seems many times there is an absence of absolutes.

The Apostle Paul does not forbid anger, but he mentions not remaining angry after the sun goes down. I was given this valuable piece of information many years ago by my grandmother. I have found it a valuable principle for a workable and rewarding marriage.

Paul also tells us anger gives the devil a foothold in our lives. We are vulnerable when we are angry and the devil waits for an opportunity such as this to inflict his arrows of negative influences upon us. Harbouring anger results in a variety of negative effects.

Spending time in prayer and asking God to give us the strength to forgive and help us rise above the thing that made us angry in the first place, brings victory.

Prayer for today

Heavenly Father, sometimes I find myself getting angry about small things that don't really matter. I know this is wasted energy and not your will for my life. With your help I know I can overcome this. Help me to realize what is worth getting upset over and what I need to ignore or handle with sensitivity and gentleness.

In Jesus's name. Amen

Friday
overcoming the use of abusive language

Don't use foul or abusive language. Let everything you say be good and helpful, so that your words will be an encouragement to those who hear them.

Ephesians 4:29

I have delightfully discovered my conversations lack cuss words or abusive language. I've often found myself judging others who use bad language.

My students used to tell me it was okay to cuss when they were angry because they couldn't help it. I replied quite sarcastically with, "That is not a valid or acceptable excuse and perhaps you should strive for more variety in your vocabulary."

The Lord showed me this verse, which not only says to abstain from using foul language, but also instructs us to let our words be an encouragement to others as well as good and helpful.

I remember entering into conversations in the staff room that were destructive and sarcastic toward others, and I realized I was as guilty of abusive language as the students who used bad words.

I had some repenting to do and have since asked God to help me to be an encourager at all times. I now have the strength, most of the time, to abstain from gossip and sarcasm, and instead, I exert my energies to uplift and speak kindly about and to others.

Let the words of my mouth and the meditations
of my heart be acceptable to you,
Oh Lord.

Psalms 19:14

Prayer for today

Oh Lord, I ask you to guide my speech and help me to utter words that will bring encouragement. Keep me from entering into abusive conversations, remembering you created everyone, all are acceptable in your sight, and you love each and every one you created. Give me a heart that's filled with love, make me more like Jesus and give me words that will bring joy and encouragement to those around me.

In Jesus's name. Amen.

A Weekend Read

Kate's blessing

As a teacher in a public system, I was not allowed to share my beliefs or speak of my faith.

I spent much time in prayer asking for wisdom and direction in this area and God heard my prayers and gave me many opportunities to witness for him, even in this restricted area.

One year I was blessed beyond measure when I discovered a student in my classroom was attending confirmation classes with her church. She proved to be a missionary in the classroom many times, and somehow God granted me wisdom to ask the right questions to open up opportunities for her to speak freely. It was quite permissible for the students to speak freely but not the teacher.

I was experiencing a trial that involved my daughter, the mother of three boys. She had been diagnosed with thyroid cancer. After many weeks of tests and apprehension, finally the day arrived when she was scheduled for surgery to remove the diseased thyroid.

As I entered the classroom that day, my concern must have been evident and this wonderful student asked me, in front of the class, what was wrong. I took the time to inform the class of my concern.

Immediately after my sharing, Kate jumped up and said, "Everyone bow your heads, I am going to pray for Mrs. Paget's daughter now." Kate was a natural leader and when she asked the class to do something, they obeyed. She began to pray in the classroom, a prayer with conviction and innocent faith. The moment was truly inspired by the Holy Spirit and brought tears to my eyes and I realized what a great blessing this was for me.

Needless to say, she became a very special student to me in my years as a teacher. My daughter's operation was successful as well, which I am eternally grateful for.

Adena H. Paget †

The Provincial exams were easier that year as well because each morning, Kate would begin the day with everyone in prayer for the tests that day.

She truly was a child of light in the classroom that year and I pray that her child-like faith will follow her throughout her life. What an example to me and everyone else in the classroom and such a wonderful blessing from the Lord.

There were several other students in my classrooms over the years that enabled many wonderful faith conversations. I am still amazed by God's grace every day and what He accomplished in my humble classroom with the students He allowed me to enjoy.

WEEK 11

Monday
live carefully

Do not bring sorrow to God's Holy Spirit by the way you live. Remember, He is the one who identified you as His own, guaranteeing that you will be saved on the day of redemption.

Ephesians 4:30

Have you had sorrow brought upon you by someone? Perhaps someone said something to you that hurt your feelings or saddened you by a comment they made?

I am guilty of that offence myself. I remember saying something hurtful to a good friend and I didn't even realize it until much later.

We are probably all guilty of this. I also remember behaving in a way that embarrassed someone and brought sorrow to that person because of what I had done.

We need to scrutinize our daily lives and ensure we don't bring sorrow to our friends and our Creator by the things we do. As a child of God, I have a responsibility to display a life of holiness and humility, not to think, as Christians often do, that I am better than another because I am saved.

In reality, Jesus came to save the lost and I am not loved more by God because I profess to be a Christian. In fact, we are to show love to those who have trouble accepting the truth. When we choose to ignore those who don't belong to our group we are bringing sorrow to God's Holy Spirit.

Prayer for today

Dear Lord, I thank you for forgiveness because I know I am guilty of bringing sorrow to you and the Holy Spirit by things I have said in the past. Help me to show unconditional love to others and not to think more highly of myself than those that don't know you yet. I know you came to save the lost and I know you love them and my desire is to please you. Without you I am not capable of showing the love that I need to show.

In Jesus's name. Amen.

Tuesday

getting rid of the "buttons"

Get rid of all bitterness, rage, anger, harsh words, and slander, as well as all types of malicious behaviour. Instead, be kind to each other, tender-hearted, forgiving one another, just as God through Christ has forgiven you.

Ephesians 4:31-32

I have a very good friend to whom I look to for spiritual guidance. I consider this friend a true woman of God.

Her husband was a chaplain in the Canadian army for years and spent a great deal of time in prayer and listening for the voice or impression of God upon his heart.

One day as he was talking to God, he asked God to keep people away from him who had a tendency to push his buttons. He said God answered and impressed upon him to "get rid of the buttons." This proved to be a valuable insight for me.

If we can get rid of the buttons, we will not be bothered by anything anyone says to us and that will lead to an absence of bitterness, rage, harsh words, and slander and all those other emotions that keep us from the joy we are meant to feel.

I believe an attitude that enables us to overlook harsh remarks from others will help us show kindness to all even if they are not our favourite people.

The Holy Spirit will help us to rise above the hurts as we are given the strength to forgive just as God through Christ has forgiven us.

Prayer for today

Dear Lord, I need your help to "get rid of the buttons" and to get rid of all the bitterness that I harbour. Help me to show kindness and be tender-hearted and forgiving. Make me more like you, Jesus, and cause me to look beyond the hurts and rise above them. With the help of the Holy Spirit I can become what you want me to be.

In Jesus's name. Amen.

Wednesday
learning patience

Be still in the presence of the Lord, and wait patiently for Him to act.

Psalms 37:7

Waiting is one of the most difficult things to do. It makes us feel abandoned or forgotten and impatient.

When God doesn't answer our prayer in the time we think He should, we wonder if He heard us. There have been times I have barged ahead and tried to do the thing on my time, only to have it fail miserably. With maturity, we learn to wait for God's timing but it never seems easy.

Think of the priceless diamond, waiting and waiting for thousands of years to be unearthed, to be discovered, and even after it has been found it needs much more care to become a worthwhile gem. It needs to be mined, appraised, cut, and polished, and then it needs to be placed in the exact right setting to enhance its beauty.

Some diamonds are discovered and then hidden in locked safes, only momentarily opened and admired. Often only the owner knows its true beauty and value, but it is still beautiful and cherished.

Many times when we think we have been forgotten, it is only because we are being matured and polished and shaped to be used in the perfect setting that our Creator has prepared for us. He knows exactly where we can best be used for Him and even though many others may not see our talents, He knows where we are and He cherishes us until we are completely equipped and ready for His purpose.

Prayer for today

Father, I am so thankful that you know exactly where I am, not only physically but spiritually as well. Even though I feel useless sometimes,

I know you are in control and when you have something else for me to accomplish, you will let me know. My desire is to be used by you for your purpose and my prayer is that I may hear your voice when I need to. Help me be patient until you know I'm ready for whatever you have for me to do.

In Jesus's name. Amen.

Thursday

road of life

Don't be impatient for the Lord to act.
Travel steadily along His path.

Psalm 37:34.

Road trips with our five children were often tests of patience and perseverance, and my husband has always been ultra-cognizant of speed limits and road rules.

After we had sung all the songs, and played all the games we knew and many originals, my patience often grew thin and I would think maybe just this once we could pick up speed or stop for the afternoon or treat ourselves to a luxurious stay in a hotel. My husband always kept steadily driving along while I fought to stay patient, and inevitably we would arrive at our destination at the designated time without added expenses.

Our journey along life's roadway could be analogous to our family road trips. We need to realize the path of our destiny is guided by our Heavenly Father and He will bring us safely to our planned destination at precisely the right time.

Impatience only leads to confusion and perhaps losing our way or having to tread through a difficult detour that would otherwise have been smooth and straight. We need to wait on the Lord, because His timing is perfect.

Prayer for today

Lord, grant me patience to wait for you. You are the one constant in my life, the one who never changes and who consistently loves me and sticks by me. You, Oh Lord, are ageless and unchanging and I need to learn to be steady and patient while waiting for you to guide me further along the journey of life.

In Jesus's name. Amen.

Friday

the blessing of giving

Give your gifts in secret, and your Father, who knows all secrets, will reward you.

Matthew 6:4

Many years ago, I asked the Lord who should receive some money that I had designated to God. He gave me a beautiful dream.

I was sitting in a church pew behind a lady I knew very well. She was a single mom, who had been struggling financially for some time. Soon after I sat down, she turned around and laid her hands on me and started praying for me. I was extremely blessed by this. After a few moments she rose from her seat and came and stood behind me and anointed me with oil. As she continued to pray, I felt an inner warmth, which I knew, was the Holy Spirit flowing through me. I was blessed beyond words and then I awoke.

I knew God wanted me to give the money to this woman. I thought maybe I should give her some of it, but I knew I would be hindering the full blessing the Lord wanted to give me. I wanted the entire blessing, the warmth that came with the oil, so I knew I needed to give it all. In obedience to God I visited her the next day and gave her the gift. She was very grateful and in need. What a blessing to be used by God in this way.

Years later I met this same woman in another city. I had forgotten my gift to her, but she reminded me and said she remembered praying for help to make ends meet shortly before I arrived at her door.

Perhaps you have felt a twinge or urgency to perform a charitable act. It could be the still, small voice of the Holy Spirit calling you to perform some service for the Lord.

One day we will be rewarded for the gifts we give in secret. There may not be tax receipts or recognition from anyone on earth but your Heavenly Father knows and will reward you.

Prayer for Today

Heavenly Father, thank you for prompting us to do things for you so that we can reap your blessings. Help me to be sensitive to the still, small voice and obey it.

In Jesus's name. Amen.

A Weekend Read

obedience and trust

I have heard people caution others not to pray for patience, because it hurts when God teaches you.

While we experience testing, we know God never gives us more than we can handle and He promises to walk through the flames with us. When the lesson is complete, we exit with a maturity that wasn't there before.

In my own life, I believe, my patience was increased many times by waiting for God to answer my prayers. I am naturally an impatient person, being born with a desire to see my wishes and hopes appear instantaneously. As I grow older, I realize that these expectations are immature and unrealistic.

I believe God must have a great sense of humour. He realized my impatient personality and blessed us with five children. If anything in this world can try one's patience, it is definitely children. My patience was tried constantly, but each time we encountered a dilemma, we realized we were becoming more equipped to handle (almost) any problems. Our home was often in chaos but somehow, through a miracle, our children all grew up and became responsible citizens.

One particular night, my husband was away on a business trip and our son, Drew and his buddy wanted to sleep in the back yard in a shack they had spent all day building. I didn't see any problem with this and consented.

About 4:00 a.m. I was awakened by a ringing phone. It was the City Police asking me if I knew where my son was. I said, "Yes, he's sleeping in the back yard." They asked me if I was sure because they had a ten-year-old boy, who said he was my son, in custody. He had been caught taking money out of the neighbourhood milk chutes.

Adena H. Paget †

(Milk chutes were little boxes built into houses beside the back door with a little door from the outside and a little door from the inside. You left the milk money there and in the morning the milkman took the money and left your milk.)

Sure enough, my little darlin' and his buddy were guilty, and I had to take the bus downtown to the police station to collect them. Was God trying to teach me patience?

It was a devastating discovery and my trust in Drew needed time to be renewed, but I believe this little escapade, like many others, helped me realize my children weren't beyond breaking the law. I needed to be aware of that, but it also helped me gain wisdom and understanding of the awesome job of parenting that God entrusted to me.

Many times I have been able to see the wondrous love and patience of my Heavenly Father through my relationship with my children.

So often I have disobeyed and realized that on my own, I fail time and time again.

Just as my son needed my help to get him out of his predicament, I need my Heavenly Father to rescue me. As our son matured he realized the importance of obeying his parents and the law.

As I mature I realize the importance of following the precepts that God has ordained and the joy that comes by being an obedient child and listening to His voice. I am so thankful my Father in Heaven is patient and forgiving to me, because I am often a negligent and immature child.

The goal for me this week is to ask God for wisdom and listen to His gentle voice when I forget to wait. I desire to grow in patience.

WEEK 12

Monday

producing fruit

You didn't choose me. I chose you. I appointed you to go and produce fruit that will last, so that the Father will give you whatever you ask for, using my name.

John 15:16

This verse makes me feel very special. The first time I told my story to a group of women, the Lord gave me this scripture to use as my text.

After I had written down what I felt I should say, I realized how very much that little verse meant to me. It told me how special I was to God and let me know He loved me enough to choose me as His child and give me the privilege of bearing fruit for him.

This verse became especially dear to me when I started going on mission trips, because it made me realize it was God's doing and not my own. It also made me realize that perhaps this was an opportunity to produce fruit for Jesus.

Even though you may not travel to a foreign country or even have an opportunity to speak to strangers, what you say to your children and spouse and neighbours each day produces fruit as well.

There is no greater mission on earth than to be a parent who brings up children to know who Jesus is. Being a spouse who displays God's love produces fruit as well; fruit that will last.

Prayer for today

Dear Lord, Thank you for choosing me to be your child. I am so blessed to know your love and call you my Father. Thank you for the privilege of taking your word to those who do not know you. Thank you for blessing us with wonderful children, who are a joy to us. I pray, Lord, that I may use every circumstance that you give me to show your love so that I may bear fruit for you.

In Jesus's name. Amen.

Tuesday

doing God's work

So dear brothers and sisters, work hard to prove that you really are among those God has called and chosen. Doing this you will never stumble or fall away.

2Peter 1:10

I believe God has called us and chosen us to do His work. Each one of us has been called for a different purpose and we need to know what that purpose is. There is a wonderful worship chorus that goes like this:

This is my desire, to honour you,
Lord, with all my heart I worship you.
All I have to give you, I offer praise.
All that I adore is in you.
Lord, I give you my heart, I give you my soul.
I live for you alone

Every breath that I take,
Every moment I'm awake
Lord, have your way in me.

If our desire is to be used by God, then I believe He will show us what He wants us to be and where He wants us to go for him. We don't need to worry and fret that God is not using us.

It says in the scriptures we may be entertaining angels without knowing it so don't you think that God may be using us for His purpose without us even being aware of it sometimes? Keep on doing what the Lord has called you to do even if it does not seem important to you, because if we work to do what God has called us to do we will never stray from Him.

Prayer for today

Dear Lord, I want to be used by you to fulfill my purpose on earth. I know you chose me to be your child and I know you love me more than I can comprehend, and I want to be in the center of your will. Help me to be a student of your word, to understand what it is saying to me. And help me Lord, to hear your voice guiding me in the direction you have planned for me. Let the words of my mouth and the meditations of my heart be acceptable to you, oh Lord.

In Jesus's name. Amen.

Wednesday

you are very special

For I have chosen you and will not throw you away.

Isaiah 41:9

Did you know you were chosen by God to be His child? And furthermore, He will never leave you or abandon you. When I'm feeling lonely or having a bad day, I remember God loved me so much, He chose me to be His own.

It reminds me of my relationship with my husband – we may have disagreements now and then, but when we made our vows at the altar, we pledged to stay with each other through sickness and health, whether rich or poor, and we have managed to keep that promise for over fifty years. After this length of time, I can't imagine my life without him. We are sure of our love for each other; it is unconditional and always evident and I know he would not leave me and he is sure of my love as well.

If we can experience this kind of love as earthly human beings, imagine how very much God loves you, to choose you to be His child. If you are feeling alone or abandoned, just remember how very special you are to God and how very much He loves you.

Prayer for today

Dear Lord, I am in awe of your great power and majesty and yet it humbles me to think that you love me enough to choose me to be your child. I am thankful that you promise to keep me and not throw me away. Your promises make me realize that I will always be your child and nothing can sever the relationship that you and I have. Thank you Lord, for loving me.

In Jesus's name. Amen.

Thursday
speaking up

For they loved human praise more than the praise of God.

John 12:43

This verse speaks of the Jewish leaders who were afraid of being expelled from the synagogue if they admitted to believing that Jesus was the Messiah. The fear was ~~that~~ the Pharisees would shun them and they would not be admitted to the synagogue.

Have you ever been in this predicament? When I was employed as a teacher in an elementary public school, I was often intimidated by what was conceived to be politically correct. Instead of standing up for my Christian beliefs, I would either stay out of the conversation or even agree with beliefs that I knew were unacceptable to my faith.

Sometimes it is expedient to keep your mouth quiet, but often we don't speak because we're afraid others might call us prejudiced or biased or, Heaven forbid, we may be accused of being politically incorrect. Why are we afraid? Is it more important for us to be accepted by our peers than to please God?

Today is a good day to bring acknowledgement and glory to God in some way.

It is time we, as Christians, became active voices for the Lord and biblical principles instead of practicing apathy because we are afraid to create waves.

Are we afraid of being expelled from the worldly inner circles? I am not advocating speaking without wisdom. We need to ask for wisdom in order to be able to discern when the right time is for us to speak. If we charge ahead without the Holy Spirit prompting us, we may find our total mission debunked.

Adena H. Paget †

Prayer for today

Lord, today I ask you to help me speak up for you and Christian values and principles. I know I have no need to be afraid because the Holy Spirit has been given to me to help me say the right words at the right time. I ask for a discerning spirit to help me know the right time, and I pray that you will place an opportunity before me to speak for you, Lord.

In Jesus's name. Amen.

Friday
to be humble

But those who exalt themselves will be humbled, and those who humble themselves will be exalted.

Matthew 23:12

Jesus is speaking about the religious leaders who wore extra-wide prayer boxes and long prayer tassels to show that they were religious and deserved respect and places of honour at banquets and other gatherings. Jesus said to listen to them but not to behave like them.

This is a lesson for today, as well. When we exalt ourselves above others, we lose credibility, instead, it is far better to work at what you need to become and let someone else offer the accolades and the credibility for you.

This seems contradictory to what the world is telling us; we often hear it is important to blow your own horn because no one else will blow it for you or tell others about your accomplishments so they will respect you. This is against what Jesus taught.

I am not advocating a lowly attitude or a fear of being able to stand up for yourself when you need to, but you should also not be afraid of displaying an attitude of humility instead of a self-righteous outlook.

It seems that this life on earth is very short compared to eternity, and I would prefer to store up my rewards for eternity rather than experience them on earth in this short life. Wouldn't it be wonderful to be exalted in Heaven by the King of Kings?

Prayer for today

Today, Lord, help me to be humble even though I am privileged to be a child of God and that makes me feel special and loved. Help me to remember your Son when He humbled himself to become a servant to others and help me to remember His teachings when He told us to take a back seat instead of exalting ourselves. My desire is to exalt you, oh Lord and you alone. Help me have a servant's heart for you.

In Jesus's name. Amen.

A Weekend Read

a humbling experience

Pride goes before destruction...

Proverbs 16:18

...humility precedes honour.

Proverbs 15: 33

Sometimes my life becomes a comedy of errors. Many times, just when I think I'm mastering a new skill, or have accomplished more than I hoped for and I develop a sense of pride, it is followed by a humiliating experience in that very area.

I have been golfing for several years and if anything can humble a person, it is golf. Some years I spent weeks practicing and other years I just played and hit a few balls before each round. One year I took some refresher lessons to improve on distance and accuracy. That is the year I broke 100 for the first time.

I thought I would keep improving in that direction, however, the next game opened my eyes to the possibility I was not ready for the pro-circuit tour yet.

During the years of my golfing career, our group usually consisted of twelve to fourteen people. Mostly, the women golfed together and so did the men, so I didn't get to play with my husband many times a season.

One year I had been golfing particularly well and I couldn't wait to show my husband how much I had improved. He and I planned a golfing holiday after I had been bragging about my low scores. I even agreed to play for dinner in a fine restaurant as a sure bet that I could beat him (using handicaps, of course).

The first drive, I dribbled the ball off the tee, second shot, scuffed it, third shot, hit it fat, and fourth shot hit a pretty good one, at least it landed close to the green. One more shot to get on the green and another four putts to finally put the ball in the hole. From there I didn't improve much and ended with a very high score. That ended my haughty conversation about how much I improved.

I was, to say the least, humiliated. This has happened many times in the game of golf and I have finally learned not to say anything about my game and just play and hope I don't embarrass myself.

Sometimes my games are good and sometimes they are downright ugly. But at least I have learned not to predict what I will shoot.

I find this is also true in everyday experiences of life. When we spend time bragging or building ourselves up, it almost always leads to embarrassment or a humbling experience.

It also bears true in fault-finding. No one confides in a fault-finder. Each time we pass judgment on someone else, it displays haughtiness in ourselves and we appear to think of ourselves as better than that person.

As time marches on, I am discovering it is better to keep quiet about my accomplishments, and it is also better to look for the good things in others. It brings me joy to dwell on the positive side instead of dwelling on the negative.

Discovering humility in myself is a gift that enhances. The Bible tells us to humble ourselves before the Lord and He will lift us up in honour.

I used to look at the following scripture in confusion, but as I discovered its relevancy in my life, it makes perfect sense to me.

How can you think of saying, "Let me help you get rid of that speck in your eye," when you can't see past the log in your own eye?

· Matthew 7: 4

WEEK 13

Monday
forgiveness

But you offer forgiveness that we might learn to fear you.

Psalm 130:4

"Fear" is a word with two meanings:

- *To have reverent awe of God*
- *Dread or alarm in facing danger*

In this instance, I believe it refers to the first definition.

I believe the analogy of being accepted and forgiven by a friend who forgives and still loves me can be compared to God's forgiveness in a human sense. I think of many times in my life that I needed to be forgiven for a wrong I committed. I remember a good friend who I wronged by breaking a trust.

I agonized and lamented the act before I even considered admitting that I had broken this trust. When I finally went to my friend, admitted my mistake, and asked forgiveness, I was reduced to a new depth of humility by being forgiven and accepted.

If I felt this way in a human sense, I am in awe of the great depth of the forgiveness of God, who has the capacity to forgive the sins of the world because of what His son, Jesus Christ, suffered on the cross.

The act of forgiveness is a wonderful thing to experience but to realize the glorious forgiveness of a Heavenly Father who created Heaven and Earth and everything on it and in it and around it, is beyond my comprehension.

Prayer for today

Dear Lord, thank you for forgiving my sins. I am in awe of your greatness and because you could not accept the ways of sinful man, you made an all-time sacrifice so that you could accept me and see me without blemish or sin. It is only the sacrifice of your Son, Jesus Christ, that allows us to come to you clean and totally forgiven and be accepted by you as justified. I ask you to keep me from temptation so I will not be a stumbling stone to anyone or bring pain to anyone. Help me to give you all the praise and honour for the perfect peace I have because of you.

In Jesus's name. Amen.

Tuesday

multiple forgiveness

Then Peter came to him and asked, "Lord, how often should I forgive someone who sins against me? Seven times?"

"No." Jesus replied, "Seventy times seven."

Matthew 18:21 – 22

Jesus is saying we should forgive anyone who sins against us. Not just once or twice or even seven times but again and again.

How often have I said, "I'm not going to put up with this anymore?" Especially when I have been hurt by someone. If we follow the teachings of Jesus, we don't keep track of how often we have been sinned against.

This is hardly ever possible in our own strength, but with God all things are possible, even to forgive our enemies.

In the Lord's Prayer, Matt. 6:12, we are told to pray for forgiveness of our sins just as we forgive those who sin (or trespass) against us. If it is not possible to forgive within ourselves, then we are at liberty to ask for help. Jesus never gives us more than we can handle and He doesn't expect us to fend for ourselves. He is always close and waits for us to ask for help.

Prayer for today

Father, help me to forgive those that trespass against me. Help me not to keep track of how many times I have been sinned against but to keep forgiving just as you have instructed us to do. Thank you Father, for forgiving my sins and accepting me just as I am, sin and all. Give me strength to be more like you, Jesus, and to show more love and forgiveness to my fellow human beings, especially those who are close to me.

In Jesus's name. Amen.

Wednesday
hindering blessings

> *But when you are praying, first forgive anyone you are holding a grudge against, so that your Father in Heaven will forgive your sins, too.*
>
> Mark 11:25

When we do things in violation of the teachings of Jesus or against God's Word it is called sin. This act drives a wedge in our relationship with Christ.

The above scripture verse tells us not to expect a perfect relationship with Christ if we are harbouring a grudge against someone else. We are hindering the blessing from God when we let bitterness and hurt come between us and our relationship with someone else.

As long as this hurt is in us, we cannot possibly expect to be used or blessed to the fullest capacity by God. The bitterness we harbour is a stumbling block to perfect harmony with our Lord Jesus Christ. It is impossible for him to work in our lives the way He desires to when we cling to ill feelings, for they hinder the perfect harmony and orchestration of the Holy Spirit.

Prayer for today

Dear Lord, help me not to harbour any resentment or bitterness against anyone. I desire to be fully alive and abundantly blessed by you, and I know this is not possible as long as I have unforgiving thoughts I have not dealt with. Help me to forgive others just as you have forgiven me. Let me walk in the light of your love, which is only possible through total forgiveness and having the ability to forgive.

In the precious name of Jesus. Amen.

Thursday

the ultimate sacrifice

He is the one all the prophets testified about,
saying that everyone who believes in Him will
have their sins forgiven through His name.

Acts 10:43

We are all sinners. All have sinned and
come short of the glory of God.

Romans 3:23

Jesus never refuses to forgive and He is our model and example to imitate and strive to be like.

Before Christ died on the cross, forgiveness of sins required sacrificing perfect animals or specific grains as outlined in Deuteronomy. It was a long arduous task and the preciseness of the act was exact, as God gave instructions.

Human beings were not capable of carrying out the plans of God and soon faltered under the law by negligence or becoming ultra-legalistic. The sins of the people were only covered by the blood of the sacrifices.

God, in His mercy, provided a way for us to be without blemish in His sight, by sacrificing the ultimate perfect Lamb, His son, Jesus Christ, who made it possible to remove our sins completely.

For us, it is easy but the price that was paid was the most costly sacrifice. We can never underestimate the sacrifice that was paid for our redemption.

Prayer for today

Thank you, Father, for the ultimate sacrifice of your Son who took all my sins upon Himself so that I could be forgiven by accepting your Son, Jesus Christ. I can't even comprehend how much love you displayed for me, to sacrifice your only Son so that I would be blameless in your sight, because you could not look upon the sinfulness of man. Help me to strive to be what you want me to be and seek your face every day to know you more and be in your perfect will.

In Jesus's name. Amen.

Friday
freely forgiving

If we say we have no sin, we are only fooling ourselves and refusing to accept the truth. But if we confess our sins to Him, He is faithful and just to forgive us and to cleanse us from every wrong.

1 John 1:8-9

The Bible tells us we are all sinners and if we think we have no sin we are lying to ourselves.

Everyone needs to experience repentance and forgiveness by Jesus Christ before being able to claim the gift of eternal life with Jesus and a personal relationship with Jesus on earth.

In the book of Romans, the Apostle Paul says we are all sinners because of Adam's sin. It was Adam's sin that brought death to all.

It was Jesus Christ who brought forgiveness to all through God's bountiful gift. And the result of God's gracious gift is very different from the result of that one man's sin.

We have the free gift of being accepted by God, even though we are guilty of many sins.

God, in His mercy, knew humanity would never be capable of following the rules and so He made it very easy for us to enter into the Heavenly realms by sending His own son, Jesus Christ, as the ultimate sacrifice for our sins. It is only by the shed blood of Jesus that we can enjoy a personal relationship with our Creator by having our sins forgiven just by asking. What a gracious God we serve.

Prayer for today

Father, thank you seems like such a small token for what you have done for me. How can I ever thank you enough or praise you enough for your generous and glorious gift to me? I don't even deserve to be forgiven but you have made it possible for all my sins to be completely erased from my file, as far as the east is from the west. I will forever praise you and thank you for you are my healer and redeemer and Saviour and Friend. Help me to be a witness for you and to live each day for you.

In Jesus's name. Amen.

Adena H. Paget †

Weekend Read

trust the trainer

In the early days of my grandparents' and my father's time, many unique tasks were performed by horses. A well-trained horse was a valuable asset. The horse was a very important commodity to running a farm and a delivery service in the city. It meant transportation and therefore a lifeline. It was used to plough the land, plant the crops, and harvest them. It was used to round up the cattle and control them.

It required a patient and persevering trainer, who understood the temperament and make-up of the individual horse's personality.

For some horses the training period was long, while others learned quickly and easily. Some had stubborn natures and needed the same lessons and consequences time after time, again and again. Others seemed to have giving, kind spirits, which submitted easily to the authority of the trainer.

If the training was too lenient, the horse wouldn't be useful because it wasn't obedient and became used to doing its own thing. If the trainer used harsh discipline and tried to beat the lessons into the horse, the horse became fearful and skittish and could seldom be trusted to perform the requirements of his purpose.

A valuable animal was one that consistently performed the duties expected with very little direction from the trainer. So much of what the horse became was due to the master trainer.

A horse with a willing nature, which could be trusted and was obedient turned out to be a valuable asset. On the other hand, a horse that showed continual defiance or was unable to be trained, was considered near worthless.

I remember a beautiful, silky-black team of Percherons that were lively and spirited. When my dad was controlling the reins, they knew exactly what they needed to do and followed all the instructions perfectly. When my brother was driving they often did and went where they wanted to. They knew he wasn't the master. The horses instinctively knew who was driving them. They had a keen sense of recognition from the touch on the reins and the sound of the voice.

My brother improved over time and became a gentle trainer but my dad was always the master trainer when it came to horses.

Some questions to consider:

Who is your Master?

> Is He the Master who trains you to be everything He created you to be?
> Are you attuned to His words and commands?
> Do you know His voice, His signals, His ways?
> Are you giving in to His direction or are you confused?
> Are you valuable and confident in who you are, or do you harbour a rebellious nature?
> Are you listening to the Master or are you following someone who professes to be a master, though you are not really sure who it is?

No one can serve two masters. For you will hate one and love the other, or be devoted to one and despise the other. (You cannot serve both God and money.)

Luke 16:13

WEEK 14

Monday

purpose of pleasing God

You are worthy, O Lord our God, to receive glory and honour and power. For you created everything, and it is for your pleasure that they exist and were created.

Revelation 4:11

We were created to demonstrate the glory of God and to have fellowship with the God of glory. That is what gives God pleasure. In order to be used by God according to his will we need to:

1. Learn what God's will is for our lives.
2. Ask God to plant His perfect will in our lives.

There is an old hymn that we used to sing containing the words:

Dare to be a Daniel, dare to stand alone.
Dare to have a purpose firm.
Dare to make it known.

Daniel's purpose is so clear in the Bible. He was firm in his convictions, never wavering. Even when a lie could have benefited him, he chose to obey God. He was in close communion with God, spending time with him each day.

Even though the interpretation of Nebuchadnezzar's dream meant disaster for him, Daniel knew he had to tell the truth. He must have been somewhat fearful and yet he obeyed his Creator.

His will was in complete and total alignment with God's will. His faith was steadfast, even into the lion's den. God was with Daniel because He chose to be but also because Daniel was in perfect tune with God and knew exactly what God's will was for his life. The story of Daniel is an example for us to follow when we are fearful of proclaiming who God is. I would encourage you to read this fascinating Book in the Old Testament.

Prayer for today

Today, Lord, draw me nearer to your side so that my will may be the same as yours and my prayers and hopes will be the same as what you have planned for me. Teach me your will, Lord, and make me what you want me to be. Help me to know my purpose and to stand by what your plan is for my life. My desire is to be in your perfect will.

In Jesus's name. Amen.

Tuesday

purpose of giving praise

> *Praise the Lord, all you who fear him. Honour him, all you descendants of Jacob. Show him reverence, all you descendants of Israel.*
>
> Psalm 22:23

We are created to praise God. In fact, we need to praise him in everything and revere him.

Sometimes it is difficult to praise God. Especially during the times when we are experiencing a test of faith.

When my emotions are at the lowest point and I feel like I am in the midst of a refining fire, if I take my eyes off myself and turn them upward, the spirit of the Lord descends, and covers me with a warmth that enfolds me. It erases the pain I harboured a short time before. When I praise my Redeemer, He draws near to me and helps me know He is with me no matter what.

When the cares of the world are heavy on your mind and everything seems to be bearing down and you are not sure where to turn, there is only one thing to do, take time to praise your Maker. Be assured He waits for it, He inhabits our praise and desires to bring comfort to your hurts.

Turn your eyes upon Jesus,
Look full in his wonderful face,
And the things of earth will grow strangely dim
In the light of his glory and grace.

The light of the world is Jesus and we need to turn our eyes to the light.

Prayer for today

Father, help me to see your face through my tears and to remember to praise you even when it is difficult to do. I know you delight in me when I spend time with you because your desire is to have a close relationship with me. Help me, above all, to fulfill my purpose here on earth.

In Jesus's name. Amen.

Wednesday

purpose of giving praise

Go into all the world and preach the Good News to everyone

Mark 16:15

Another purpose for our creation is called "The Great Commission"; to proclaim the Good News that Jesus Christ, The Messiah, is come.

He took our sins upon Himself as he was sacrificed on the cross, rose again to defy death, and lives today so that we too can have eternal life.

Many times I am timid at proclaiming the truth of Jesus. I think people might laugh or not believe me. I feel embarrassed and intimidated by others and do not speak openly about the message of salvation. I wonder if you can identify with me.

Jesus says:

"If anyone acknowledges me publicly here on earth, I will openly acknowledge that person before my Father in Heaven."

Matthew 10:32

A little boldness is worth the promise that one day Jesus Christ can acknowledge us to our Creator, God.

Prayer for Today

Oh, Lord Jesus, help me to proclaim your truth to others. I pray for sensitivity toward the prompting of the Holy Spirit to speak when I should and the wisdom to know when to show your love in other ways. My desire is to be used by you and to fulfill my purpose on earth. I want to know more of the heart of God by knowing you better.

In Jesus's name. Amen.

Adena H. Paget †

Thursday

purpose of communication

...asking God, the glorious Father of our Lord, Jesus Christ, to give you spiritual wisdom and understanding, so that you might grow in your knowledge of God.

Ephesians 1:17

I used to have unrealistic expectations of my husband that couldn't possibly be met, because he had no idea what they were. For some reason, I expected him to know my needs. For many years, he never seemed to fulfill my expectations. I often went into a hissy-fit and he would wonder why, never thinking it may have been something he did or didn't do, or something he said or didn't say.

One day as I was feeling particularly sorry for myself at having such an insensitive mate, I realized I had failed to communicate my needs to him in a clear way.

I started the communication connection by commenting on positive things, like complimenting him for the good things he did and making special mention of the thoughtful gifts and tender moments. I also started re-evaluating my own personality and realized that I was as remiss as he was.

I had never really spent time wondering what his needs were or asking him if I could do anything to make life easier for him. I came to the stark realization that I was far less than the perfect wife I thought I was.

Through our efforts to communicate in a clearer way, my husband started sensing my needs and I realized his. Communication is most important in any relationship.

How often do we communicate with our Lord Jesus Christ? How can we know Him if we don't spend time with Him? Even though He knows the desires of our hearts, He needs to hear it from us. We do not speak to God for His benefit. It is for our benefit, however, He loves to hear from us and to talk to God and listen for His direction, gives us a better understanding of who He is.

God created humans for the purpose of praise and worship. We need to exalt His name in praise and acknowledge that He is the King of Kings and Lord of Lords. This is what gets God's attention – it pleases Him. This is the beginning of communication with Him, and then comes the time to put forth our requests, to ask Him to fulfill our needs.

Just like my communication dilemma in my marriage, I needed to start with positive remarks and not with accusations or demands.

Since I have been openly communicating with my husband, he has become my best friend. Isn't that the relationship we want with Jesus? He says He is a friend that will stick closer than a brother. Set a time each day to talk to Him and let Him know how very much you love Him and how you long to know Him, and pray for listening ears to be able to hear what He is saying to you.

Prayer for today

Father, I thank you for being my friend. I praise you for who you are, the one and only Sovereign God, Creator of Heaven and Earth, and yet you know me and love me and want what is best for me. I love you, Lord, and want to serve you. I long to know you more and worship you more. Cause my heart to be broken with the things that break your heart and help me to know your direction and recognize your voice.

In Jesus's name. Amen.

Adena H. Paget †

Friday

being refined

Remove the dross from the silver and
the sterling will be ready for the silversmith.

Proverbs 25:4

Sometimes, it hurts to be purified, to have the dross removed so we can be ready for the silversmith.

I have a pure sterling-silver bracelet, which I inherited from my sister. When I take the time to polish it, the silver shimmers brilliantly. It has beautifully carved petals and stems that create three-dimensional images displaying every intricate detail when it has been cleaned and polished.

To be fully appreciated as the silversmith intended, requires time and effort in the polishing and buffing stages. It seems, every time I wear it, it needs cleaning, but I enjoy cleaning it and watching the intricate patterns appear, and people always comment on its beauty when I wear it.

It reminds me of ourselves and the fact that we need to come often, and ask the creator to cleanse us, so we can be what He intended us to be. You and I need the Master Silversmith to polish us so every lovely detail is evident and we need to ask Him to get rid of the dross that inhibits the true beauty of the created vessel.

It isn't always a pleasant experience because often we come face to face with something in our lives we don't want to face or change, but in order to be as beautiful as possible, it is necessary to face the truth and ask the Master Silversmith to clean and polish us to be who He created us to be.

Today's Prayer

Dear Lord, thank you for caring enough about me to take the time to clean away the "dross" so only the sterling will be evident and I will be ready for the Master Silversmith to work a miracle in me. Without you I am nothing and can accomplish very little. Help me to be ready and willing to let you have your way in my life. I know the tests are often difficult, but I also know they are all worth it to become what you created me to be.

In Jesus's name. Amen.

A Weekend Read

the Lord's prayer

My interpretation of

The Lords prayer, Luke 11

Our Father, who art in Heaven, hallowed be your name
Precious Heavenly Father, Your name is holy as you are holy. You are the creator of Heaven and earth and everything in it and on it and around it and even beyond. You, Oh Lord, are an awesome God, and yet you love me, insignificant me. Even though you sit on the ultimate throne in Heaven, you love me. May your name be praised forever-more.

Thy Kingdom come, Thy will be done on earth as it is in Heaven
May your kingdom be established in my life and in the lives of those around me. Work through me to let your glory shine to others; help me to be mouldable and supple, allowing you to change me into what you created me to be. May my goal and prayers be in perfect alignment with

your perfect and holy will. Let nothing stand between you and me, oh Lord, so that your kingdom will be in me. In Revelation 1:6, it says, you have made us your kingdom.

Give us this day, our daily bread

Thank you for this day that you have provided for me to enjoy. Help me to make the best use of it and finish it with healthy thoughts. You have so richly provided sunshine and rain and beauty for me to enjoy. I appreciate the provisions that I receive each day to keep me strong and healthy. I give you thanks for my daily food and I ask that you continue to provide.

Forgive us our trespasses as we forgive those who trespass against us

Oh my Lord, my sins are so numerous, and yet you have removed them as far as the east is from the west and you don't even remember them anymore. I need you to keep forgiving me each day because, although I don't consciously plan to sin, I know that I do. I ask you Lord, to reveal the sin in my life that I am not aware of. I know, sometimes, my attitude leaves much to be desired and often I have selfish thoughts that are not from you. I ask your forgiveness, Jesus, and for your help in striving for holiness.

Help me to forgive those who have wronged me in the past and help me not to harbour ill feelings toward them, no matter how they have slighted me.

And lead us not into temptation but deliver us from evil

And I ask you to keep me from being tempted by Satan's ploy to try and create a desire for anything of this world that is not pleasing to you. Help me keep my mind on things that are true and honourable and right and pure.

For Thine is the power and the glory forever

I belong to You, Jesus and I live to please you, praise you, worship you, and live for you every day. You alone are more powerful than anything or anyone and you only are holy and deserve all honour and glory forever and ever. Amen.

WEEK 15

Monday

take up your cross

And you cannot be my disciple if you cannot carry your own cross and follow me

Luke 14:27

I have never met anyone who did not have a cross to bear. We have all been given a cross in one form or another. Some are heavier than others and more difficult to carry and sometimes we meet someone and we think, "Wow, what a life that person has – they seem to have everything and all their needs are met easily."

While others may be able to conceal their burden (or cross) it is there. Have you ever wondered how or why some people never seem to be in a valley, and are seemingly on the mountain all the time?

And then there are those who we know are experiencing great difficulties, and yet they have an inner joy that never seems to be absent. They seem to float through the hard times and never blink an eye.

I wonder if Jesus meant that we are to carry our own crosses with joy or sorrow? I have come to the realization that whether our joy or sorrow is evident, we need to learn to put our trust in the Lord and know His word and that will equip us to carry our own cross.

Adena H. Paget †

I don't believe Jesus meant for us to carry our cross alone, because even Jesus had someone to carry His cross when He could not bear the load. I believe He provided the Holy Spirit, The Comforter, for us so we are always assured of the help we might need. I think He meant that we need to take responsibility for our cross and the way to do that is to give our burdens to Him.

Part of our responsibility is admitting that the cross is there and accepting it as our own rather than blaming others or God for it.

Friend, if your cross seems too heavy for you to bear today, give it to Jesus; lay it down and just ask Him to carry it. He waits for you to rely on Him and He will answer your prayer. Don't be like I was when I realized Jesus would carry my burdens, I gave them up and then felt guilty because I wasn't feeling heavy about not having burdens to carry.

"The cross is the symbol of Jesus's love, God's power to save, and the thankful believer's unreserved commitment to Christian discipleship. To those who know the salvation that Christ gained for us through His death, it is a wondrous cross indeed." (Nelson's *New illustrated Bible Dictionary*)

Prayer for today

Dear Lord, Thank you for your Word and the relevance that I find in every verse, every chapter, every book. You say that your Word will not return void to you and I know you are hearing my prayers and listening to my requests. I thank you for the privilege of carrying the cross that you see fit for me to bear. You know what is best for me and I know I can always rely on you for strength to carry whatever I need to.

In Jesus's name. Amen.

Tuesday
under construction

But don't begin until you count the cost. For who would begin construction of a building without first getting estimates and then checking to see if there is enough money to pay the bills?

Luke 14: 28

One day, my husband and I were enjoying a leisurely walk in an upscale neighbourhood in Victoria, BC. Most of the homes were appraised at $700,000 to over $3,000,000; they were very beautiful with magnificent views of the ocean.

As we stood and envied the fortunate people who lived here, we noticed a large lot in front of us with a huge house that was incomplete. We realized it had been started some time ago; the wood had become discoloured, windowpanes were missing, the steps were not attached to the front doorstep, and the yard was overgrown with weeds. It was very sad to realize what could have been, had been abandoned.

We wondered why anyone would begin such a huge project only to abort it before completing it. Did the builder run out of money? Was this person unable to plan and could not realize what it would take to complete the house? It seemed as if there was not sufficient foresight in planning or finances.

Then the Lord showed me the similarity between that picture and the people who profess to be His followers but don't display any Christian qualities – they are like unfinished buildings, begun but never willing to be completed by the Master Builder.

Jesus teaches us to be prepared and count the cost before immersing our energies into a place we are not prepared to go. We must be willing to follow Him, no matter what it takes.

Adena H. Paget †

Many times the road gets increasingly narrow and we wonder if we are on the right track but the Lord knows exactly what we are capable of and He will never give us more than we can handle.

God never said we would have an easy road to travel but He promises to walk with us. When we remember the road Jesus walked for us, our journey seems trivial.

My friend, we need to count the cost and if we make the commitment, we need to complete the course, no matter what it brings. Let us complete the building so it will stand to be admired by all who pass so they may see the work of the Master Builder who magnificently constructed it.

Prayer for today

Dear Jesus, thank you for persevering and not giving up on me. I am so thankful that I am on my way to becoming a house of completion. I realize there are many more finishing touches that are required before I am complete, but I know you will be with me through it all. Help me to be ready and willing to allow you to renovate or remodel as you see fit. Help me to be exactly what you want me to be.

In Jesus's name. Amen

Wednesday

building on the solid rock

But there is going to come a time of testing at the judgment day, to see what kind of work each builder has done. Everyone's work will be put through the fire to see whether or not it keeps its value.

1 Corinthians 3:13

I remember a plaque my family had hanging on the wall when I was a child – it said, "Everything here on earth will pass, everything done for Christ will last."

I heard a speaker once say, "If it doesn't count for eternity, it doesn't count."

When the time of testing comes, I fear there will be many of us who have worked superfluously in this life. We need to evaluate and do what will count for eternity and not what counts for our recognition and satisfaction while we are on earth.

Many times I have feared embarrassment for speaking out for God or even for deciding what is right or wrong. My fears stem from the idea someone may find me intolerant or self-righteous or pious. If my convictions are Bible-based and I speak truth, then my rewards will be eternal. What a glorious ceremony that will be when we receive our rewards from our Heavenly Father.

Start building on the solid Rock today, for everything else will crumble. If our work is built on a foundation of The Rock, our building will endure the tests and fires and still stand. So we need to ensure our efforts are meaningful and built on Jesus Christ and Biblical Principles.

Prayer for today

Heavenly Father, I am so thankful for your guidance in my life. My prayer is that everything I do, will be for you. I need your direction so that my energy can be used for your honour and glory. My desire is to make everything count for eternity and not to be concerned about earthly rewards that won't last. I pray that my desires will be in complete harmony and agreement with your plans and all my efforts will withstand the test of fire and time.

In Jesus's name. Amen.

Thursday

holy temples

Together we are His house built on the foundation of the apostle's and the prophets. And the corner stone is Christ Jesus himself

Ephesians 2:20

We, who belong to the Lord are a privileged people. Paul says we are His temple. He is speaking figuratively but the parallel is clear. When we think how specific and intricate the Holy Temple of God was in the Old Testament, so holy that only the high Priest was allowed inside, it humbles me to think that I can be compared to such a magnificent and Godly structure.

Christ's body is also referred to as a Holy Temple but expounded on as the fulfillment of the typology of the Temple because He is the sacrifice that brought an end to the old covenant.

In the New Testament, we have a new covenant to live by; that of the shed blood of Jesus Christ, the onetime sacrifice that enables us to have a personal relationship with the Saviour.

As we are considered the House of the Lord, we must portray the picture that invites others to taste and accept the invitation to enter this house.

It is our responsibility to mirror the peace, love, and joy that is ours with the acceptance of this new life. Many Christians go about with long faces and a solemn appearance and attitude, which don't attract others to Christianity.

If you are having a hard time displaying the joy that Christ gives, I encourage you to spend time and ask Jesus why you don't have it. It is a free gift that comes with the knowledge of being saved from sin and the indwelling of the Holy Spirit. It is truly a joy being a child of God.

Prayer for today

Lord I am in awe of the tremendous privilege of being a holy temple. Thank you for providing the solid foundation that stands no matter what happens. Thank you for supporting me with the cornerstone that is Christ Jesus, the solid Rock. Help me to be a testimony that attracts others to desire to know you.

In Jesus's name. Amen.

Friday
the body of believers

We, who believe are carefully joined together becoming a holy temple for the Lord.

Ephesians 2:21

As a temple of the Lord, we are joined together to other lovers of God to form one complete Holy temple. This tells us to fellowship with other Christians and together we make the whole.

I am discovering many people are fed up with conventional churches or have been hurt by someone in a church and find themselves without a place of worship to attend.

Friends, we need to be with others who love the Lord to gain strength and be part of a family that will pray for us and support us when we need it. We also need to be informed of who we can pray for and support, just as family members support each other. Without each other, we are incomplete, only a part of what God considers to be His Holy Temple.

Unfortunately, there is no such thing as the perfect church. There are congregations and doctrines that suit us, but because churches are made up of people, we cannot find a perfect one. No matter how hard we try, we cannot be perfected as long as we are in this earthly body.

That is not to dispute that the church will one day be raptured by Christ as perfect and unblemished, which refers to the body of believers. In the meantime we need to accept the inabilities and weaknesses in each other, and come together in His name.

And let us not neglect our meeting together,
as some people do, but encourage and warn each other,
especially now that the day of His coming
back again is drawing near.

Hebrews 11:25

Prayer for today

Heavenly Father, thank you for providing others to fellowship with. I want to join with others in order to make up one Holy Temple for you. Help me to overlook the faults and petty hurts that happen when people work together. Help me not to compromise the truth. I love you Lord, and praise you for all your wonderful provisions and promises.

In Jesus's name. Amen.

Weekend Read

horse sense

Blessed are those who fear to do wrong,
But the stubborn are headed for serious trouble.

Proverbs 28:14

When I was a young teenager, we lived on a farm. We often stabled horses for owners who were away or needed a place for the horse to live for a while.

One winter we pastured a beautiful little pinto. Sirocco was his name, which suited him very well. He was fast, he ran like the wind. He also had an evident stubborn streak in him.

Being responsible for his well being, I got the job of exercising him on a regular basis.

One winter day I was on Sirocco, trotting down a country road. The deep ditches were level with the road, filled with snow. I was very aware how deep they were. As we trotted down the road, Sirocco kept veering towards the ditch.

I kept reining him back onto the road, but the more I reined him left the more determined he was to head for the ditch. After a few tries, out of exasperation, I let him lead and he went straight for the snow bank into the ditch. It was very deep; he panicked and got stuck.

I had to get off, clear the snow, and lead him back onto the road. I'm sure if the owner had been the rider she could have controlled him; on the other hand, his stubborn streak was an issue and needed breaking. He seemed to learn from his experience, because after that he was more obedient and trusted my reining.

I've been there. I usually want to do things my own way. Often I've ended up in the ditch where it was difficult to return to the track that was easy and flat.

Adena H. Paget †

I have needed help to get back on the right track. Each time when I call for the Master, He comes and helps me and I wonder why I am so stubborn. Sirocco didn't realize the consequences and wondered why I would not let him go where he wanted to go but I knew what would happen.

God also sees the big picture and knows what lies before us and beside us. He steers our journey enabling us to stay on the right road and keeps us from veering into the ditch.

When we ask, "Why?" He knows the reason and if we pause for a while, we learn to see it too.

God always knows what we need, when we need it and He makes sure we always receive what is best for us. His timing is perfect. Learn to trust Him.

WEEK 16

Monday

awesome creation

When I look at the night sky and see the work of your fingers, the moon and stars you set in place

Psalm 8:3.

Destiny Bay is a beautiful little resort located on Kooteney Lake, B.C. My husband and I enjoyed a romantic weekend there one summer. We were impressed with the delicious offering of gourmet meals and personal service like hot muffins brought to our rooms each morning and the fireplace prepared in the evening. Two small glasses of sherry as a night-time sleep enhancer and rich and delicious chocolates were left beside our pillows. There were many little treats that we did not ordinarily indulge in, making it a very special weekend. One of our favourite luxuries was the sauna located on the beach so one could sit in the sauna and then run into the lake for a cold dip. It was most refreshing. The evidence of how much thought and effort had been exercised in building this special place amazed us.

One evening, when we walked to the sauna, we beheld a wondrous sight that man could never equal. It was the exhilarating and awesome scene of millions of stars against a clear, dark-blue canopy, lit by a magnificent full moon, reflected in the spectacular calmness of the lake, which was bordered by the silhouette of the evergreen forest and majestic mountains in the background. I thought to myself, "How could anyone doubt the presence of a Creator?"

What an awesome God we serve, Creator of this wonderful world for us to live in and marvel at. I was awe-struck by the majesty of it all and realized that nothing can compare with the wondrous works of our mighty God. No matter what man attempts here on earth, it can never be compared with the richness and glorious creations that are God's.

Prayer for today

You are an awesome God and I thank you for creating such a beautiful world. Help me to be a good and diligent steward of the things around me. Your handiwork is far more glorious than anything man-made and each day I see the evidence of your mighty hand. When I hear the notes of the bird's song or see the leaves turn color with the change of seasons, or behold the majestic mountains and the vivid profusion of the wild flowers all around me, I am in awe. Thank you Heavenly Father for all your goodness.

In Jesus's name. Amen.

Adena H. Paget †

Tuesday

infinite understanding

Don't you know that the Lord is the everlasting God,
the creator of all the earth? He never grows faint or weary.
No one can measure the depths of his understanding

Isaiah 40:28

Young moms always want the best for their children; I was no exception. When they were infants or toddlers, it was easy to make them see my reasoning but when they reached the age of four and older, they developed minds of their own and it became more difficult to persuade them to my way of thinking. Sometimes it involved an extended stay in the bedroom or a little corporal punishment for refusing to listen.

It was important for them to listen and obey, because I knew the consequences of what could happen. Immature decisions of a three-year-old can lead to harmful effects such as touching a hot stove or playing in the toilet. They need to be taught what is safe and what is not. Depending on the personality of the youngster, this can be a very frustrating stage in child rearing. The blessings come later when you realize they actually did absorb some of the instructions and advice you gave them as children.

I liken this illustration to a child of God. In Isaiah it says He never grows weary and He understands why we often make wrong choices. There is nothing that is capable of measuring his understanding.

When I raised my children, I didn't understand why they did so many foolish things. I was often frustrated and weary from repeating myself and constantly teaching, but God never grows weary or faint, He perseveres with us and teaches us over and over again until we understand. We are created with different personalities and it takes some of us longer to learn, but God is patient and ever with us, never abandoning He children. Praise His wonderful name.

Prayer for today

Dear Lord Jesus, Thank you for being patient with me and understanding my foolishness. I have touched the hot stove many times even though I know the danger of it and you continue to have infinite patience again and again. Even though you are the Creator of Heaven and earth, you still care about me. Thank you for investing your time in me.

In Jesus's name. Amen.

Wednesday
Creator

In the beginning God created the Heavens and the earth.

Genesis 1:1

Have you ever been amazed at the intricacy of our world and how it all fits together perfectly? How perfect the links of the food chain, the seasons, flowers and trees and the millions of other plants, human reproduction, the waters of the earth, and on and on. It was created by a designer, who planned everything for our survival and enjoyment. Everything was created in harmony.

The story of creation in Genesis can lead to controversy. Scholars differ over the length of creative days, claiming there is a long gap between Genesis 1:1 and 1:2. Hebrew syntax allows such a view as an exception but not always. The Bible tells us the universe had a beginning and it came into existence through God's will.

Aside from this text, there are many more that prove the account of creationism: Isaiah 40: 51, Hebrews 11:3, the latter part of the book of Job.

Genesis also teaches about numerous kinds of plants and animals, which cannot reproduce in such a way as to evolve from one kind into another.

Many in the past have tried to dispute creation by a Creator, but through their search, have realized the truth of the Biblical creation account. God says if we search for Him, we will be found by Him.

Prayer for today

Heavenly Father, you are the Creator of everything good and lovely and today I want to acknowledge you. I thank you for making our beautiful surroundings. I pray that I may not take all this for granted but give you the honour and glory for all the wonders I enjoy each day. I pray for the courage and wisdom to acknowledge you and the works of your hands before others. I love you, Lord.

In Jesus's name. Amen.

Thursday

unshakable faith

By faith we understand that the entire universe was formed at God's command, that what we now see did not come from anything that can be seen.

Hebrews 11:3

Faith helps us accept the gift of salvation and faith helps us to believe the reality of it. It is by faith we are saved and it is by faith that healing comes and it is by faith that many patriarchs in the Old Testament continued their quests and received God's blessings. Excellent examples are:

- Enoch, who was taken up to Heaven without dying.
- Noah, who built an ark without ever having witnessed rain.
- Abraham, who obeyed God when he was told to leave home and go to another land that God would give him.
- Joseph, who when he was about to die continued to believe and expressed his faith.

Take the time to read the numerous stories in the Bible of these patriarchs who had unshakable faith.

The writer of Hebrews asks us to believe God's command formed the entire universe. When we behold the intricate design, the perfect cycles, the reproductive phenomenon, and millions of unexplainable wonders around us every day, faith grows.

Prayer for today

Oh, Lord, you are God of Heaven and earth. I ask you to increase my faith. Give me the kind of faith that moves mountains, an unshakeable faith that sustains me even when I don't see the evidence of your presence. We see the evil in this world and sometimes it is difficult to know you are in control, and yet I know you are. Help me today to be an example to others and display a strong and real faith that cannot be shaken by doubters.

In Jesus's name. Amen.

Friday

being the favourite

In His goodness He chose to make us His own children by giving us His true word. And we, out of all creation, became His choice possession.

James 1:18

Out of all creation God chose us to be His favourite, His choice possession? Sometimes when I meditate on my Heavenly Father, I am so humbled that He would bless me so abundantly but then I read in His Word He loves me more than all other creation. It is far more than my human mind can conceive and the most marvellous thing of all, I don't even deserve His love or His grace or mercy. I only receive it because He is a giving and forgiving God who chose us out of everything He made, to be His favourite.

If I had to choose anything from creation to favour, I think it would be the little songbirds that I hear in the early mornings. Whether it's cold and rainy or a beautiful sunny day, the birds sing at my window and I wonder at their clear notes and sweet melody.

My roomie and I place hummingbird feeders on our window every winter and the presence of these tiny yet mighty hummers is amazing. The tiny wings flap faster than the naked eye can count. I have read they fly thousands of miles each year. When I look at how they are clothed, more beautiful in vivid color than most other things, this perfect, tiny creation causes me to marvel at the works of the Creator.

Even though there are creatures that amaze us, God chose you and me to be more favoured than these beautiful little creations that hunt for their food and feel the elements of the weather and yet sing praises, to the King of Kings. What a glorious Master we serve.

Prayer for today

Today, Lord, I am in awe again, by your sweet mercy and saving grace and now I see that I am favoured above all other creation. I am humbled by your Word that tells me this and I want to know you more and serve you more than ever before. Help me to be what you want me to be as I grow in you and fully realize your great and wondrous love for me. I love you, Lord.

In Jesus's name. Amen.

A Weekend Read

Is that all there is

A lesson learned

The other day I recognized a familiar song playing on the radio, Peggy Lee singing, "Is That All There Is?" It triggered a memory of a family road trip when our children were young.

Our children were thirteen, twelve, ten, nine and three years old. We had agreed on this vacation on my behalf, to give me an opportunity to return to my birthplace in Northern Saskatchewan, a little corner called Ratner, which was basically just a post office and store. I pride myself on my vivid memories of my childhood. Some would say they are somewhat enhanced, however, they are my memories.

As we drove along the once familiar highways and side roads watching for landmarks, I noticed how dilapidated some of the farmyards and buildings were. Many places that used to seem magnificent to me as a child, now showed signs of neglect and age; some had been abandoned and appeared to be forlorn and sad.

After listening for many years to my childhood stories of beautiful landscapes, country roads, and magnificent farm homes, the expectations were lofty. Our children, instead of being impressed kept repeating the phrase, "Is that all there is?"

I assured them the destination of my childhood home would be worth the effort and patience of driving down dusty roads and getting lost and the continued search would be rewarded by the final view.

After much confusion and several disagreements, we finally arrived at the homestead site, only to find a golden field of waving grain where my beloved farm buildings had once stood.

I remember the huge disappointment I felt as we stood there speechless. My husband and children said, "Is this all there is?"

After allowing myself a few moments of grief, I announced the intent of visiting the hub of the community, the local co-op store where one could buy everything under the sun, which also housed the local post office. I started sharing memories of a special aunt who was fortunate to live across the road from the store.

As we drove down the sandy country trail, I lost myself in memories of years past riding down this very road in a horse and buggy with my grandfather during the long summer days and winters, riding in an enclosed wooden van with slick runners crunching through the snow, pulled by two beautiful black Percherons named Bubbles and Spark.

I recalled simpler times that were filled with warm family sing-a-longs, board games, and other activities that fostered harmony and cherished memories.

Soon our arrival jolted me into reality when on the corner of a cross-road, I beheld

a small grocery store with faded lettering above the door, spelling out the word

CO-OP

I was relieved to see it was still operating, but as we entered, I noticed more changes. The black-oiled floors had been replaced with new black and white floor tiles and the old cash register was now a state-of-the-art computer. Where the cloth bags of flour and sugar had been stacked, there were food freezers and Coke machines. It had a look of an older 7-11 and my family said, "Is this all there is?" I too was asking the same question.

The next stop was my coveted aunt's home, a huge two-story house across the road from the store. When we drove into the yard, I thought we were at the wrong place because the house had diminished in size and the out buildings were badly in need of repair.

I was relieved to discover my aunt at home and I knew she would have delicacies that I had envisioned in my mind and my taste buds.

She was very happy to see us and our family of five children. After a short visit she informed us we were going to my cousin's, her son's, for supper.

My cousin and his family lived on a new farm not far from the old place but unfamiliar to me.

We were served a wonderful, old-fashioned farm dinner and our children had a good time with their second cousins. As for me, I was disappointed that things were not what they used to be and I asked, "Is this all there is?"

As we drove into the town of Nipawin, I waited in anticipation to see the familiar sights of my memories. I quickly realized nothing stays the same in this world.

As we came to rest in front of my old school, even it had been abandoned. The roads were changed and the old bridge across the Saskatchewan River was now a modern, new bridge with a four-lane highway running across the river. The little store where I had walked to purchase Popsicles and candy bars was just a gas station. I questioned, "Is this all there is?"

Finally, after numerous disappointments and defensive comments to my family, it was time for us to return to our campsite. As we drove in quiet reserve, the children napping, I realized the futility of putting one's hope of happiness in memories of the past.

I still have wonderful memories of times spent with my family as a child and of love and acceptance and warmth, but the material memories of those times have changed and become distant and distorted.

I soon realized my happiness was around me and my blessings were numerous at that time, in that place, and in that car with my own family.

I learned to accept my life in the here and now and appreciate and be thankful for the blessings I receive every day

It was a valuable lesson for me not to live in the past but to be thankful for my present life.

I was reminded of the promise, God never changes. He is always the same and no matter how wonderful our memories are, there are greater promises still in store for us as we grow in Him and allow Him to work in us.

I learned to put all my trust in Him who is always with us and never disappoints us. I also learned memories and past activities are not all there is. The reality and joy of living is the assurance of a personal relationship with Jesus, who never changes, never disappoints us, and will never leave us alone.

There is an old hymn I'm reminded of:

Yesterday, Today, Forever, Jesus is the same.
All may change but Jesus never.
Glory to His name. Glory to His name, Glory to His name
All may change but Jesus never, Glory to His name.
Jesus Christ is the same yesterday, today, and forever.

Hebrews 13:8.

I am so thankful this life; what we see now and what we experience is not all there is. There is coming a time of great joy and fulfillment when the wondrous word of God will come to fruition and we shall see Jesus face to face to abide with Him forever more. Praise the wonderful name of Jesus.

WEEK 17

Monday

Father, Son

Christ is the visible image of the invisible God. He existed before God made anything at all and is supreme over all creation.

Colossians 1:15

God knew we, as human beings, were having a difficult time following His decrees and laws, which were rigid and seemingly unforgiving. He made a way for us to simply accept the gift of salvation.

Sometimes I think God wanted to know exactly what He had created, so He decided to come down and live amongst us to experience first hand what it was like to be totally human. But we know why He came and it was much bigger than that.

He came down in the form of a tiny babe, who would one day be the perfect sacrifice for all sinners. His blood, shed on the cross of Calvary became our salvation.

There is much evidence of the life of Jesus Christ, in reputable history accounts as well as in the Word of God, the Bible. His life on earth was filled with rejection and suffering. He experienced earthly emotions and feelings just as we do.

We accept that Jesus dwelt with God before He came to earth and returned to be with His Heavenly Father after He rose from the grave as the first but not the last to be resurrected. That is why we can be assured of being able to follow Him into Glory where we will forever be with Him if we accept Him as our personal Saviour.

Adena H. Paget †

Prayer for today

Precious Jesus, I am so thankful you came to earth to sacrifice yourself on the cross for me. I cannot comprehend how deep and how wide and how high your love is. I only know I am blessed to be your child and you have forgiven me because I asked you to. I can't imagine leaving Heaven to dwell with humans on earth but you did it and it proves your love for us all. I love you, Lord and I ask you to help me draw closer to you. You, who are supreme over all, came down to rescue me from sin.

Thank you, Jesus. Amen.

Tuesday

strength – endurance – joy

We also pray that you will be strengthened with His glorious power so that you will have all the patience and endurance you need. May you be filled with joy.

Colossians 1:11

Some days we wonder if God is hearing our cries of despair and longing. When we've been up most of the night with a sick child and morning brings the list of must do's, or when we have been praying for a loved one who seems to be farther away than ever, we wonder.

I assure you, the good and encouraging news is that God is hearing and He cares.

In this letter Paul wrote to the Corinthians, he continues to assure them of his prayers for patience, strength and endurance. We know these qualities are available to us today.

In my life, I have discovered praying for someone else brings peace to my heart. When I take my mind off myself and start asking God to help someone else, my worries and impatience and sorrow are replaced with patience, endurance, peace, and joy. It draws me closer to Jesus.

Try it today. Even if you are burdened down, give your problems to Jesus and start praying for someone else.

Prayer for today

Dear Jesus, Thank you for your blessings and your holy spirit in my life today. My mind seems to be on my problems today, and I am so thankful you are aware of them. Help me Lord, to release them to you and take my eyes off myself. I know there are so many who are needier than myself and today I want to lift up ___________ to you and pray your special blessing upon them.

I ask you to meet their needs today and fill them with joy and contentment. Thank you for being my Saviour and friend and caring for the ones I love. Help me to love others and reflect your joy and peace.

In Jesus's name. Amen.

Wednesday

growing strong

Let your roots grow down into Him and draw up nourishment from Him, so you will grow in faith, strong and vigorous in the truth you were taught. Let your lives overflow with thanksgiving for all He has done.

Colossians 2:7.

I love spring. I remember the excitement of digging my garden patch, pulling the weeds, creating perfect rows and meticulously dropping in the tiny seeds. Then carefully covering the seeds with the rich soil and attaching the seed package at the end of each row to proudly display what was planted there. Watering the new plants deeply encouraged the roots to descend deeply for a strong plant.

The backbreaking job was keeping the weeds down while the new plants grew. Weeds had to be pulled and hoed because they would quickly choke out the new plant. The most rewarding part was to watch the tiny green chutes springing up as a promise for delicious eating in the fall.

If I scattered the seeds into the dirt at random and just hoped they would grow, I would not be rewarded. Perhaps a few shoots would grow despite my neglect, but certainly not the crop I anticipated by nurturing and caring for my garden.

Paul instructs us to draw nourishment from Christ Jesus by letting our roots go down into Him. If we desire the blessings and closeness of a personal Christ, we need to spend time, nurturing our relationship with Him. There is only one way to do this and that is by reading His Word and talking to Him. Paul tells us to let our lives overflow with thanksgiving for all He has done.

A close relationship requires care. A close relationship with Jesus is no exception and we tend to neglect this relationship more those we share with our earthly friends. Let's encourage our roots to be strong and descend into His Word.

Prayer for today

Dear Lord, Forgive me for neglecting my relationship with you. I need you so desperately all the time, and it seems I am always asking for things or crying to you for an injustice or hurt. Forgive me as I attempt to praise you more, love you more, and offer to be what you want me to be. Help me to be a fountain, overflowing with thanks for all you have done for me.

In Jesus's name. Amen.

Thursday
trusting

Let Heaven fill your thoughts.
Do not think only about things down here on earth.

Colossians 3:2

I often get wrapped up in my troubles and forget to let Heaven fill my mind.

Many times it is difficult for me to trust God and live as though He is truly in control. I often worry about trivial things, things that rarely come to pass.

I forget God is the ultimate one in charge of my life and what He allows is ordained by Him. We know trials happen but we forget they are necessary lessons to enable us to grow and become stronger for a purpose.

If we keep our thoughts on Heavenly things, we do not need to worry about the difficulties we encounter. We know there is evil around us and although we cannot see the purpose of some tragedies, we can rest in the fact that God is always and ultimately in control. Yes; it does require faith but as we know Him more we become stronger in our faith and learn to lean on Him.

Adena H. Paget †

Prayer for today

Dear Father, thank you for being in control of my life and everything around me, even the big tragedies that happen in this world. Forgive me for not recognizing your sovereignty in the midst of terrible events in the world and spending needless energy worrying about things that are out of my control. You are Lord of everything and everything is in your hands. Thank you for being my Saviour too, and even loving me and caring about me in the midst of everything else.

In Jesus's name. Amen

Friday

forgiveness

You must make allowance for each other's faults and forgive the person who offends you. Remember, the Lord forgave you, so you must forgive others.

Colossians 3:13

Does anyone else ever have a critical spirit, like me?

The Bible says to make allowance for the faults of others. Is it possible, we are not perfect ourselves?

We are often critical of others because they don't think the same way we think or because they say or do something that hurts us. We certainly see signs confirming the imperfection of human beings.

I remember being privy to a disagreement that caused a rift so harsh it ended a longtime relationship: a deprivation of a loving relationship that both had enjoyed for years. I know some who have actually ended relationships with grandchildren and children because of what one or the other said many years ago.

It is often because neither party is willing to forgive. With Christian love, given by the Holy Spirit, it becomes easier to ask forgiveness than to carry a grudge that becomes a deep, bitter wound. The Bible says, others will know we are Christians by our love.

A wound caused by human error not only severs a human relationship but drives a wedge between us and our relationship with God, which widens as time lengthens. If there is a problem with forgiveness, ask God to grant the wisdom to move forward in a forgiving and healthy way.

Prayer for today

Dear Jesus, I thank you for forgiving me each time I ask. I need your grace to forgive those who have hurt me. Help me not to harbour ill feelings toward anyone else but to be accepting of those who might see things differently than I do. Help me to know when to make an issue of things and when to allow for differences. With your help I know I can forgive and show grace and mercy to others as you do for me.

In Jesus's name. Amen.

A Weekend Read
forgiveness

Several years ago I became an active participant in a little church I had attended for several years. After leading worship for a few years, I

Adena H. Paget †

accepted the pastoral care position. It was here I learned how to become a better listener.

I had an interesting experience with a mature woman, who often confided in me. As we became better acquainted, I realized she seemed to harbour a bitter spirit towards some of her family members.

She had recently been blessed with a new granddaughter by her son and daughter-in-law, who often accompanied her to church. After the birth of this beautiful gift, a spirit of dissension became evident between mother and daughter-in-law. Her unforgiving attitude towards her daughter-in-law, reminded me of a similar situation.

Several years prior, I had an experience with my own daughter that was nasty and hurtful until we determined to mend the brokenness and get on with life. I have been thankful for our healthy relationship ever since. Because of my personal experience, I thought perhaps I could offer help to mend this woman's relational struggle as well.

As we spoke, she admitted struggling with an issue that had become a mountain in her thoughts. The parents of the new baby required the new grandchild to be baptized with water in their church, and my friend thought it should only be a service of dedication in her church.

She was so distraught by this, she actually rejected the entire experience of seeing her grandchild baptized or dedicated.

I listened and gave sympathy to her concerns, but I could not agree with her actions in the matter. I couldn't believe how anyone could jeopardize the privilege of a loving relationship with family members, especially a new grandchild, by not accepting a differing opinion on such a thing as this.

To me it did not seem terribly important because ultimately, it would have no bearing on the baby's spiritual life, but she could not let it go.

We talked many hours about the dilemma without resolve. I encouraged her to pray about it and seek God's council and she said she would but her spirit seemed rigid.

Soon she stopped speaking to me and finally started attending another church. I felt responsible for her hurt and yet I could not agree with her.

My follow-up indicated that feelings had become irreparably hurt after the baby's service, and my friend's family had become distant to the extent of becoming estranged. This new grandmother had deprived herself of a beautiful experience.

I wonder and pray and hope they were able to mend the relationship at some point. As for me, I learned a valuable lesson through this experience about forgiveness.

> Jesus forgave when asked to do so. His response was always to forgive with instructions to go in peace and sin no more. He dealt with the sin, loved the sinner, and forgave with grace and acceptance.
>
> Never once is it written that He held a grudge against someone. We are aware of the wondrous work of the Holy Spirit when we come for forgiveness to Jesus and when we ask, we find He gives us the ability to truly forgive others and it seems to come from deep within, from the presence of God in our hearts.
>
> The result is a feeling that covers us in a balm of healing and newness. Jesus says we are to forgive seventy times seven, the same person, if they keep asking. It is indeed blessed to forgive and it is blessed, as well, to ask forgiveness of someone else. It is usually a two-way street and we are often expected to make the first move.
>
> Jesus tells us a wonderful story depicting forgiveness in Matthew 18:23-25:
>
> *For this reason, the Kingdom of Heaven can be compared to a king who decided to bring his accounts up to date with servants who had borrowed money from him.*

> *In the process, one of his debtors was brought in who owed him millions of dollars. He could not pay, so the king ordered that he, his wife, his children, and everything he had be sold to pay the debt. But the man fell down before the king and begged him, "Oh, sir, be patient with me, and I will pay it all."*
>
> *Then the king was filled with pity for him, and released him and forgave his debt. But when the man left the king, he went to a fellow servant who owed him a few thousand dollars. He grabbed him by the throat and demanded instant payment. His fellow servant fell down before him and begged for a little more time. "Be patient and I will pay," he pleaded.*
>
> *But his creditor wouldn't wait. He had the man arrested and jailed until the debt could be paid in full. When some of the other servants saw this, they were very upset. They went to the king and told him what had happened. Then the king called in the man he had forgiven and said, "You evil servant. I forgave you that tremendous debt because you pleaded with me. Shouldn't you have mercy on your fellow servant, just as I had mercy on you?"*
>
> *Then the angry king sent the man to prison until he had paid every penny.*
>
> *That's what my Heavenly Father will do to you if you refuse to forgive your brothers and sisters in your heart.*

Jesus promises us forgiveness if we forgive those who need forgiveness. Forgiving certainly seems like the best alternative, doesn't it?

WEEK 18

Monday
just because we love

When you obey me you should say, "We are not worthy of praise. We are servants who have simply done our duty."

Luke 17:10

I have often witnessed parents who reward their children for a good report card or good behaviour. Apparently this motivator works for some children.

I confess, we also tried this method with one or two of our own children and discovered it simply did not work. We realized a child is naturally motivated or not. Some excel in school while putting forth a great deal of effort while others, who may even be more capable, slip through by a narrow margin because of less effort. No matter what the ability, we discovered learning took place in all our children.

When we realized money was not an effective motivator, we simply implied that school was their job and the expectation was to do their best without extrinsic rewards.

I believe this is what we are asked to do for the Lord, not to expect extrinsic rewards because we are, in fact, just fulfilling our duty.

We are expected to carry out God's plan and it is our duty to obey without grumbling or expecting praise.

Today, if you feel the Lord has a job for you to do, do it without expectations of rewards but because it is a requirement and your desire is to please God.

Adena H. Paget †

Prayer for today

Dear Lord, I am so thankful for your faithfulness and never-ending love and it is my desire to please you and serve you. Help me to accept the duties you want me to perform without hesitation and help me Lord not to expect praise or instant rewards but just to serve you because I love you and my desire is to please you.

In Jesus's name. Amen.

Tuesday
living water

For I will give you abundant water to quench your thirst and moisten your parched fields. And I will pour out my spirit and my blessings on your children.

Isaiah 44:3

I knew it had been an exceptionally dry summer in Western Canada but as we headed toward the west coast in our motor home, the scenes were sad and disheartening. Many of the roadside sloughs and wetlands were parched and cracked from lack of water.

I believe God showed me the analogy of the scene, comparing it to the many precious souls who are suffering in the same manner, parched and dying from lack of water. In North America, we do not suffer from lack of earthly water but human souls are craving for spiritual water and God tells us He has an abundant supply if we ask.

If we live as He ordains, He promises we will be like a well-watered garden, an ever-flowing spring (Isaiah 58:11). And this promise is for our children as well.

In the last few years, the world's people have been searching fervently for spiritual fulfillment to fill the empty void in their spirits. As someone who knows the answer, I can say with confidence, only a personal relationship with Jesus Christ can satiate that deep emptiness.

Jesus waits for us to ask Him to fill that desire, He is the one who bridges the gap between us and God.

Prayer for today

Heavenly Father, I thank you for your words of comfort to fill me with spiritual water; your promise to quench my thirst and longing and be filled with total satisfaction and peace that only your presence can provide. Today, I ask you to fill me so full that I'll be bubbling over so others may see the joy and fullness you freely give.

In Jesus's name. Amen.

Wednesday
reach out to Jesus

> *Jesus asked the man to reach out his hand. The man reached out his hand and it became normal again.*
>
> Luke 6:10

This man suffered from a withered hand when he encountered Jesus.

Can you imagine how useless he felt? He probably wasn't able to work to provide for his family. There were possibly many negative repercussions because of his malady. In those days, there were no prostheses or trained medical personnel to perform corrective surgery. We cannot possibly understand how devastating this would be to someone in that day. His only means of support was to be a beggar.

Can you imagine his surge of hope and excitement when he heard of the man, Jesus, who was performing healing miracles? In faith, he hoped that this miracle worker might touch Him.

Jesus simply asked him to reach out his hand and the man was healed, his withered arm was restored because he did what Jesus asked.

Do you feel useless today? Is there an area in your life that needs the miraculous touch of Jesus?

Today Jesus is asking you to reach out your hand. He will heal that affliction, even if it is not visible. Even if it is an inward hurt that might be crippling your ministry or your life. Listen to the Son of God, Jesus Christ who is still saying, "Reach out to me and I will heal you."

Jesus is the same yesterday, today, and forever. His promises and healing power are still here for us to accept.

Prayer for today

Dear Lord, I am so thankful you care about me, even my hurts and pains. I want to reach out to you because I know you will touch me in a new and miraculous way if I reach out. Help me, Lord, to toss away my pride and freely give myself to you including all my sicknesses. I know you can heal physical and emotional pain, and so I trust you Lord, to take it all from me.

In Jesus's name. Amen.

Thursday
moving on

...Stand up, pick up your mat and go home because you are healed.

Luke 5:24

Jesus was being questioned and accused of blaspheming God for forgiving the sins of this man who was crippled. The Pharisees were always looking for an excuse to kill Jesus. They were afraid people would follow Jesus and they would lose their power over them.

This man was brought to Jesus for healing. First Jesus forgave his sins and then He healed his affliction. Is it a prerequisite to have our sins forgiven before healing can take place? Maybe not, but if we are full of sin, it stands to reason, we would also be riddled with guilt. Sin and guilt go hand in hand.

I believe it is easier to accept healing if our hearts are clean, whether it be for a physical or emotional ailment. When we are full of sin we feel ashamed and unworthy to accept the gift of healing and when our conscience is free, our self-concept is more apt to receive gifts.

Often just the act of asking forgiveness is a healing balm and brings relief to heaviness and physical ailments. I wonder if the mat is a metaphor for the burdens the man was weighed down with or for the unforgiven sins that plagued him? Jesus simply said, "*Take your mat and go home.*"

If you are burdened down with past sins and are being weighed down by a heavy conscience, Jesus is saying to you, "Take your mat and go home." If you have asked forgiveness, don't continue to lie on your mat of sorrows. This man immediately jumped up, picked up his mat and went home praising God.

Adena H. Paget †

It is important to accept forgiveness and move on, be thankful, and praise the Lord in order to find total freedom from the chains of affliction.

Prayer for today

Precious Jesus, I come before you asking forgiveness for suppressing things I need to face and deal with. Thank you for loving me and waiting for me to see things I need to confess. Help me to pick up my mat of pity and self-indulgence and find my way home to you.

In Jesus's name. Amen.

Friday
Jesus never changes

The lepers' cry was, "Lord, if you want to, you can make me well again."

Luke 5:12-15

Lepers were outcasts, they were forced to walk through the streets shouting, "Unclean, unclean," so people could distance themselves from them. Imagine the devastation and isolation a leper experienced; totally ostracized from family and friends.

It stands to reason why this person approached Jesus with the words, "If you want to."

But Jesus had compassion and answered, "I want to." and the man was healed.

Jesus is still the same. It pleasures Jesus to heal us and bless us. If we ask in faith and are willing and open to accept His touch, we can be healed. He is able to heal us from physical sickness and emotional sickness.

"At the touch of Jesus, blinded eyes shall see,
Broken hearts are mended, spirits are set free.
When He speaks the mountains move at His command,
At the touch of Jesus, ruined lives can stand."

Prayer for today

Dear Jesus, you are beautiful beyond description, too marvellous for words and I am so thankful you are still the same today as you were when you walked this earth. You care about our afflictions and our ailments and you wait for us to accept your healing touch. Our ideas may differ from what you desire of us and I know that you know what is best for me, always. I am thankful you want to heal me. Lord help me to be willing to allow you to work in me and heal me from anything that might hinder my relationship with you.

In Jesus's name. Amen.

A weekend Read

loss and comfort

Our wishes may differ from God's plan

I was eight years old when I realized the truth about my mother's illness. She had been sick for many weeks, but I was never really informed of the severity of her illness.

I was in second grade, when my mom and dad picked me up after school one memorable day. We did not drive to our home, we proceeded to the doctor's office.

I patiently sat in the waiting room until my mom returned; she was very distraught and on the verge of tears. When we were back in the car, she spoke in hushed tones as she relayed the terrible news to my dad. She had breast cancer. This was in the early 'fifties and treatment for cancer was almost non-existent.

My childhood faith was not shaken. I had been taught that Jesus was the healer and if we came to Him in faith, He would heal. My parents also believed this and we started to pray.

In the next few agonizing years, her situation became more severe and she was in constant, excruciating pain.

We attended different evangelistic healing meetings, sometimes driving all night to a different city because we'd heard of a healing minister in that place. Although we thought we were doing everything we could, my mom was not improving. My parents fasted and spent hours in prayer and we often had all- night prayer vigils in our home.

After three years of suffering, finally my mother agreed to go into the hospital for a radical mastectomy. By this time, the cancer had spread to other parts of her body and there was little hope for her recovery.

I remember awakening in the night to hear her moaning and crying for release from the terrible nightmare she was in. After suffering for an unbearably long time, she finally allowed herself to drift into a coma that helped her deal with the pain.

One night, my dad called a doctor who administered medication to ease her suffering. Several hours after the doctor left, I heard my dad quietly enter the bedroom where my sister and I slept. His news was sad but also a relief. Our mom had passed on to be with Jesus.

I vividly remember not knowing how to deal with this loss, and so, instead of a reply, I refused to acknowledge the situation and feigned sleep. I fought with the dilemma of what my reaction should be.

In a way I was rejoicing for her because I knew she would be rid of her pain forever and, in fact, never have pain again. I knew she was in Heaven with her dad and those who had gone before. I also knew I would never be able to replace her.

It was the day before my eleventh birthday and I knew I was too young to be without a mother.

Somehow, even at this young age, God sent comfort and helped me through the entire ordeal with this devastating loss and the meaningful but emotional sympathies of my classmates and relatives and family.

It was an early lesson for me that taught me God is Sovereign and we cannot make Him do what we want Him to.

Even though Jesus is the same yesterday, today, and forever, it is not always his will to heal or to fix things as we see fit. I learned it is not a reflection of what we have done or lack of faith not to have our prayers answered as we see fit.

We do not always understand the reasons for the way things happen but we have the assurance that He is in control and He will help us through all the trials and tribulations that come into our lives.

The Lord has always provided Christian mentors in my life and I have learned to fully trust Him no matter what.

I also acquired a new family less than a year later and experienced much joy and many great experiences.

Adena H. Paget

†

WEEK 19

Monday

being rich

I advise you to buy gold from me – gold that has been purified by fire. Then you will be rich.

Revelation 3:18

Are we relying on the world for riches?

Riches mean different things to different people. To some it might be money, to others, children that excel, and to others large houses and land. According to this scripture, to be truly rich is more than earthly riches.

How then is this richness achieved? Jesus Christ went through the fire, not to be purified because He already was perfect and pure. Why, then did He have to suffer? Because He took my sins and your sins and, in fact, the sins of the whole world upon Himself so that we would not have to sacrifice animals or shed blood in order to buy redemption. Jesus did it all.

That is not to say we don't need the experience of going through the fire. We will likely suffer many fires but not for the sake of redemption and justification.

We need the fires to learn and mature, in order to be able to help someone else.

God's Son is the pure one and has suffered the "fire" for you and me. It is that gold we need to embrace and rely on for our riches, which are yet to come. If we have the Holy Spirit, we are rich already – far richer than the riches this world has to offer, and the promise of one day being with the Lord, is the greatest wealth we can ever hope for.

Prayer for today

Dear Lord, I thank you today for paying the ultimate price for my salvation. You are the gold that has been purified and you provide it to me, freely. While I wait for your return, you give me peace and comfort in the midst of life's storms. Thank you for providing me with the presence of the Holy Spirit that fills me with love, joy, and hope for the future. Help me to give you all the honour and glory because you are God.

In Jesus's name. Amen.

Tuesday

free salvation

...and also buy white garments so you will not be shamed by your nakedness...

Revelation 3:18b

The garments mentioned in today's scripture signify purity, which God sees in us when we ask forgiveness from His Son, Jesus Christ.

Our sins are buried so deep that God does not see them anymore. When we communicate (pray) to God, He sees us as perfect in white garments. We cannot do anything to earn these white robes – they are provided when Jesus becomes our personal Saviour.

Many people I know are trying to be good enough to earn a place in Heaven, but in ourselves we can never accomplish enough "goodness" to be worthy of Heaven. Often there is no joy in performing good deeds, but the goal keeps us doing it.

How sad that we wear ourselves out trying to accomplish earthly perfection when it is impossible. Even though perfection is required to enter into the Heavenly realm, the only way to accomplish this is to accept the free gift of salvation.

Acceptance is simple; ask Jesus to forgive you and come into your life and live in you. As you do this, the Holy Spirit enters your spirit and dwells in you thereby enabling you to live by the faith that is given and, in God's sight, we become perfect, clothed in pure-white garments that hide our nakedness or impurity and enable us to enter into the Holy Kingdom.

Prayer for today

Father God, how I thank you today for making it so easy to be welcomed into your Kingdom. You have enabled me to become perfect in your sight. I am so thankful I don't need to earn my way into Heaven but you have made it possible for me to accept your free gift of salvation by simply acknowledging Jesus is Lord, and through this action my sins are forgiven and you see me as perfect in your sight. Help my unbelief and increase my faith.

In Jesus's name. Amen.

Wednesday

clearly seeing

...and buy ointment for your eyes so you will be able to see.

Revelation 3:18C

The unconditional love that Christ gives enables us to see with love.

It is only the ointment that Christ gives that can dim the hurts we have experienced and help us to forgive those who inflicted us. With Christ we are able to forgive, to see the good things and to forget the negative.

Many things I used to think were important have decreased to small annoyances or changed into insignificant issues. I often fought petty battles and won, only to discover I'd actually lost the ones that mattered. My energy was wasted.

It is an awesome thing to realize many things don't really matter in the big picture of life. Mountains turn into anthills when we weigh them against important issues.

When we come to rely on the Holy Spirit to lead us and truly let Him have control, we can relax and start to enjoy our earthly life.

I learned to carefully examine and pray about the things that used to drive me around the bend and began to see them for what they really were – trivial annoyances.

It was a successful and relaxing day when I let go of the drama and faced the real world.

Prayer for today:

Father God, thank you for placing your ointment on my eyes and leading me to see more clearly. Forgive me for creating a fuss over the little things in life. Often I build things up in my mind and create mountains out of anthills. Help me to keep uncertainty in perspective and allow the things that don't really matter to pass without creating a situation that may cause dissension.

In Jesus's name. Amen.

Thursday

gossip and apathy

I am the one who corrects and disciplines everyone I love. Be diligent and turn from your indifference.

Revelation 3:19

The Lord says He is the one who will correct and discipline. When we take it upon ourselves to correct someone, we are saying that God is not capable of tackling this problem and we will do it for Him.

When I look back at some of the blunders I made in these areas, I feel petty and ashamed for my behaviour. I know the answer is always in prayer and giving the situation to the Lord instead of tackling it myself.

In today's scripture, The Holy Spirit, through John, the writer, is addressing the Church of Laodicea, which had become apathetic in the ways of God. Although this scripture was written many years ago, I fear our culture is falling into the same abyss. We have become indifferent to the ways of the Lord.

Very often, I find myself in silence when I should speak and defend my faith. I often accept language that used to offend my ears. Our television sets and movies are numbing our ears to cuss words and gutter language unacceptable just a few years ago.

The same attitude holds true in our laws, which are moving towards more tolerance and loose morality and coming against biblical principles. I feel we need to pray against a spirit of indifference and apathy in this area.

In North America, we are often afraid to say anything against the worldly ways as long as they do not affect us directly. I fear the effects will be evident in our offspring and our grandchildren.

Prayer for today

Dear Lord Jesus, thank you for the wisdom in your Word. Forgive me for speaking ill of others for my own edification. Help me to know when I should speak and when I should be silent. Help me, also, not to become apathetic when I may be compromising my convictions or your holy precepts. Grant me wisdom in these areas, Lord, and make me what you want me to be.

In Jesus's name. Amen.

Friday
an invitation

> *Look. Here I stand at the door and knock. If you hear me calling and open the door, I will come in and we will share a meal as friends.*
>
> Revelation 3:20

Why would Jesus stand at the door and knock? He is surely capable of entering wherever and whenever He wants? I am reminded of something a special lady told me about Jesus. He stands at the door and knocks because He is a gentle man and never forces himself upon anyone or intrudes in anyone's life unless He is invited.

When our children left home to set up housekeeping, I remember asking for their house keys. They were somewhat surprised but we explained to them, while they would always be welcome at home, we would expect when they came to visit, they would ring the doorbell and be invited to come in. By the same token, I would never walk into their homes without knocking or being invited.

Isn't it comforting to know that Jesus has the same respect? He never barges in, He waits to be invited. If you have felt Him tug at your heart, invite Him to come in so you can enjoy the fellowship that is available by knowing Him. To experience a close and intimate fellowship with someone who will stick closer to you than a brother, the Lord Jesus Christ, is the ultimate joy.

Prayer for today:

Dear Lord Jesus, thank you for loving me enough to wait for me to invite you into my life. My relationship with you is the most important thing, and I know you will never let me go. Create in me a clean heart and renew a right spirit within me so you will always know you are welcome in my heart and in my life.

In Jesus's name. Amen.

A Weekend Read

only a homeless man

A fictional story

There was a chill in the air and sheltered places to sleep were scarce.

He had managed some hot food at the shelter, but there were no beds left so he wandered aimlessly until it became too dark to search any longer.

He remembered a place under an overpass where pipes ran over land. There was warmth and he recalled leaving a good piece of cardboard with some old coats there several nights ago. He made his way to familiarity.

As he lay down on his makeshift bed, it wasn't long before he craved sleep. Perhaps a time of pleasant dreams when things were different would bring comfort and much needed sleep.

He wasn't sure why he was even still alive. What gave him this undisputed will to go on – to hold on to the sanctity of life? It seemed as if ending it all would be the reasonable answer. Who would care? Who would miss him?

His thoughts continued to return to another time…

The party was jumping, the booze tasted sweet, and the women were voluptuous. The evening was young and he was in celebration mode.

The career had fallen into his lap and he was a success. He knew he was climbing the corporate ladder, soon to be one of the top execs in the company.

Sure, there were a few things that bothered him but he was learning to ignore them and keep looking ahead to larger payouts.

His mind had diminished the nagging conscience that used to hound him and get in the way of his success. He learned to avert his thoughts and eyes and dwell on other aspects of the operation, telling himself that everything was fine.

As he continued to climb, the company flourished and his lifestyle became a succession of parties, women, booze, and drugs…

It was times like this when he allowed his thoughts to wander, to remember the good times – he thought it kept him sane.

He experienced recurring memories of one special woman who was different than the other party girls. Jenine was her name. Funny how he could always recall her name. He couldn't put his finger on it but there definitely had been something about her… something that brought him comfort in his despair.

"Why" he wondered?

His thoughts drifted to the horrible court scene where he was charged with embezzlement and he vividly remembered the eighteen-month jail sentence.

Most people thought that after eighteen months behind bars, a person would learn and be able to recover, but it wasn't that way with him. The only job he could find was washing dishes in a greasy-spoon cafe.

He remembered thinking he was too good for this kind of employment and refused to do it any longer. It was the beginning of the spiral that led him to where he was today.

His only companions were his thoughts and memories.

Each day was lonely but the nights were indescribable. How could he have let this happen? The unfortunate thing was, he knew exactly why things were as they were. He relived it every day.

He seldom allowed himself to remember further back, to when he was a child.

His boyhood had been happy. That word was certainly foreign to him now, but he had been happy when he was at home with his family. He had been loved but their rules and regulations were beyond following and they left little room for independence and creativity.

When he was offered the job before he'd graduated from college, he knew he had to accept it. He also knew his father was relying on him to carry on the family business; but surely they did not expect him to refuse this offer.

He had a quick mind and this offer would allow him to use it. Besides, the salary, a new car, and an unlimited expense account were nothing to scoff at.

The position had been described as a business offer that could lead to a partnership in a short time with a new and vibrant company. It involved shuffling papers and moving huge amounts of money from one account to another, often from one country to another.

As time progressed, he became proficient at what he was expected to do and advanced into a respected member of the company. What did his parents know about big business anyway?

And so he threw himself into his new career and forgot about his parents. It had been years since he had seen them or even bothered to visit. He was absolutely finished with the family rules and their beliefs, which had come from that intolerant church they were attending. And what about this God that his parents worshipped anyway? Where was he now?

He awoke with his head throbbing and the never ending drumming of incessant rain pounding on the surrounding concrete. His "bedroom" was being invaded by rivulets of water soaking into his "bed linen."

He soon realized his state of weakness from hunger, cold, and neglect to his physical being, was overtaking his body. As he slowly managed to lift himself from his despair, he began his ritual search for a morsel of sustenance to help him face another day of meagre existence.

He forced himself to stagger up the steep embankment to the street, where he could make out the forms of others who were slowly making their way to the shelter as well. He approached the mission and heard beautiful music and singing that seemed trancelike and didn't belong here in this area.

The call of the melodious notes beckoned him until he was standing inside the little mission, which he had so often ignored. The singing was coming to a close and he felt like he should move on, but just then he overheard the introduction of a woman called Jenine.

A strange sensation welled up inside him as he realized this was the Jenine of his past. His thoughts ran rampant – the last thing he wanted was for her to recognize him. He felt like he should run but his feet seemed to be nailed to the floor and it was impossible for him to move.

As she started to speak, it was as if she was directly speaking to him. The words were only for him, and they were not words of condemnation but comforting, forgiving, invitations of love from God himself.

He heard the love story of how Jesus came and sacrificed his life so that everyone could be forgiven and have eternal life and a relationship with Jesus himself. He remembered hearing similar messages like this before, but it had never been for him. Never like today by this woman from his past.

He felt an urgency to ask for forgiveness; to approach the altar and kneel. He tried to ignore this urgency but it was as if open arms were calling to him. It was difficult to wait until she finished speaking before he ran up the aisle. The most important thing was to be forgiven by this Jesus. She had said He was willing to forgive no matter what one had done.

The tears were streaming down his face, tears he had not allowed himself to shed for years. They came as a flood and he remembered begging to be forgiven. After that came the calmness and peace that defied understanding. It seemed he only had to lie there and accept this love surrounding him. Soon the angelic voices began to sing once more and the next few hours were a blur but he knew he would never be the same again.

Jenine came to him and related how she had been praying for him for several years. It seemed she had spent time on probation after the company dissolved. During this time she became a believer and spent her spare time giving her testimony to whoever would listen.

After spending time with the people at the mission, he found himself thirsting for more of Jesus. It seemed he could not get enough of him. He knew his sins were forgiven and the burdens of the past were gone.

After several weeks, he and Jenine became more than friends, and he knew that this was not coincidence.

One day, he felt compelled to look up his family. Jenine was by his side when an ageing white-haired man opened the door. There was no hesitation, the physical outstretched arms of love were once again around him and he knew he was exactly where he should be.

His father's reaction was a familiar phrase, " My son, who was dead is alive again."

WEEK 20

Monday

waiting....

Wait on the Lord, be of good courage,
And He shall strengthen your heart;
Wait, I say, on the Lord.

Psalm 27:14

"Oh Lord, How long?" Have you ever asked this question? Have you prayed for something or someone forever, and it seems as if God is deaf to your particular request?

Perhaps it is an intercessory prayer for healing for someone, perhaps it is an unsaved loved one, or maybe a financial burden.

We all have unanswered prayers and I know how difficult the waiting period is.

It is during the waiting time, I have learned valuable lessons. If our prayers were always answered immediately, what would we learn?

We need to wait on the Lord and realize His perfect will is accomplished in His time. In the meantime, He is using the waiting time to teach us.

Adena H. Paget †

Our question should be, "What can I learn while I am waiting?"

Prayer for today

Oh Lord, help my unbelief and forgive my impatience. Help me to trust you and rely on your timing and your answer. I want to be on your timetable and not on my own, because I know you know what is best for me. Help me to wait on you and for you and rest in the knowledge that you are in control and you can see the "big" picture while I only see a small section. I know you are trying to teach me and I pray that you would help me be a willing learner.

In Jesus's name. Amen.

Tuesday

understanding

And we know that all things work together for good to them that love God, and to those who are called according to His purpose.

Romans 8:28

Have you ever felt overwhelmed by an unexpected malfunction in your life? It might be an illness, a death of a loved one, a wayward child, or something else that causes us to stop dead in our tracks.

Many times the situation does not make sense to us and we wonder why God would allow a calamity like this. In this last statement, lies the answer; "God allows it," and if God is in control and allows this to happen, then we can have the assurance that no matter what happens, all is well.

When I look back at some of the tragedies in my life, I always see God's purpose. While I am in the midst of the calamity, though, it is difficult to understand or comprehend.

In the lives of Job and Joseph in the Old Testament, are two vivid pictures of overwhelming tragedies. Job was a very rich man who lost everything, including his children, and Joseph was wrongly accused of a crime and held captive. They must have wondered where God was when life became unbearable during their ordeals. We know God had a purpose because we are privy to the end of the story.

If God had Job and Joseph in his almighty hand, He will do the same for us today. He is an unchanging God, the same yesterday, today, and forever. He always knows exactly what is happening in our lives and is with us even when we can't see Him.

Prayer for today:

Dear Lord, I know you are in control and I know that you know what is best for me. I am asking you to keep me in perfect peace and to help me keep my mind on you. I want to trust you for everything in my life and surrender my will to you because you say that all things work together for good to those who love you. Lord, I want to love you more, I want to serve you more, and I want to praise you more. Take my life and let it be consecrated, Lord, to thee.

In Jesus's name. Amen.

Wednesday

is God sovereign?

Let the Heavens be glad, and the earth rejoice.
Tell all the nations, "The Lord reigns."

1 Chronicles 5:18

Man has been discussing the sovereignty of God and how it applies to us, for thousands of years. If we believe God is sovereign, meaning in control of all things, we have nothing to ever worry about.

We know God loves us. Believing this, we need to accept the idea true love allows for freedom of choice. This is where the dilemma often starts.

I have a friend who likens God's sovereignty to a classroom and teacher. As a teacher, there are times when the classroom can become chaotic. Everyone seems to be louder than usual and out of their desks and as you look around, you see the confusion and turmoil and chaos, but you know you have the ability to bring it under control. You glance around and see that everyone is safe and there is no danger of anyone getting seriously hurt.

I have allowed my students to become somewhat unruly and found it gave me a good insight to their personalities. It was beneficial for me to be an observer.

I think this is a particularly good illustration because it brings to light that we are not puppets controlled by a Master Puppeteer. We have free will to act on our own until, in wisdom, God intervenes and urges us to move away from harm.

We are just like the children in the classroom who have the choice to listen to the voice of the teacher or to continue to be rebellious and boisterous and disregard the warnings and instruction of the teacher.

Prayer for today

Oh Lord, help me today to be silent enough to hear your voice. I am thankful for all that you have done for me and for watching over me. Thank you for loving me enough to allow me to make wrong decisions from time to time but thank you even more for letting me know when it's time to let you guide me in my decision making. I can only see a small portion of my life but I know you can see the whole picture so help me to be thankful, always and rely on you in every circumstance.

In Jesus's name. Amen.

Thursday

safe journey

The Sovereign Lord is my strength. He will make me as sure-footed as a deer and bring me safely over the mountains.

Habakkuk 3:19

There are times when we stray from the perfect will of the Father. Those are the vulnerable times when we think we know where we're going, and then we stumble.

I liken it to hiking up a mountain on a trail that is not well marked. I have a friend who climbed Fisher Peak in southern British Columbia. Two male friends whose legs were much longer than hers accompanied her. Their stride was wider and this made it possible for them to climb up footholds that were far apart, whereas she could not reach some of the steps they used.

She relates the climb as being difficult and scary until she decided to follow the safer, less treacherous trail. It was longer and had loose shale, but these obstacles were easier for her to manoeuvre than the steep and wide short cut she had been led on previously.

When she returned to the path that was right for her, the climb became easier and less frightening.

I believe this is what happens when we stray away from the path that God has prepared for us. When we are close to the Lord, the Holy Spirit guides us and makes us as sure-footed as a deer on a mountain trail. Our feet will not slip and we will safely make the climb to our destination. God is our strength and helps us complete the journey.

Prayer for today

Thank you, Lord for guiding my steps. Keep me close to you so I always know exactly where you want me to step. Help me not to wander off the trail you planned for me. With you as my guide, I know I can climb any mountain that might be in my way. Thank you for loving me enough to bring me safely over.

In Jesus's name. Amen.

Friday

sceptical

Then the Jews complained about Him, because He said, "I am the bread which came down from Heaven." And they said, "Is not this Jesus, the son of Joseph, whose father and mother we know? How is it then that He says, "I have come down from Heaven?"

John 6:41

We have an advantage over the people who lived when Jesus walked the earth, we are able to see the whole story.

I understand why the Jews in Jesus's day were sceptical and how difficult it must have been for them to accept this man, Jesus, as God.

I often wonder if I could have believed that Jesus was the Messiah if I had lived during that time.

For us, there is no excuse not to believe. We have the inspired Word of God, the Bible, where history is recorded from the beginning to the end of the earthly coming and ministry of Jesus.

The Prophets in the Old Testament all point to the coming of Messiah and the New Testament records the fulfillment of the coming. When we realize the wonder and truth of it all we can, with assurance, accept that Jesus is the, I Am, Very God, Messiah, Saviour and King. They only saw a small portion of the big picture and had blind minds to the fulfillment of the Prophets they worshipped.

Still today, we see only a small fragment of what Christ sees, but we have an advantage, we have the Bible and we know how the wonderful story ends.

I am thankful He orchestrates our lives when we walk in the footsteps He prepares for us. Trust Him to know what is best for you today.

Prayer for today

Heavenly Father, thank you for the revelation of your purpose on earth. Help me to understand you more fully and to see more of your power.

In Jesus's name. Amen.

A Weekend Read

a personal dream

I dreamt I was walking through a very long tunnel.

It was a pleasant experience with many windows along the way letting in a goodly amount of light. The light continuously illuminated a portion of the road ahead.

It was the light at the end that I was striving for, the ultimate daylight that warms and shines bright in full splendour. I could imagine the scene in the distance and I knew one day I would see it.

Every so often I came to a turn and thought I could almost see the brightness of the end of the tunnel, but it didn't seem to be time yet. I knew I was in this situation because of the choices I'd made.

I experienced many advantages here. I was safe from harm because nothing could discourage me from the assurance of knowing one day the light would illuminate around me perfectly.

I knew which direction to travel, one of two; forward or backward. I had no desire to go back, which left a clear direction to travel – forward.

I was also aware of a close commandant who was near to support me and keep me from becoming lonely. He appeared as though he didn't want this experience to end. He was very happy and content where we were and it was as if there was a fear of the unknown.

I remember thinking,

> *There are many people who just want to remain in their present situation because they know how to behave and what to expect. They enjoy the familiarity of each day and week and year. They are not sure what might be expected of them in a new situation and so they prefer to stay where they are.*

Perhaps it is fear of the unknown or being unsure of what others may think if there is a change in attitude or lifestyle.

As I moved along, I waited in anticipation of the moment when we would reach the light.

Until then, I remained beside the partner that my Master blessed me with.

He shared my intimate moments, my emotions, my hurts and my elation. I knew we would be together until the day when we both came to the end of the journey, when we would both share the glory of the true light together. I refrained from urging him to hurry, for fear it would lead to injury and hinder our progress.

As we walked on, I found myself enjoying his company and sensing that I was exactly where I should be.

Although my goal was to reach the end, I knew we would reach it together. In order to do that, I knew I must continue to move at the exact right speed, not so slow I lagged behind, not too fast, in case left him behind, but right beside him each step of the way. That way we could help each other if one should stumble.

I also knew our Guide, sent by the Master, was not far away and would not allow anything to happen that might hinder reaching the ultimate goal.

I strain to reach the end of the race and receive the prize for which God, through Jesus Christ, is calling us to Heaven.

Phil.3: 14

WEEK 21

Monday

the temple

> *Now seek the Lord your God with all your heart. Build the sanctuary of the Lord God so that you can bring the Ark of the Lord's Covenant and the holy vessels of God into the Temple built to honour the Lord's name.*
>
> Chronicles 22:19

In the Old Testament, the Jerusalem temple contained no idols, only a box called the Ark, containing the two tablets of the law with the symbolic worshipping cherubim above, and specific vessels used in the ritual worship. It was known for the lavish beauty rather than the size and had been built to exact specifications. The purpose of the Temple was to house the Ark of the Covenant and as a Holy place of worship.

The central place of the temple in the religious life of ancient Israel is reflected throughout the Bible. Only the high priests were allowed to enter the inner court of the temple, called the Holy of Holies. Ordinary people were never allowed to enter into this area. A curtain divided the temple into two distinctive areas.

In 587 BC, the temple was destroyed by the Babylonians and rebuilt by Herod later as a much bigger structure in 37- 4 BC.

When Jesus was crucified, the curtain that divided the temple was rent in two, symbolizing the destruction of the division between the Jewish Priests and Christians. The sacrifice of Jesus on the cross destroyed the division and now everyone was welcome to come into the Holy of Holies. This event opened the possibility for everyone to have a relationship with God and enter into His presence. The temple was burned when Jerusalem fell to the Roman armies in August AD 70. In the New Testament, the word temple is used figuratively in a number of ways, which we will read about further as this week progresses.

Prayer for today

Dear Lord, Help me to understand your Word and the importance of the symbols used to convey the message of hope and promise. As I learn to use and respect my body as your Holy Temple, may you become the focus of my life so that your love may be seen in me. I realize you, oh Lord, are the giver of wisdom and understanding and I pray that your covenant will be evident in my life as I strive to live for you.

In Jesus's name. Amen

Tuesday

we are a temple

God will bring ruin upon anyone who ruins this temple.
For God's temple is holy and you Christians are that temple.

1 Corinthians 3:17

Here the Bible says, as Christians we are a holy temple, to be used by God.

When we accept Christ into our lives and allow the presence of the Holy Spirit to fill us, we become a Holy Temple.

If we choose to let sin into our lives and continue to do this, we will bring ruin into this holy temple. We have a responsibility to keep our temple holy and acceptable to God.

Adena H. Paget †

If anyone else contaminates the holy temple that person is responsible for his or her actions.

If we hinder anyone from entering into the presence of God, it is like bringing ruin to God's temple.

Prayer for today:

Oh, Lord, today I praise you and thank you for allowing me to be considered as your Holy Temple. Help me not to neglect my Christian duty as a chosen person in your courts. I am so thankful you considered me to be a vessel for you to show your love and compassion and hope to those who have lost hope. Help me to be an encourager to those you put in my path.

In Jesus's name. Amen.

Wednesday

honouring God

Don't you know that your body is the temple of the Holy Spirit,
who lives in you and was given to you by God?
You do not belong to yourself for God bought you with a
high price.So you must honour God with your body.

1 Corinthians 6:19-20

As Christians, we are the temple of the Holy Spirit, given to us by God.

Even though salvation is free, it was bought and paid for with the highest price imaginable, a perfect sacrifice of God's only son, Jesus Christ, who was given (not taken) for our sins so that we might have the benefit of His precious gift. Having been bought with the highest price, we belong to God.

I remember purchasing a loaded SUV with all the bells and whistles imaginable. We needed reliable transportation to make trips across wintery mountainous roads and it was advertised to fill our expectations. We were very satisfied with the performance it offered and did not object to the high price tag because of its performance. We appreciated and liked this vehicle a lot. We kept it clean and polished it diligently. The leather upholstery received the best and most expensive leather treatments. We owned it for three years and when we sold it, the newness had been maintained and we were able to sell it for a good price. It was a pleasure to drive and many people commented on the quality and looks.

I like to use this as an illustration of how important our bodies should be as vessels of God. We are tri-dimensional, consisting of physical, spiritual, and intellectual beings. As such, we need to make sure we minister to all three dimensions. I usually find myself being more diligent in two of the three of these parts. It's usually a different dimension at one time, which is a good thing, I think. Our bodies belong to God, so we need an awareness of all three parts and must strive to be good stewards of our whole body.

Prayer for today

Heavenly Father, Creator of all things, I am so thankful you created me and as your creation, I want to be all that I can be, fully alive. Help me to fulfill my duty as your child and creation by taking responsibility for my whole self. I need to care for my whole body, physically, spiritually and intellectually. Help me to fill this responsibility.

In Jesus's name. Amen.

Thursday

being a team member

Don't you realize that all of you together are the temple of God and that the Spirit of God lives in you?

1 Corinthians 3:16

We who believe are carefully joined together, becoming a holy temple for the Lord.

Ephesians 2:21

Here the term temple is used symbolically as a group of Christians coming together.

Paul says we all need to do our part as being one of the group. Working together, we can be used for God's glory.

Whether we are called a holy temple as an individual or as part of a group, we still have the awesome privilege of carrying out the responsibility of being a part of God's plan of creation.

I have noticed in any organization, there are usually a handful of people doing all the work. This is not the way God planned it.

Are we, as part of the family of God, taking our responsibility seriously enough for God to use us to our fullest potential? Are we willing and available to be used in the group or living for ourselves?

Prayer for today

Heavenly Father, I am so thankful you care about your Church. As part of your plan, help me to be available and willing to be used by you. Help me not to shirk my duty to you or cower in the corner when I am asked to do something. As part of your family, let me be all that I can be and willing to do whatever you have for me. Help me not to overdo things as well but to know exactly what your will for my life is. I want to give you the honour and the glory for everything and not be puffed up or egotistical with your gifts.

In Jesus's name. Amen.

Friday

cornerstone

Come to Christ, who is the cornerstone of God's Temple…

1 Peter 2:4

In order for a structure to withstand calamity, like storms, weaponry, erosion, or other attacks, it must have a solid and invincible cornerstone. Even if the walls and roof are solidly constructed, a building is only as good as its cornerstone or foundation.

With Christ as our cornerstone, we can withstand physical, emotional, or spiritual threats. Whether we work individually or as a group, we can combat any storms or weapons or anything else that may work to hinder our Christian testimony and our walk with the Lord.

If we truly learn to rely on Christ, the Solid Rock, our convictions for truth will not be compromised by lies or deceit. In order to grow closer to God, we need to admit that we are sinners, to commit our lives to Him and then learn to rely on Him to lead us and guide us in His ways.

Prayer for Today

Heavenly Father, I am so thankful you are the cornerstone on which I can plant my feet and my life. I never need to worry about you changing for you are an unchanging God and I never have to worry about abandonment for your Word tells me, "I will never leave you or forsake you." I love you, Lord, and ask you to help my unbelief and increase my faith.

In Jesus's name. Amen.

Weekend Read

the four mitts

A Christ-centered lesson – in four stages

1. Admit – admit that you are a sinner.

> For all have sinned: all fall short of God's glorious standard.
>
> Romans 3:23

We are all sinners and we all need forgiveness before we can stand in the presence of God, redeemed and perfect.

When we admit we are sinners and ask forgiveness with a desire for a relationship with Jesus Christ, He comes in and cleanses us.

Jesus is the mediator between God and us so when God sees us, He sees us as perfect. It is only through the shed blood of Jesus that we can be cleansed and forgiven.

To begin the transformation, we have to admit we are sinners.

2. Submit – submit our will to God.

My Father. If it is possible, let this cup of suffering be taken away from me. Yet I want your will, not mine.

Matthew 26:39-42

Once we admit we are sinners and ask forgiveness, we need to consciously submit our will to God.

Even Jesus, in the Garden of Gethsemane, asked to be relieved from the suffering, which lay ahead of Him, but He followed His plea with submitting to God's will.

In Mark 14:36, He asked His Father to take the task ahead away but again, He submitted to the Father's will.

In Hebrews 5:8, the writer tells us that even though Jesus was God's son, He learned obedience from the things He suffered.

If Jesus yielded in total submission to His Father and became the High Priest, who is the source of eternal salvation for us, how much more do we need to be willing to submit our will to Him who loves us more than we can comprehend?

3. Commit – commit your life to Christ – pledge your entire life to Him.

Commit everything to the Lord. Trust Him, and He will help you.

Psalm 37:5

If you desire to have a life filled with all the blessings that God wants to give you, it is important to commit every part of your life to Him. Let Him guide and direct your every move.

That is not to say that we should forget about using the brainpower God gave us or common sense.

Solomon was the wisest man who ever lived; evidence of him using common sense and wisdom in his decisions is significant. He spent time in prayer asking for wisdom and God granted him his request.

Living a life of prayer and Bible study, results in gaining the ability to ask for wisdom to make decisions that are in line with God's plan for our lives. If we commit our entire being to God, He will be able to use us for His glory and honour.

4. Transmit – transmit the love of God and the free gift of salvation to others.

Therefore go and make disciples of all the nations...

Matthew 28:19.

Being a disciple of Jesus Christ is more than just being a convert. Many are converted to Christ and that is the first step.

In order to fully transmit God's love to the fullest, we need to become disciples and learn how to nurture others to be disciples as well.

Being a disciple of Christ is similar to being an apprentice; practicing while learning and reaping the benefits.

Teach these new disciples to obey all the commands
I have given you and be sure of this: I am with
you always, even to the end of the age.

Matthew 28:20

Usually the best teaching method is achieved by modelling the desired behaviour. Teaching how to live as a Christian is no exception, if we want new believers to know what a Christian life looks like, we need to live a Christ- centered life ourselves.

One reason Jesus lived among people on earth was to show what God expected from us. Our lives need to be modelled after the life of Jesus, always demonstrating the love of God. This will attract others to become followers of Jesus Christ. To live a Christ-centered life requires much prayer, a close relationship with Jesus and a desire to show love and acceptance, meeting others where they are.

WEEK 22

Monday
loving others

But I say, 'love your enemies, Pray for those who persecute you."

Matthew 5:44

Most times, it is difficult to love our enemies.

In my life, I'm not sure I have ever had any enemies that I was aware of. I have had some friends who hurt me emotionally. Sometimes the hurts were so deep that I thought of that person as an enemy, but they never really were.

I realized if I spent time speaking against that person, the hurt festered and increased. The more I talked about the incident, the hotter the issue became because fuel was added to the embers and the intensity increased until the heat became so intense, the embers ignited and became destructive flames.

When I became mature in years and spirituality, God showed me how much more effective I could be by exerting my energies to pray for that person who hurt me. When we start praying for someone, it becomes impossible to hate them.

Prayer is the healing balm that soothes the hurt and makes it disappear. Jesus says, "Pray for those who persecute you."

Prayer for today

Father, I thank you for being a forgiving God who knows and understands my shortcomings. I ask you today to forgive me for gossiping about others.

Adena H. Paget †

Forgive my selfish attitude and self-absorption when I think someone has hurt me. Help me to love those who have caused me hurt and enable me to forgive them. Help me to keep my eyes on you and my thoughts pure and loving.

In Jesus's name. Amen.

Tuesday

unconditional love

If you love only those who love you, what good is that?
Even corrupt tax collectors do that much.

Matthew 5:46

How is it possible to love everyone, Lord?

Some people may call me naive because I often see hurtful comments as humour or mistaken words uttered without thought, or I refuse to think they were meant for me. I seldom allow my feelings to be hurt by passing statements.

I know I'm not such a wonderful person whom everyone loves all the time, and I realize there are those who say negative things about me or to me. I also know God's love surrounds me at all times and helps me to be unaffected by the derogatory remarks meant for me.

There was a time in my life when I became angry if anyone said something slightly hurtful or sarcastic to me. As I realized my anger only affected myself, I accepted the futility of spending my energy in this way.

When I lift my feelings to Jesus and repent of my selfish attitude, Jesus always works a miracle and heals the emotions. He creates a clean heart in me. Only with Jesus, comes the ability to love our enemies and those who persecute us.

I have come to the realization hurt feelings are self-centered emotions, which often lead to a lonely pity party.

Let's practice projecting our thoughts towards, doing good to others, helping someone in need or praying for people who say hurtful things. Take the focus off ourselves and suddenly we'll find less hurts to deal with.

Prayer for today

Heavenly Father, thank you for allowing me to be forgiving to those that might hurt my feelings. Help me to love those that may not love me. Give me a heart that's filled with love for all whom you have created.

In Jesus's name. Amen.

Wednesday
responsible love

If you are kind only to your friends, how are you different from anyone else? Even pagans do that.

Matthew 5:47

As Christians, we have a responsibility to show kindness to all, even to our enemies or those who hurt us.

It is easy to be kind to our friends and the words of Jesus challenge us to practice kindness beyond easy, to stretch our faith and Christian love.

I encourage you to take some time in the next few days to do something nice for someone that is not a particularly good friend. Perhaps even someone who is a challenge to you. Ask the Lord to show you who it should be. You will be blessed by your action.

Prayer for today:

Dear Lord, thank you for showering your love on me every day. I know sometimes I am not exactly what you would want me to be and yet you love me and bless me. Today, Lord I ask you to help me show love to someone whom you choose. Lord, even if I don't care for that person, help me to see their good points and dwell on those. Help me to see them as you see them and give me a desire to reach out and love them as you do.

In Jesus's name. Amen.

Thursday

acceptance

Stop judging others and you will not be judged. For others will treat you as you treat them. Whatever measure you use in judging others, it will be used to measure how you are judged.

Matthew 7:1-2

When I was younger, a spiritual babe, I often judged others. Many times it was because of their appearance or the church they attended or perhaps because of the way they spoke or habits they had.

It took maturity and experience and learning about the life of Jesus on earth, to make me realize that it was not my job to judge others.

When I came to the realization of my attitude and repented of being that way, I started to see potential in people.

I started to see beyond the faults and into the hearts. I soon realized that most people are not malicious and do not intentionally harm others. I learned to look beneath the immediate action or words that I found offensive.

It taught me a valuable lesson about judging others. I also learned to accept others for who they were and where they were in their journey of life and spiritual maturity.

When we take the time to understand who people really are and accept them, we find everyone has good side to them. Sometimes it may take a worthwhile bit of time and searching.

When we take the time, life becomes easier and the blessings increase because we give up the need to be defensive. Soon we discover our enjoyment for others increases and we discover blessings by knowing them.

Prayer for Today:

Father, thank you for loving me and having patience with me, even when I am judgmental of the people you love and have created. Please forgive me for neglecting to see good in all people. I realize when you see us, you see potential in every one of us. Help me to be more like you, Jesus, and see others as you see them. Help me to love as you do.

In Jesus's name. Amen.

Friday

mercy

So whenever you speak, or whatever you do, remember that you will be judged by the law of love, the law that set you free. For there will be no mercy for you if you have not been merciful to others. But if you have been merciful, then God's mercy toward you will win out over His judgment against you.

James 2:12- 13

Mercy: An act of divine favour or compassion; withholding of the punishment or judgment our sins deserve.

James is urging us to show mercy to others so the promise of receiving mercy will be granted to us.

Jesus is merciful and we need to strive to become Christ-like. This is a good area to work on, and with the help of the Holy Spirit we can become more merciful.

Some people are easier to show mercy to than others, but it is the one who we find difficult to be merciful to who needs it most. When we ask the Lord to help us and grant wisdom, He provides discernment and success in the circumstance.

Prayer for today

Dear Lord, thank you for showing mercy to me, a sinner, who does not deserve it. But you are a merciful Saviour and even though I am a sinner, you forgave me and showed mercy to me. Forgive me for being negligent of being merciful at times. I pray for the ability and wisdom to show mercy to all.

In Jesus's name. Amen.

Weekend Read

who's in control

Sometimes it takes a great deal of time and teaching to become what God can really use. Some of us were created with stubborn natures and controlling personalities.

Genetics are an interesting phenomena but I believe we cannot use this as an excuse to be less than we are capable of being.

When I was teaching, many times, I heard, "Well my Mom can't spell so I guess I inherited that from her." Or, fathers would tell me, "Well, when I was his age, I was quite a scrapper so I guess he comes by it honestly." I always cringed when I heard things like this because it provided an excuse for a child to stop trying and accept the shortcoming of whatever area the parent excused the behaviour in.

After hearing the same excuses they become self-fulfilling prophecies and children begin to think they are incapable of hurdling that obstacle.

I finally realized, in my life, that God wanted to change some of the inherited traits I was blessed with, and through the process of letting go I am becoming what God wants me to be.

As a young person, I thought there was nothing I could not control and if I made up my mind about something, I would harass, nag, cajole, and work until it came to be.

God allowed many difficult situations into my life to help me realize I really didn't have control over everything.

When my mother became very ill with cancer, it never dawned on me that she would not get better. I had an innocent, childlike faith that would not accept the possibility that she would not be healed. After all, my family believed in divine healing and surely God would honour that faith.

Memories of my mom involve sitting at her feet listening to stories of her childhood in Siberia. Sometimes I was privileged to hear her beautiful soprano voice, and we would sing together as she taught me new songs. The songs she taught me as a young child are still precious memories.

I remember sitting beside her in church and laying my head on her lap to nap when the sermon became too boring for a young child to bear.

Mothers are good with this, fathers, on the other hand don't realize this is important.

We don't know why God chooses to call his children home at a young age, my mom was just thirty-eight years old, but I believe that was the beginning of my realization that I did not have the power to control everything.

She went home to be with Jesus the day before my eleventh birthday. It was a huge loss and a very difficult lesson, but as I look back I realize difficult lessons began the process of moulding and shaping me into what I needed to become in order for God to be able to use me.

I realize my mom's passing was not only for the benefit of teaching me, but it was the first of many lessons that finally brought me to a place where I knew I needed to rely on my Heavenly Father for comfort, guidance and direction in all areas of my life and let Him control instead of me.

I believe if we use the valleys or trials in our lives as learning experiences and reflect upon them as opportunities to grow spiritually, and even ask God what He wants us to learn, we often find they bring us to a place where we become pliable and willing to give up stubborn traits that hinder our closeness with God.

I have learned time and time again, as Paul states, "Don't worry about anything, instead, pray about everything. Tell God what you need, and thank Him for all He has done," and through the pain in tribulation ask, "What are you teaching me, Lord?"

Today, I still mourn the loss of my mother, but not as the world mourns. I know she has been transported to a glorious place that I am not capable of comprehending at this stage in my life.

The righteous pass away; the Godly often die before their time...God is protecting them from evil to come. For the Godly who die will rest in peace.

Isaiah 57:1- 2

This verse has always been my comfort and so is the fact that one day I will see her again and sit by her feet and listen to her tell me stories and sing me songs. What a glorious promise to look forward to.

WEEK 23

Monday

hiding place

For you are my hiding place and, you protect me from trouble. You surround me with songs of victory.

Psalm 32:7

I find it comforting to know about David's struggles, imperfections and pleas for forgiveness. I'm sure many of us can identify with David's life and the tragic events that occurred.

After every struggle, we find passages of elation and thankfulness experiencing victorious songs and peace.

The God who forgave David is still on the throne today, ready to forgive our transgressions and make us new.

When He forgives, we are justified, just as if we had never sinned. God promises to remove our sins as far as the east is from the west. When we arrive at the crucial crossroad where we make the choice of confessing or continuing in our sin, we can take a lesson from David who knew confession brought songs of victory, peace and complete forgiveness.

That is where we find David in this psalm, singing songs of victory and knowing he is protected from trouble. God will shelter us in a special way, called a hiding place in David's mind. The same promise is still true today and available for us time and time again.

Prayer for today:

Heavenly Father, thank you for being willing to forgive all my sins, even the ones I don't talk about. I know you are aware of every sin in my life I have not dealt with and if there are any sins that are keeping me from abiding in your perfect will, help me to remember them and bring them to your alter of forgiveness so I may have songs of victory. Help me, also to be forgiving as you are forgiving.

In Jesus's name. Amen.

Tuesday

a caring God

The Lord says, "I will guide you along
the best pathway for your life.
I will advise you and watch over you."

Psalm 32: 8

My friend, how often have we disregarded God's plan for our lives and decided to go our own way?

Many times, we believe God doesn't really care about us or the little things in our life. Sometimes it seems as if God is very far away or has even abandoned us.

In this psalm, God promises to show us the best path to follow and advise us while we journey. Walking on the path God planned for us guarantees His presence and protection.

-When it seems as if nothing Godly is happening in our lives, perhaps we are to learn patience and wait.

-When the valley is dark, perhaps it is only then we look to our Heavenly Father for strength.

-When we are in despair over the loss of a loved one, perhaps we will be able to avert our eyes to someone else to extend comfort.

-When we think God has abandoned us we can take comfort in knowing He has the pathway planned and we can rest in the assurance He knows exactly what He is doing.

Prayer for today

Father, God, Thank you for having a plan for my life. Even when it seems you don't care or you are far away, I know you are with me and you DO care about my life and me. Help me to remember how much you love me and let me rest in that assurance, always. I am so thankful you chose me to be your child and I know you will never give me more than I can handle. With you as my guide and advisor, I will be victorious in this life until that glorious day when I see you face to face.

In Jesus's name. Amen.

Wednesday
songs of victory

Let the godly sing with joy to the Lord,
for it is fitting to praise Him.

Praise the Lord with melodies on the lyre; make
music for Him on the ten stringed harp.

Sing new songs of praise to Him; play skilfully
on the harp and sing with joy.

Psalm 33:1-3

Music is a gift from God. When I recorded my CDs, I found great enjoyment in every re-take and re-do and rehearsal because I love to sing

In the first book of the Bible, Genesis, we read that Pharaoh's courts sang praises about Sarai because of her beauty. This tells us music was used as an expression of love and admiration even then.

I have discovered a song to the Lord changes my demeanour. When sad thoughts bring me down I know music causes my blue mood to disappear, and my attitude changes to one of joy and elation.

David loved music. The Psalms are a wealthy collection of praise and worship.

God inhabits our praise, He is pleased when we sing praises to Him.

Singing praises is an important component of worshipping the Lord. We are instructed to sing praises and play instruments to honour God and glorify Him.

Prayer for today

Thank you for our voices, Lord, they enable us to sing praises to you and to glorify you. Help me to be more like David, who was uninhibited by

peer pressure trying to squelch his public praises. He was overflowing with joy and displayed his joy by playing instruments and singing and dancing for your glory. Lord, you are great and greatly to be praised, help me to praise you with everything I have and bring honour and glory to your holy name.

In Jesus's name. Amen.

Thursday

benefits of song

Let the whole world bless our God and sing aloud His praises.

Psalm 66:8

Why are we instructed to sing aloud His praises? We know God knows what is in our hearts, so why are we to praise Him out loud?

It is for our edification and well-being that we openly and audibly sing praises. The devil cannot read our thoughts, but he when he hears our voices and our praises to God, he flees from us.

Our praises also lift our spirits and diminish the despondency. When our surroundings seem dark and gray, the sound of praise and worship causes the darkness to flee.

I liken it to lighting a match in a dark room. It's amazing how the light from a little match can illuminate an entire room, isn't it? That is exactly what the sound of praise to God does for a weary and dejected spirit; it lightens and brings a joyful peace to our being.

Even if you don't feel like singing or being joyful or thankful, I encourage you to start and see what happens.

Adena H. Paget †

Prayer for today

Oh Lord, thank you for the gift of song and praise. Without it, Lord, we would never know the joy that is possible. Help me to remember to sing praises unto you even when I don't feel like it. Sometimes, I know, Lord, it takes initiative on my part. Help me to remember that singing praises to you brings peace and happiness in the midst of the storm. You are great and greatly to be praised.

In Jesus's name. Amen.

Friday

replacing despair with joy

He will give beauty for ashes, joy instead of mourning, praise instead of despair...

Isaiah 61:3

This promise was given to the Children of Israel, who mourned and were often in despair, and this promise is also for us today.

I have seen the transformation of despairing, mourning people who have finally turned to the Lord and allowed Him to heal.

I have witnessed lines on worried faces disappear and stooped statures become erect with the acceptance of the love of Jesus.

I have observed the healing power of the stripes suffered by Christ in the life of a young woman who was burdened with weak and crippled legs. She came for prayer and received love and support and prayers and was able to accept the healing balm of the Saviour. Many who witnessed this miracle were in awe at the work done in this hurting soul by the power of prayer and love. She went on to become a physically healthy mother and wife again.

God's promises are as valid today as they were thousands of years ago, because He is the same yesterday, today, and forever. We are included in the promises He gave to the Israelites. The Bible says to ask in faith and then accept the love, the beauty, and the joy, and replace despair with praises.

Hide this verse in your heart and claim His promises today as a child of the King.

Prayer for today

Father God, thank you for loving me and offering healing power for my mourning and despair. I realize sometimes I complain more than the Children of Israel did long ago, and yet you still loved them and kept your promises. I also know your promises are just as valid today as they were then. Lord you are beautiful and you can even make sinners beautiful. Thank you for performing a miracle in my life by helping me trust in you and accepting your forgiving power and love.

In Jesus's name. Amen.

Weekend Read

a personal journal entry

For my son, Drew

February 22, 1961 - October 6 1998

I have suddenly lost a son. Our third son, Drew was taken from us in a fatal car accident. He fell asleep at the wheel of his van as he was returning to his home in Cremona, Alberta. About one a.m. he missed a crucial curve in the highway. The RCMP did not find his body until five a.m.

Our family is still reeling from this, but there is an amazing peace as well.

Drew has two beautiful children who will miss his games, hugs, love, weekend fun, and kisses and so much more they enjoyed doing together. They are young and that is a blessing.

My prayer is that Terri (mother) and Ken (her significant other) will be a loving couple and provide the laughter and love and discipline in their young and impressionable lives.

As a mother, I can't describe the deep hurt of this terrible loss, and yet God gives me peace in the midst of this storm. I have been able to withstand even though my hurt is indescribable.

My dearest, youngest son, my love for you is very special. You held a place in my heart that no one else can possibly fill and now that you are gone, the place in my heart that was yours is very empty.

I had room for your hurts and laughter and long chats on the phone and the cute little telltale signs of your visits when we weren't home. You always left a message, like placing the broom in front of the door.

There are many memories and I am thankful for each one, but the hugs and the phone calls are gone. I shall miss you more than words can say.

You were a unique individual and I was very proud of you, for many reasons.

You were a wonderful father, your children always came first in your life and you were always loving and affectionate.

Oh, my son, you were not perfect, none of us are but you were trying so hard to be a better person. Some of your efforts were evident, like the anger management classes that you attended and donating your talents and time to Habitat for Humanity.

Not long ago you took me out to dinner to Chianti's. We had a wonderful visit, as we often did.

What can I do with this hurt? I know in time it will become easier but that emptiness will always be there.

A treasured memory is my retirement party – you wrote a silly song on a napkin in tribute to me and even though there were hundreds of people there, you asked if you could get up and sing it into the mic. I pretended to be embarrassed but I was really very proud of you for doing that.

I have a beautiful brooch that you gave me one Christmas. I wear it a lot and love it even more now. It is a precious gift and keepsake from you.

You had so many wonderful qualities that I shall miss – but, my son, you also experienced extreme emotions and when I think about the hurts you were experiencing in your life, I am thankful that you never have to suffer hurtful emotions ever again.

When you loved, you loved with all your heart and soul and mind, and when you hurt, you hurt with such a very real and deep hurt.

I take comfort in the fact that you will never be hurt again, emotionally, and physically or any other way.

I know it hurt you because dad and I were not a bigger part of your children's lives, I have no excuse except we did not know how we could be more than we were. For many years, your life was far removed from us because you were such a free spirit. When it was time to rein in, we didn't know how close you really wanted us to come.

Adena H. Paget †

You were an idealist and I know we didn't measure up to your ideal standards. We are not perfect either and I know you didn't let that disappointment come between your love for us and for that I am truly thankful.

So many times, you expressed your love for your dad and me. You were a wonderful son and your absence will never be understood.

I take great comfort in knowing you gave your heart to Jesus and I have no doubts that one day we shall sit together and I'll be able to hear you say,

"I love you, Mom." This is a great comfort and I am so thankful for the promises God makes to us in his word.

And so my sensitive, loving son, until that glorious day, I know your spirit has truly found freedom to soar. I know you are in the presence of perfect love where there are no tears or hurts and I am deeply happy for you.

I will continue to trust God for the well-being of your children. I pray they will grow in the knowledge that God loves them and is with them even though you can't be. We will love them and be as much a part of their lives as possible.

So good-bye for a little while

Love Mom

WEEK 24

Monday

promises – promises

It is better to say nothing than to promise something you don't follow through on.

Ecclesiastes 5:5

The Bible is relevant today and offers a wealth of information including common sense. Common sense is always a valuable practice and Solomon, who wrote the book of Proverbs, offers us much sense and wisdom. It is a great book to read and absorb.

I had an aunt who always made wonderful promises to our seven-year-old daughter. She promised her outings, jewellery, and special times, none of which ever transpired. As a result, our daughter grew to mistrust this person because it became evident the promises were empty and meaningless.

I have often heard parents promise children wonderful things for different reasons. Sometimes promises are made to encourage a desired behaviour or action. Often those promises are forgotten after the promise is made. This kind of discipline models deceitfulness. Unless a promise is kept, it is useless and children soon discover the truth about that person.

Solomon warns us not to do this. Jesus says our yes should be yes and our no should be no. He even says that our adding a promise to our word shows something is wrong. (Matthew 5:37) We make a mockery of this instruction when we fail to stand by our word.

Let us encourage each other to use caution when we speak so we don't mislead others into disappointments by our words.

Adena H. Paget †

Prayer for today:

Dear Lord, thank you for not ever making empty promises. Your word is as true today as it was when it was inspired thousands of years ago. Forgive me for the times I have flippantly made a promise I could not keep. Help me, Lord, to think before I make idle promises. Let my yes be yes and my no be no and help me refrain from compromising on my word in the eyes of you or others.

In Jesus's name. Amen

Tuesday

stop preaching

...in quietness and confidence is your strength...

Isaiah 30:15

Although I have been married to my husband for over fifty years and our love is strong as close friends as well as lovers, we do not share the same faith. He is a logical man who needs to see things in black and white and the Bible tells us faith is the thing hoped for and not seen.

For many years I thought I could talk him into sharing my faith and I talked a lot about it, left Christian literature lying around for him to read, and tried to convince him over to my way of thinking. I came to realize the more I talked, the less he listened and in fact, he grew to resent my preaching.

One day in a Christian bookstore, I happened to see this verse on a wall plaque and the Lord opened my eyes to what I had been doing. I realized I was taking the total responsibility for saving someone else's soul, rather than leaving it to God. I decided to stop talking about my Christianity and start living like a loving wife, leaving the soul-saving to God.

I asked God to help me live a more Christ-like life that would enable me to walk the talk rather than, talk the walk. It took some time but soon I began to see a new respect for my faith from my spouse.

My husband has become my best testimony, telling others about my Christian walk. He is proud of who I am and of my faith.

Quiet confidence in my faith in God, allowing him to do the work, and me to do the loving, has enabled us to celebrate fifty-eight years of a happy marriage.

Prayer for today

Dear Lord, thank you for the deep peace that enables me to be silent instead of prattling unnecessarily. Thank you for the confidence I harbour in your presence. Let your love and kindness and acceptance of others be seen in me and help me to portray your love to others.

In Jesus's name. Amen.

Wednesday

chatterboxes or not

Don't talk too much, for it fosters sin. Be sensible and turn off the flow.

Proverbs 10:19

I find this a difficult proverb to follow, and yet as I look back on my life, I see many instances where my submission to it, would have greatly benefited me.

Sometimes, we say things that are deemed as wise and this is where we should stop. Many of us don't need much encouragement to continue on and on and on… and soon we destroy and muddle the initial message by superfluous prattle.

When this happens, our listener is soon turned off and forgets what the kernel of wisdom even was. The entire message is lost in the saga of our advice.

Sometimes it proves wise to keep totally silent and pray for wisdom before answering or advising. In doing this, we discover our advice is not required. This moves us out of the way of God's plan and allows the other person to learn what God is teaching them. We often reap more benefits by listening and keeping quiet than by sharing advice.

Prayer for today

Father, God, you know how foolish I can be sometimes when I disregard the inner voice inside that tells me to keep quiet. Help me to remember that other people are blessed with wisdom and I don't know as much as I often think I do. Help me to be a better listener and less of a talker unless you require me to say something.

In Jesus's name. Amen.

Thursday
quiet confidence

...but Mary quietly treasured these things in her heart and thought about them often.

Luke 2:19

Mary had a quiet confidence. She knew the baby she was carrying was the Saviour of the world, the Messiah. Even though this was true, she did not boast about being chosen, but treasured the knowledge in her heart.

When the Lord showed me this quality in Mary, I realized He wanted me to be more like this. When God blesses me, as He does each day, I want to tell the world, but I discovered by doing this, I was often being offensive. My attitude almost sounded self-righteous or like I thought God favoured me more than others, somewhat of a braggart.

When people are going through rough times, the last thing they want to hear about is your abundant blessings. That is not to say you should never tell when God has blessed you, but we are to practice discernment before we open our mouths.

I have a friend who used to remind me not to give advice, just listen, when she shared her concerns with me. As I grow in years and wisdom, I have learned to be more sensitive to the feelings of others and to harbour the blessings in my heart until God impresses upon me to share them.

Prayer for today

Heavenly Father, thank you for your abundant blessings. Each day you send me new blessings and you make me feel so very special. I also want to thank you for the rough times in my life because that is then when I grow in you. Help me to be sensitive to others when they are going through valleys and to not sound self-righteous by expounding on my good fortune. Help me to be a better listener and not feel obligated to talk so much.

In Jesus's name. Amen.

Friday

listen, listen

It is foolish to belittle a neighbour; a person with good sense remains silent.

Proverbs 11:12

There is a wonderful line in the animated movie of *Bambi,* when Thumper's mom says, "If you can't say anything nice, don't say anything at all." It seems as if this is a paraphrase of Prov.11:12.

We often fall into the trap of joining those around us who belittle or speak against another person. I have found myself doing this numerous times, and each time I feel repentant for my wrongdoing, because, in fact, it is wrong.

I have also learned that people who speak harshly of others to you will do the same about you to others. As I seek to draw nearer to the Lord, He grants wisdom and gives me strength to refrain from speaking negative things about others, and as I strive to please Him, I am discovering fewer and fewer negative thoughts entering my mind.

He helps me rise above the nastiness of those who love to bring dissension between friends.

Prayer for today

Dear Lord, help me to see potential in others and build them up when I think about them. Help me to speak with edification and to see them as better than myself. Help me to remember that you created everyone and everything and it is not my place to judge when I may be guilty of the same thing. Thank you for having patience with me when I neglect to think before I speak and even when I speak ill of someone you love.

In Jesus's name. Amen.

Weekend Read

quiet confidence

In quietness and confidence shall be your strength.

Isaiah 30:15

I love silence – blissful, beautiful silence…

The whole earth seems to be filled with noise. Some noises are pleasant. I enjoy good music, many kinds of music, all genres; blues, classical, country, gospel, some rock. I like vocals, solos, trios, quartets, groups, choirs, harmony, unison, etc. etc.

There is a man in back of us in the RV park where we spend our winters, who practices his guitar about eighteen hours at a time, each day, which of course, leads into the wee hours of the night. I have noticed an improvement over the last couple of months, which is more pleasing to my ears and must be encouraging to him. It is not so loud it disturbs us but we can hear his diligent perseverance.

My husband and I almost always have music playing in our home, whether it is in our motor home or in our stationary home. When I am not listening to the radio or CDs, I often haul out my keyboard and play and sing for hours at a time. So it's not as if I am obsessed about quietness.

We love to walk, perhaps two or three days a week. We like to walk where there's no traffic. Walking in silence is most enjoyable. It increases my senses and appreciation for nature and it enables me to hear the diverse and delightful song of the birds or the breeze rustling through the leaves. I love the subtle melody of creation.

When we're driving in a vehicle, we often listen to music, but my favourite drives are in the majestic mountains where there are no radio signals. We drive for hours lost in our own thoughts. We seldom know what the other is thinking, but it doesn't matter because we are at peace with each other and comfortable after so many years of being together.

I silently talk to God and wait for Him to plant thoughts and ideas within me; and He does. I understand there are couples that feel compelled to talk to each other almost always but we are very comfortable riding in serene silence.

When we are with our children and grandchildren, I enjoy listening to the excited voices as they almost always all speak at the same time. There is an air of excitement when all eleven of the cousins are together. These are very special occasions, which only happen two or three times a year. It is a great blessing to be the gramma at these gatherings. After a few hours everyone disperses and returns to their own homes.

My husband and I are alone once more and even though the silence is deafening and contrastive to the day, it is also refreshing and restful. As we sit together, just the two of us, we reminisce quietly over the highlights and treasures of the past several hours.

Then we rejoice because we can revel in our serenity once more.

In my quiet, alone time, I almost always talk with God. I know He hears me and He cares about me, and it enables me to continue in the hustle and bustle of life in this world where we must dwell.

In the quiet I gain confidence as I ponder the promises that are written in His Word. I also spend quiet moments asking for clarity as I search His word for guidance and direction in my everyday life. This quietness is important because it provides the confidence I need to continue, the confidence that confirms my uniqueness in the knowledge that I have been selected to be special because I am a child of God.

Although sound is necessary and I am thankful I have the ability to hear, I am also encouraged to enjoy the silence because it is during these times, I can hear what the Lord is saying to me. Silence is important and a quiet time in your life each day may be what it takes to enable you to face today or tomorrow.

I have a very good friend who spends much time listening and conversing with God. She has very little ability to hear, only about five percent in one ear. I knew her for several months before I realized her challenge; she is an exceptional lip reader. After we became better friends, I once asked her if there was surgery available that would help her loss of hearing. She replied, "Actually, I am content and happy in my silent world." I was surprised to hear that comment but I think I understand it and love her dearly for being honest with me.

In the stillness God speaks in a voice that can only be heard by me.

Adena H. Paget †

WEEK 25

Monday
unfailing love

*Praise God, who did not ignore my
prayer and did not withdraw
His unfailing love from me.*

Psalm 66:20.

Did you know? Did you realize God never withdraws His love from us?

When I think He has withdrawn His love from me or I feel He is far away, it is never God who has moved, it is always me.

Each time I sin, and sin comes in many forms, I place a wedge between God and myself. The separation begins subtly, hardly even noticeable but a repeat offence drives the wedge deeper, creating a wider gap. As I continue to sin, it is I who drive the wedge still further and soon I start to wonder why God seems far away. It is when I realize my neglect in our relationship that I go to Him in repentance.

He always waits for our communication and He always hears us and forgives so we can, again, experience and enjoy the closeness and comfort of His unfailing love.

Prayer for today

Father, today I want to thank you for being patient with me and always forgiving me when I come to you. You are an awesome God and I know I don't deserve your unconditional love. I praise you, almighty God, for you are great and greatly to be praised. I ask you to help me become what you want me to be, to strive to be without sin, even though I know I can't attain this while I am here on earth. Help me to be more Christ-like. Only in God is my soul at rest – in Him is my salvation.

In Jesus's name. Amen.

Tuesday

enduring love

Give thanks to the Lord for He is good.
His faithful love endures forever.

Psalm 106:1

God's love is too vast for us to comprehend, but as a parent, I can sometimes experience an inkling of how great His love must be.

When our three sons were growing up, it seemed one was always in trouble. I'm sure they intentionally took turns, it was as if they had secret meetings each night to decide who would be the tester the next day.

As they grew older, their shenanigans escalated into more serious offences until, one day their disobedience became serious, and we were compelled to inform two of them they could no longer live in our home. They were being blatantly disobedient and refused to follow the rules of our home and we were out of options. I remember being extremely frustrated and angry in my disappointment with them, but in spite of this, I never stopped loving them.

Regardless of how deep our love was for them, we could not allow or accept the choices they insisted on making for themselves. Although my heart broke when they moved out, I knew in my mind, we were doing the right thing.

Even though we took this drastic step, our love for them endured and one day they made the decision to change their ways and share in the faith of knowing Jesus Christ, which enabled our family ties to grow.

I am thankful for this experience because it gives me a glimpse of what our Heavenly Father experiences when we sin and when we choose to go our own ways. I also have an inkling of the unconditional love my Saviour, my Abba Father has for me and I know He is ready to forgive when I ask Him to.

Prayer for today

Father, I am so thankful for your forgiveness and never-ending love. Thank you for allowing me to go through the valleys that enable me to see a glimpse of your love for me. I love you, Father and I am sorry for the hurts I have often brought to your loving heart. I thank you for your faithfulness and pray that I could be more like you.

In Jesus's name. Amen.

Wednesday

daily mercies

Great is His faithfulness, His mercies begin fresh each day.

Lamentations 3:23

The Lord provides enough grace and mercy for each day. We never have to be afraid there won't be enough. We never have to reach back to yesterday or save some of today's mercy for tomorrow: He gives enough for each day.

If we are replenished every day, why do we worry? Trusting God should alleviate our worries, right?

Worry is a selfish emotion and happens when we turn our eyes inward, towards ourselves.

When we worry, we are defying God's Word because He tells us not to worry about anything. He provides new mercies every day and He is faithful.

I like to think of this verse every morning with an expectation of experiencing God's new mercies during my day. Sometimes they are huge and other times, I need to look for them but they are always there.

Prayer for today

Precious Lord, I know you are a merciful God and provide all I need, every day. Forgive my selfishness and anxiety. Help me to keep my eyes on you and trust you for each day's provision of whatever I need. Help me to familiarize myself with your promises and learn to live by them.

In Jesus's name. Amen.

Thursday

faithful one so unchanging

If we are unfaithful, He remains faithful,
for He cannot deny himself.

Hebrew 2:13

Because God is undisputedly a faithful and true spirit, He cannot be a liar or even untruthful.

It is always the created one that becomes unfaithful; it is myself, not ever God.

Years ago there was a cartoon strip in the daily newspapers called, *Pogo*. A classic line from that creation has remained with me; it's when Pogo says,

"I have seen the enemy and the enemy is us."

God is forever faithful and loving and cannot be anything else because that is who He is. I am always the guilty one who becomes unfaithful and less loving.

We can take great comfort in this promise and it has been proven over and over again. As I look back on my life, I can see the times when God was a faithful God even though I chose to ignore His desire to be near me and I neglected the close relationship we had for a long time.

When the time came for me to rekindle my first love, my Lord and Saviour, Jesus Christ, He didn't bring up past sins and accuse me of neglect, He simply accepted my repentance and forgave me and welcomed me back into His fold. Because He is a faithful God.

God's faithfulness is as sure as His love and forgiveness. If you feel God has abandoned you, read Hebrews 2:13 and believe what you read.

Prayer for today

Dear Lord, I am so very thankful that you are a faithful God who never gives up on me. Even though I cause you hurt and neglect you, you are always here for me to talk to and draw near to. I want to thank you for being who you say you are, and I know I can always rely on you no matter what, for you have promised to be closer to me than a brother. Thank you for loving me, always. Help me to stay close to you and be faithful to you and your word.

In Jesus's name. Amen.

Friday

being faithful

Unless you are faithful in small matters, you won't be faithful in large ones.

Luke 16:10.

Several years ago, I attended a little church that met in a community hall.

There was an elderly gentleman who faithfully arrived early every Sunday morning. He spent time clearing the snow, turning the heat on, and placing the chairs in rows. He performed this labour of love each week for several years.

Everyone was impressed by His faithfulness and dedication to such a mundane task.

One day he died, unexpectedly and very suddenly. I felt privileged to be able to sing at his service. We all missed him and it took us some time to find someone who could do the required tasks as well as he had.

I often think about him and how diligently he did what needed to be done. I imagine him now, readying a Heavenly chapel with authority because I know the Lord will lavish His rewards on him.

Sometimes we see early rewards given to those who are faithful in small matters, working their way up the ladder. Other times, small duties are not recognized and go on and on without intrinsic rewards. Staying faithful in small matters is always recognized by God who is preparing a place for those who love Him and are called according to His name.

Prayer for today

Heavenly Father, thank you for trusting me to do your work. Sometimes I feel what I do is not important, but I pray that you will help me do my duties as unto you and not to impress someone here on earth or to achieve

Adena H. Paget †

recognition. Help me to do the little things that you entrust me with as well as I possibly can and not to neglect them. Thank you for loving me even when I fail at the responsibilities you ask me to perform.

In Jesus's name. Amen.

Weekend Read

scripture passage

Lamentations 3:22-33

The unfailing love of the Lord never ends
By His mercies we have been kept from complete destruction.
Great is His faithfulness
His mercies begin afresh each day.
I say to myself
The Lord is my inheritance
therefore I will hope in Him.
The Lord is wonderfully good
to those who wait for Him and seek Him.
So it is good to wait quietly for salvation from the Lord.
It is good for the young to submit to the yoke of His discipline,
let them sit alone in silence beneath the Lord's demands,
let them turn the other cheek to those who strike them,
let them accept the insults of their enemies.
For the Lord does not abandon anyone forever
though He brings grief.
He also shows compassion according to the
greatness of His unfailing love.

For He does not enjoy hurting people
or causing them sorrow.

WEEK 26

Monday

claiming victory

For every child of God defeats this evil world by trusting Christ to give the victory.

1 John 5:4

Where does victory over defeat come from? When you are experiencing loneliness, hurt, rejection, where or who do you turn to? We often go to a close friend or a pastor or counsellor, and that is good but usually it isn't enough.

Sometimes our troubles overwhelm us. John says we will be victorious in this evil world by trusting in Christ. Even though it often seems as though God is not listening, He does have the answer.

I encourage you to go to Jesus the next time you are burdened with the inevitable cares of this world, heartache, loneliness, or perhaps sickness. He will give you rest and He gives victory if we are willing to give Him our burdens and troubles and concerns.

I know this is true. It took me years to truly give my worries to Jesus. When I finally realized He could not take them from me if I was not willing to give them, I found true victory in living each day and overcoming the worries that we experience in this world.

Adena H. Paget †

Prayer for today

Dear Lord, you are great and greatly to be praised. I want to thank you for the promise of receiving the victory even though my life seems to be riddled with problems and worries. Help me to realize the benefits of being able to lay my burdens at your feet. You say we can defeat this world and receive the victory, and I claim your promise today. Increase my faith so I may learn to trust you implicitly and truly give you my worries.

In Jesus's name. Amen.

Tuesday

safety

God arms me with strength: He has made my way safe.

Psalm 18:32

When we travel in our motor home on precarious mountain roads and highways or park in high winds, it seems as if there is very little keeping us stable.

The strong winds tend to rock the motor home from side to side and when the winds are really strong, we wonder if our little abode will be able to withstand the force.

The same feeling occurs when things go awry in my life. I experience fear and there is very little to keep me stable, and then I remember I don't have to rely only on my own strength.

My strength comes from God and He is the one who will make my way safe. Just as He enables us to stay on the road through the mountains, He gives us stability in the winds of life. He gives us strength to withstand the strife in our lives and make our way safe.

Prayer for today:

Dear Jesus, today I want to thank you for keeping me safe, even when my life tends to become unstable. Thank you for making my way safe in the midst of the storm. Help me to realize that you are with me, and in you there is safety from any dangers this life may confront me with. Help me to accept your peace and know that I am protected with you as my helmsman.

In Jesus's name. Amen.

Wednesday

the planned path

> *The Lord is my strength and my song; He has become*
> *my victory. He is my God, and I will praise Him.*
> *He is my Father's God, and I will exalt Him.*
>
> Exodus 15:2

This is the song Moses and the people of Israel sang after the escape through the Red Sea. I am always surprised when I read about the Children of Israel and learn about their rebellious ways.

All through the journey, they complained and bickered against God and each other and Moses. Each time God provided their needs and forgave them. The evidence of being victorious is in this verse.

They seemed easily led to be worshippers of idols and other gods. They built golden calves to worship in the absence of their leader.

I lose respect for them and I wonder why they insisted on having their own way. Then I realize this is a picture of us. We tend to complain and take on a bad attitude when things don't go as we planned.

Just as the Israelites did, we want our own plans to work and don't realize God sees the whole picture and knows best.

As long as we are adamant to follow our own way and refuse to listen to God, we cannot be victorious. It is only through seeking God's plan for our life that we can experience victory.

We are similar to the Israelites because we are just as human as they were. We desire riches and set up idols that prohibit us from hearing the voice of God. Perhaps it is time to admit our reliance on worthless things and to start to rely on God, who always knows what's best for us.

Prayer for today

Dear Jesus, Forgive me for following my own path many times when I knew it was not the right thing to do. You are a God of wisdom and love and you always want what's best for me. Help me to learn from my past mistakes, to fully trust you and strive to hear your voice and follow your perfect will. Keep me close to your side where I will be sure to hear you.

In Jesus name amen.

Thursday

power of the Bible

And you will know the truth, and the truth shall set you free.

John 8:32

If we truly want to experience the victory that comes from a guilt-free spirit, the knowledge of total forgiveness of all our sins, and the assurance of salvation and eternal life, and if we desire to live a Christ-filled life that will speak to those around us, and if our desire is to live victoriously while on earth, what do we need to know? The truth.

This scripture has the answer, it is the truth that sets us free, victoriously.

The question is then, how do we find the truth? Jesus says it is from obeying His teachings. How do we know what the teachings of Jesus are? From His inspired word that He gave us exactly for this purpose. When we read His Word with prayer and a desire to know the truth, our eyes are opened to what we need to see.

I remember when I started to encourage our oldest son to read the Bible. He agreed and read it as a novel, he said. He hadn't read very far into it when he discovered it was more than a novel. It is the very essence of life and everything we need to know about living a Christian life is contained in this Holy book.

If you are wondering about living a full life for Christ, get yourself a Bible that you can understand and a concordance that will give you instruction on how to study and you will be on your way to living a victorious life for our Lord.

Prayer for today

Dear Lord Jesus, Thank you for giving me your inspired Word so I can know the truth. Help me to spend more time in your Word so that I may be able to speak with authority about you and your teachings. Give me a new understanding when I spend time in the Word, and open my eyes to see what you want me to see and do what you want me to do. I love you Lord and desire to follow you every day of my life and I desire to have your peace dwell in me forever.

In Jesus's name. Amen.

Friday

despair – hope – blessings

I know the Lord is always with me.
I will not be shaken for he is right beside me.

Psalm 16:8

Maybe you are having a less than perfect day today, maybe you are having a downright bad day. Some days it is difficult to wake up praising the Lord. It is true, some situations bring us down and cause despair. I want to remind you of the promises in God's Word.

When days are sad or tragic, we can identify with King David, as he often experienced tragedy in his life. His saving grace was the knowledge that God was with him. Even though David committed many seemingly unforgiving sins, including murder and adultery, he knew God forgave and continued to love him and stay with him.

David also had times when he felt betrayed and lonely and held pity parties for himself. When our thoughts remain on ourselves we only see the distress, which never leads to a successful solution.

There are many Psalms that depict King David as a man of despair, however, when he turns his eyes to the Lord in praise and thanksgiving, we see the victory.

These are the Psalms that give us hope in the midst of our sorrows and stresses. We know the Lord has promised never to leave us or forsake us especially in the midst of our troubles and sin,

He is here. Just as He honoured David and brought release and joy to him many years ago He wants to do the same for us today.

Prayer for today

Dear Lord Jesus, I am thankful that you want to bless me today. Help me to turn my eyes upward and look at you for my answers. I often tend to pity myself, forgetting my numerous blessings, forgive my selfishness. You have promised a victorious life and I claim your promise today. Help me be all that I can be, to be where you can use me for your honour and glory.

In Jesus's name. Amen.

Weekend Read

prayer poem

During times of testing and trials, what a comfort it is to know others are praying for you.

During our grief after our son was killed, I know the prayers of our friends and family brought us the peace and comfort we experienced.

In the months following his death, I was inspired to write several songs and poems.

This is dedicated to all those who prayed us through the ordeal.

Adena H. Paget †

Your Prayers Matter

1999

Don't think your prayers don't matter
I know they do, my friend
For when my name is lifted
I'm on the other end
And often when I walk in sorrow
Burdened down with cares
the clouds are lifted
The sun shines through
I'm floating on your prayers

Don't think your prayers don't matter
I know they do, my brother
For in His Holy Word it's stated
To pray for one another
I know when days are dull and dreary
And I'm caught in Satan's snares
The valleys seem to escalate
I'm floating on your prayers

When you think your prayers don't matter
When it seems God never hears
Don't give up or be discouraged
I am floating on your prayers.

WEEK 27

Monday
sweet smelling fragrance

Then Mary took a twelve-ounce jar of expensive perfume made from nard, and she anointed Jesus's feet with it and wiped His feet with her hair. And the house was filled with fragrance.

John 12:3

Olfactory glands have great importance. Often when my house smells stale or musty from cooking odours or has been shut up for a time, I light candles or bake cookies. The aroma from these wonderful-smelling fragrances makes the house smell inviting, warm, and welcoming.

My daughter is a representative for a very successful essential-oil company. She diffuses natural oils all the time, which makes her house smell warm and inviting.

I believe the house of Lazarus smelled invitingly warm after Mary anointed Jesus's feet, but I am more impressed by the symbolic tender affection and extravagant love that Mary displayed for Jesus by this gesture. It truly was a symbol of unconditional love and everyone benefited from her action.

It was only the "betrayer" who called her down for doing it, and he was later duped by Satan and became the one who sold Jesus to the soldiers.

Our heart could be considered our personal houses. I often wonder if Jesus feels as loved by dwelling there as He did in the house of Lazarus by Mary's show of admiration and love.

Adena H. Paget †

Our hearts need to reflect a pure love such as this with the sweet aroma of goodness, acceptance and devotion. This kind of environment makes Jesus feel welcome.

If you need an attitude adjustment, perhaps it is time for a display of love towards Jesus. Wrap yourself in the sweet fruits of the Spirit so Jesus will feel loved and welcome while dwelling in your heart. Offer him an inviting fragrance to dwell in.

Prayer for today

Dear Lord, I pray I will always be a sweet fragrance for you to enjoy. Forgive me for the times I have made you feel less than welcome by having a musty attitude. Help me be like Mary, who made you feel loved and welcomed by her sweet fragrance.

In Jesus's name. Amen.

Tuesday
discipline

For the Lord disciplines those He loves,
and He punishes those He accepts as His children.

Hebrews 12:6

Discipline is imperative to becoming all we can be.

God is the best teacher. When we need to learn a lesson, He allows something to happen to teach us. Does He do this because He enjoys watching us suffer? No. He does it because He loves us and wants us to be all that He created us to be.

As a parent and teacher, I sense many parents lack the incentive or energy to apply basic rules in order to teach valuable life lessons to offspring. Some parents want to be friends with their children or believe in natural consequences to the extent of omitting teaching altogether.

To allow a child to behave in a disobedient way without a consequence, is a gross injustice to a child. It is vitally important for a child to understand some rules cannot be broken or ignored without consequences. To be taught respect is an important life-long lesson, a valuable principle of great benefit.

How is it possible for a child to grow up and learn to respect God's authority if they have never been taught how to respect someone in an authoritative position?

God is our Heavenly Father and disciplines us when necessary.

Sometimes the lessons are difficult but in the end the result is refined gold.

Prayer for today

Dear Heavenly Father, I know you are a loving God and want what is best for me, your child. I find it awesome that you even love me at all. I seem so insignificant in this wonderful world that you created. I also know that I am far from what I can be and I'm so thankful that you care enough about me to take the time to teach me valuable lessons I need to learn.

I know your way is best and I want to be on your agenda not my own. Help me to learn from the daily lessons and thank you for your love and acceptance.

In Jesus's name. Amen.

Wednesday

keeping fit

Physical exercise has some value, but spiritual exercise is much more important for it promises a reward in both this life and the next.

1 Timothy 4:8

How many times have I promised myself to exercise diligently and consistently? Usually, one thing or another hinders my promise to myself.

When I stay on a regime of exercise, I feel better and many of my aches and pains practically disappear. I also feel better about myself and seem to gain confidence in every situation. I definitely know regular physical exercise makes me feel better and look better.

If we know the benefits of physical exercise, how much more do we require spiritual exercise? Many times I forget this life is a training ground for the life everlasting awaiting us after this life is over. If we remember we are three-dimensional creations, we should also know that physical and emotional wellness is not enough for a successful existence.

Our spiritual dimension needs nurturing and it is the one we often neglect. In Hebrews, the writer reminds us not to neglect that very important dimension of our lives, not only because it benefits our earthly bodies but because the rewards will be there for us in the next life as well.

Prayer for today

Dear Lord, Thank you for helping me to realize the full dimension of myself. You have wondrously made me to be a thinking, feeling, and physical person. Help me to realize the importance of keeping spiritually fit and seeking your face and will in my life.

In Jesus's name. Amen.

Thursday
speak up

For God has not given us a spirit of fear and timidity, but of power, love and self-discipline.

2 Timothy 1:7

Have you ever felt a twinge of urgency to speak to someone about Jesus or share an experience you had in your Christian walk?

I'm not sure if you feel the same way I often do when I'm prompted this way, but many times I have ignored the instruction.

The Apostle Paul tells us we should not be timid or fearful, and yet we often cringe and display fear at sharing Jesus with others.

I remember observing a young woman cautiously enter the church I attended and sitting a few rows from me. I felt empathy for her and watched her as the pastor spoke about the love of Jesus. At the end of the message, there was an altar call and I felt I should go and offer to walk up the aisle with this young woman but I didn't do so. I was in a hurry to go home and cook a family dinner.

This neglect bothered me until the mid-week prayer service where I felt an urgency to share my feelings of remorse and ask forgiveness for ignoring the voice of the Lord. I know I am forgiven, but ever since then I try to be more in tune with the still, small voice of the Holy Spirit, because I never want to feel the heaviness of neglecting His direction again. A willing and obedient heart, God expects.

Prayer for today

Heavenly Father, thank you for that person who was not afraid to speak to me when I accepted you as my personal Saviour. I am grateful you were not afraid to follow the purpose of your life on earth and I ask you to help me to be bold for you and not afraid or timid when I am urged to speak or act for you. Help me to be in tune with your direction and hear your still, small voice when you speak.

In Jesus's name. Amen.

Friday
free gift

He saved us, not because of the good things we did, but because of His mercy.

Titus 3:5

God's mercy is unfathomable for our minds to perceive. There is nothing we can do to earn our way into Heaven and live with Jesus for eternity. It is only by His mercy that we can be saved.

It is a free gift, so no one can boast about what he or she has done to gain entrance into God's presence. Knowing that we are all the same in the eyes of God, puts all of us on the same level. It does not matter who we are, when we come to Jesus in repentance, we can rest in the assurance that He forgives and invites us to a home in Heaven after we pass from this earth.

When we become children of God, our attitude is made anew and our desire is to do good and please Him. We look for opportunities to perform pleasing tasks that bring comfort and encouragement to others. It is a matter of wanting to share God's goodness with someone else.

Prayer for today

Dear Jesus, I am so thankful today for your redeeming grace that saved me from my sins. I know you see me as pure and sinless because your blood washed my sins away when you died on the cross. I am so thankful your salvation is free and your love is abundant for me. Help me to show your love in my life so others may also know your love and see you in me.

In Jesus's name. Amen.

A Weekend Read

abandonment

A fictional story

Create in me a clean heart, Oh God. Renew a right spirit within me. Do not banish me from your presence and don't take your Holy Spirit from me.

Psalm 51:10-11

She valued her relationship with her father. Close to him she felt safe and protected. She knew He would shelter her from hurts, pain, and poverty. She cherished the intimate moments when they could be alone and always practiced complete honesty with him.

Several times she had wandered toward the lights and music but always kept her father in sight. There was a curiosity about the activities and sounds she heard from there, it was a world she had never experienced.

She remembered the strange feelings of fear and loneliness the day she wandered far enough to lose sight of her father for a brief time. Even though she felt fearful, there was a sense of excitement and wonder at the brightly coloured lights and loud laughter. She remembered the twinge of curiosity and a desire to see more.

One morning, she made a decision to satisfy her insatiable curiosity to know what was beyond the lights and laughter.

As she started on her journey, she tried to keep her father in her sights and she looked back often, but the road twisted and turned and soon she lost sight of him.

She felt she should turn back but her curiosity urged her to venture farther away from familiarity. There was a tug inside her that kept her going. She struggled to make the right decision and appeased her indecision by convincing herself she would return as soon as she could get a glimpse at this other world. Her decision made, she forged ahead and decided to resolve her curiosity.

The sounds continued to increase and soon she was able to hear music like she had never heard before – and the lights – oh the lights. The brilliance was dazzling with zany colors, which led to strange shadows and shapes on the walls surrounding her.

As she looked around, she noticed many tantalizing activities and she wondered if she should participate in any of them and which ones could bring resolution to her unanswered questions?

Very soon, while she was still wondering, there stood beside her a handsome escort with a most alluring voice and demeanour, who assured her he would take care of her and show her the sights.

“My goodness,” she thought, “what a coincidence, to have someone show me around like this, and someone who seems to know just where to go.” And she became quite comfortable in the new situation. Soon she realized she was laughing and having a great time, forgetting where she came from and her father.

As time progressed, she started sensing weariness with the frenzy and endless activities that were now becoming repetitious and even boring. She found herself wishing she had not come this far.

Soon she felt an urgency to return home but when she tried to leave, her escort, in his honey-smooth manner, persuaded her to stay with him a while longer. He sounded lonely and made her feel guilty at wanting to leave so she felt obliged to stay.

As the experience progressed, she lost track of time and her thinking became fuzzy. She didn’t have a clear idea of how long she had been gone but she knew one thing – she wanted to return to her father.

As she shared her desire to return home, she noticed her escort becoming fidgety and impatient with her. The more she tried to leave, the more impatient he became until she knew if she did not leave soon, it would be too late and she might never find her way home again.

As her desire to leave became even stronger, the idea of leaving the lights and music and her escort became her only goal. She waited for his eyes to wander to someone else that appeared to be new… and started to run.

As she fled, she realized the way home had become obscure and she wasn’t sure where to go or which street to take. They all looked alike and she was becoming more and more confused. Soon she became panic stricken.

Every corner had more lights and more alluring attractions but she only wanted to find the road that led to home and the safety of her father.

In utter rejection, desperation, and abandonment she sat down on a near-by curb and started to sob. She wondered why she had ever been curious about this unknown world and thought about the quiet times with her father and the place of safety that he provided.

The longing she experienced could not be compared to anything she had ever felt before. She only knew if this was what it felt like to be part of this world and away from her father, she could never bear it.

She could never live in this dark, lonely world where no one really cared or loved. She had never experienced a loneliness like this and now she felt something new, which she had never known before. She was unfamiliar with this strange emotion but in the back of her mind she knew it must be guilt.

This emotion made her feel unloved, unforgiven, and totally alone. As she looked around, she became aware of others who seemed to be in despair like herself. She asked if they knew where she could find her father and none seemed to understand what she was talking about. In total desperation, she finally cried out, "Father, Father, Daddy, Father, where are you? I need you."

When she looked up, she couldn't believe her eyes – there he was standing before her with outstretched arms, saying, "Come home with me."

She ran into his waiting arms and collapsed. He picked her up and carried her home to the safety of his secure presence, back to the peaceful world she had so loved before her wandering. She begged forgiveness and promised never to wander away from this beautiful world again.

The realization of the deep love that surrounded her and the peace she felt were overwhelming and caused her emotions to well up. Unable to contain her own love and thankfulness, she allowed the tears to flow while he held her close. She knew this was where she belonged and wanted to stay forever.

WEEK 28

Monday
trusting the captain

Trust in the Lord, always, for the Lord God is the eternal rock.

Isaiah 26:4

The wind was fierce, the waved were turbulent, the ship was precariously tossed to and fro like a kite in a gale. It seemed futile and the crew thought their ship would not withstand the force of the storm. At the perfect time, the captain gave the order to drop the anchor.

As the command was obeyed, the ship became steady and all knew that they could now outwait the storm. Even though the little ship rocked, it remained anchored and stable. The captain was confident for he had assured himself that the anchor was reliable and firm as a rock, in order to withstand even the fiercest of storms. The passengers and crew were calm because they had complete trust in their captain. They had been on this ship before with him.

We are often faced with one storm after another, some stronger and fiercer than others. If we have an anchor that holds and is trustworthy, we can be assured of being able to withstand any storm that might develop.

The Lord God is that rock. Whatever storm you may be in right now, give it to the Captain and let him take care of it for you. Jesus Christ is the Captain you can trust and put your faith in. He will never let you down or let you drown when you ask him for help.

Adena H. Paget †

Prayer for today

Dear Jesus, I thank you for being my Captain in life's storms. I know I can depend on you no matter what happens. I pray I will learn to trust you and rely on you and not try and solve life's problems by myself. Help me to give you my fears.

In Jesus's name. Amen.

Tuesday

the strength of the Lord

...Be strong with the Lord's mighty power

Ephesians 6:10

She worked hard at this relationship, and yet it appeared as if it was a losing battle. The daughter she had put so much trust in was straying from all she had taught her.

She had tried to be an understanding mom with listening ears, careful not to fall into the shock-mode reaction at anything. She had spent time with her daughter, taken her for dinners and movies and made a special effort to be a friend. Now she felt betrayed, almost abandoned because she had done everything her own mother had neglected to do and for what?

She opened her Bible to Ephesians 6 verse 10 and there was the answer. As she read, God opened her eyes to the realization that it was not by her own power that anything could be accomplished but his Word instructed her to be strong with *The Lord's power.*

She had been carrying the burden to no avail, and there was no need to carry it anymore because Jesus had already borne all the burdens when he carried the cross to Mount Calvary. She knew she must give it to the Lord and allow Him to take care of it.

She immediately cried to God with a repentant heart and asked him to take her burden. Immediately, the load was lifted and she knew she could be at peace about her daughter. No matter what would happen next, the Lord had already carried the burden so she did not have to.

We need to give our burdens to Jesus because he has already taken care of them and left them at Calvary. He knows our needs and waits for us to accept his answer. Everything is ultimately in His hands if we allow Him to take it.

Prayer for today

Heavenly Father, today I want to give you the weight of my burdens. You are my strength and you are a mighty power and you can handle anything I submit to you. Forgive me for thinking I can solve problems and change people on my own. Thank you, Father, for taking my worries and giving me peace.

In Jesus's name. Amen.

Wednesday

praying without disappointment

...I am placing a stone in Jerusalem, a chosen cornerstone, and anyone who believes in Him will never be disappointed.

Peter 2:6

A stone personified. Only the Lord Jesus Christ can be called a "Stone" because he is:

- everlasting
- steadfast
- in every area and part of the world
- strong enough to kill giants
- small enough to carry with us everywhere
- found in all shapes, colors, sizes, and weights.
- solid

The scriptures say, he will never disappoint us. Put your trust in the Cornerstone because when we truly believe in him, there are no disappointments or let- downs.

However, we need to be careful not to confuse this promise with a fictitious genie that grants wishes. What we wish or what we desire, is not always in our best interest.

We are not able to see the big picture but God sees it all. If you have been asking God for something and it seems like he's not hearing, remember prayer that does not line up with God's will, may not be answered as you expect.

Ask yourself if this request is in your best interest and would this request be God's will for your life? When you examine the answer, perhaps your prayer will be changed.

Prayer for today

Heavenly Father, help me to be in your will so my prayers will be what you desire for me. Draw me closer to you. I want to know you more. I want to follow your plan for my life. I need you, Lord, more than the air I breathe, more than my next heartbeat, more than anything. Help me to be what you want me to be.

In Jesus's name. Amen.

Thursday
strong cornerstone

We are His house, built on the foundation of the apostles and the prophets. And this cornerstone is Christ Jesus himself.

Ephesians 2:20

The house was magnificent, every detail had been deliberately and professionally planned. The designer had been highly recommended and the interior decorator was the best in the area. After many months of waiting, it was finally complete and ready to be occupied. The furnishings were perfect. This was the dream home they had so painstakingly planned and waited for, and now it seemed to be a reality. The excitement of actually living there was exuberant.

Soon after they moved in, the rains came; a huge deluge of water poured incessantly and with the rain came great power. As the rain came down, he could hardly believe his own eyes but there, on the hillside on which they had insisted the house should stand, which gave them the glorious, panoramic view of mountains, valleys, and ocean, the earth was eroding.

It became evident that soon the dream home would crumble if something wasn't done immediately. He realized then, the builder had neglected to ensure the strength and stability of the cornerstone that was required to withstand the elements of the weather on this coastline. The task before him loomed large.

Often, our lives reflect this dilemma as well. If our principles or cornerstone are not grounded on the Word of God, we begin to crumble when the storms of life come.

We need Christ as our cornerstone and when the dark clouds and rains begin to pour down, we simply let him take the deluge and trust him to be the Rock that helps us stand firm in every situation.

Adena H. Paget †

Prayer for today

Precious Heavenly Father, I am so thankful you are the Rock on which I base my faith. You are The King of Kings and Lord of Lords and you are able to withstand all the storms that come my way. Help me to build my life on you and you alone. I want to trust you as my anchor in the storms in my life.

In Jesus's name. Amen.

Friday
cleft in the rock

Then I pray to you, O' Lord. I say, "You are my place of refuge. You are all I really want in life."

Psalm 142:5

The hike was longer than we expected, and almost straight up the mountain. In the Canadian Rockies, one needs to be prepared for abrupt weather changes.

As we watched the black clouds advance, we anticipated a mountain shower and a drop in temperature. We were prepared for anything but did not expect the fierce and powerful snow and hail storm that began. We ran for shelter under a canopy of a cleft in the rock. We were thankful for having taken the time and effort to be prepared for similar situations.

Our refuge was quite wonderful and as we munched on muffins and fruit and enjoyed hot tea, we marvelled at the panoramic view of the landscape. Soon the storm subsided and the sun appeared in a blaze of glory.

We continued on our trek, richer for having had the experience.

Our lives are constantly battered by unexpected storms, but our protector is always available to shelter us in the shadow of his hand. He provides protection, a safe place; our cleft in the rock.

Jesus Christ is the Rock where we find the cleft of protection. Our responsibility is to be prepared to rest and wait and trust that he will keep us safe until the storm passes.

Prayer for today

Dear Father, I am so thankful you are the Great Protector. Help me to remember it is you who provides the Cleft in the Rock when I need protection in life's storms. Please, Lord, give me assurance that you will be there for me when the storms come. Help me to trust you more and more each day.

In Jesus's name. Amen.

Weekend Read

the tugboat and barge

Several years ago my husband and I were enjoying a wonderful vacation on the Sunshine Coast in British Columbia, Canada.

We stayed at a delightful little bed and breakfast on the shore of the Pacific Ocean in Seachelt.

The sky was clear as crystal, azure blue, and the water was as calm as a mirror. It was a perfect day to sit on the beach, watch water traffic, and listen to the gentle slap of the waves on the rocky shoreline.

As we sat on the beach, enjoying this magnificent part of God's creation, I noticed a little tugboat towing a barge in the distance with what looked like an entire city of huge logs trailing behind.

The little tug was moving at a snail's speed and took forever to pass my vantage point. As I watched it working to transport the logs, it reminded me of many people who carry much weight with them.

The scene inspired me to write this poem.

Give up the weight

1998

There's a small working barge sailing by in the sea
It's going so slow it may never pass me
The task it has chosen seems unrealistic
Destination is far out on the Pacific
The captain is confident, he knows what to do
Take the route that is easy and we will come through.
It's quite like some humans that travel this life
Towing the burdens of everyday strife
The task becomes heavy, too much to bear
Would Jesus accept them? Does he really care?
Let it go, feel the freedom
Give it up, spread your wings
Don't harbour the baggage,
Give it air, hear it sing
Live life to the fullest
Drop your luggage, lose the weight
Learn to love and receive it
Drop the gossip, lose the hate

Give it up, learn forgiveness
Don't take pity on yourself
Be light-headed, run more freely
Drop the pain and hurts you've felt
You'll be amazed what life can offer
If you choose to look ahead
You can meet your days with laughter
You'll know joy where you are led.

WEEK 29

Monday
steep paths

But for those who are righteous the path is not steep and rough. You are a God of justice and you smooth out the road ahead of them.

Isaiah 26:7

I learn valuable lessons every day.

I recall times in life when the path was steep and rough, and I realize it was then I grew in the Lord and really learned to trust him.

I know the protective hand of God has been upon me through every part of my journey. Many times my experiences could have ended tragically because of foolish choices I made. I know God rescued me often, and smoothed out my path, enabling me to change direction and go on.

Even though we make foolish choices and go down detours that were never meant for us to take, God continues to look at the heart that desires to please.

Even when the flesh is weak and the result is poor choices, if we ask forgiveness, he forgives and sees us as perfect and righteous.

When we are seen as righteous God fixes the path and makes it smooth and easier to follow. This is God's justice, which is promised to his children. Isn't it wonderful to be a child of God?

Prayer for today

Heavenly Father, Thank you for smoothing my paths and seeing me as righteous. I am your creation and I know you love me unconditionally, even though I make foolish choices. Help me to use wisdom and continue to trust you to smooth the path I walk daily.

In Jesus's name. Amen.

Tuesday

perfect and righteous

We are made right in God's sight when we trust in Jesus Christ to take away our sins. And we can all be saved in this same way, no matter who we are or what we have done

Romans 3:23

As a teacher, I often found it necessary to lecture myself regarding students who took advantage of me. I remember a grade six boy who inevitably would do things to annoy me. He had gained a reputation in the school as a trouble- maker. Many times I struggled with my attitude towards him.

I asked God for the desire to forgive this boy's pranks and escapades. I believe God directed me to invest time getting to know him. As I became better acquainted with him and his family, I realized why he behaved this way. When I changed my attitude about him, significant behaviours began to change in him.

By Christmas, I had gained enough trust for him to realize I would treat him fairly and we started on the road to a healthy and cooperative relationship.

It gave me great pleasure to present him with a report card filled with positive comments. I saw potential success in his future.

I believe God sees us as potential successes when we come to Christ for forgiveness. We are all guilty of sin in our lives – no one is perfect. No one can ever do anything to erase that sin from our lives. It can only be done by the one and only sacrifice of Jesus Christ, who shed his perfect blood for each one of us.

When we ask forgiveness, Jesus takes all our sins and makes everything right between God and us. There is forgiveness for everyone that comes in repentance. Praise Jesus for his unspeakable gift of righteousness that makes us clean and able to stand before God in confidence.

Prayer for today

Heavenly Father, I am so thankful you see me as righteous. Thank you for sending Jesus, who forgives all my sins. Help me to remain in Christ who is the forgiver even now, of all sin. In your eyes I am perfect even though I'm not. I want to praise you more, love you more, and serve you more.

In Jesus's name. Amen.

Adena H. Paget †

Wednesday

the gift of peace

Therefore, since we have been made right in God's sight by faith, we have peace with God because of what Jesus Christ our Lord has done for us.

Romans 5:1

A repentant heart leads us to ask for forgiveness and we are made right with God. This not only assures us of an eternity with Jesus but an abundance of benefits while we live here on earth.

One special gift is the peace that comes to our hearts, peace so wonderful and deep that it is indescribable, peace that passes all understanding. This peace is given to us with the simple act of receiving Jesus. The forgiveness we receive is accompanied by the presence of the Holy Spirit, who comes and fills that void that we are all born with.

That longing is inherent in everyone, and people spend many years and mega dollars attempting to find something to fill this emptiness. Nothing on this earth can fill that void, only salvation through Jesus Christ meets the need of true fulfillment.

Jesus never forces himself on anyone, he requires an invitation and a welcoming spirit, but once he is asked to enter, the peace that fills us is more than wonderful because we are made right with our Creator.

Prayer for today

Heavenly Father, I don't know how to thank you for forgiving me all my trespasses and making me righteous in your sight. Thank you for the peace and the assurance of knowing I will one day be with you in eternity. You,

Oh Lord, have given me more than I could ever imagine and because of you I can live each day to its fullest.

In Jesus's name. Amen.

Thursday

faith is believing

...by his faith he condemned the rest of the world and was made right in God's sight.

Hebrews 11:7

This verse speaks of Noah, who continued to obey God even though everyone laughed at him and probably thought he had lost his mind. Imagine someone starting to build an enormous ark to float on water when no one had even experienced the sensation or reality of rain. Noah believed God and performed an act of faith and trusted God despite what the world thought.

After confession and repentance, comes faith. We must believe that Jesus has forgiven us and in faith, go forth and tell others what he has done for us.

Yes; there will be rejection, ridicule, and condemnation, just as Noah experienced, but the rewards far outweigh the actions of the world.

Faith cannot be seen, it is a hope and belief in biblical truths, the substance of things hoped for but unseen.

Prayer for today:

Heavenly Father, I believe you have forgiven me and I am your child. Just like the centurion in the Bible I am asking you to help my unbelief and increase my faith so that I may be able to tell others about salvation and the promises you have given to us. Help me to spread the Good News about your saving grace even when others ridicule or laugh at my beliefs.

In Jesus's name. Amen.

Friday

answering the judge

He will judge the world with justice and rule the nations with fairness.

Psalm 9:8

God is God. God is sovereign. He can do whatever he wants but his Word tells us he is just and fair. We know God cannot make a promise without keeping it. This would be against all he is. We know he rules in justice and fairness.

His Word tells us, one day we will stand before him to be judged. How can we avoid the awesome fear that comes with this knowledge? Our desire is to be seen as perfect and forgiven. Because of Jesus and what he did for us, we can stand before God as perfect.

When we stand before the Almighty Creator, we can do so with the assurance that he will accept us. We cannot comprehend the greatness of God or understand all his actions but we can be assured of his love for us and his fairness in judging us.

He will also judge our nation. This is a call to pray for our nation.

I encourage you to take some time out of your busy schedule to pray for your country, your province or state, your community, your home and family, and finally yourself. One day we will be required to give an account of ourselves and part of that account will include our community and country.

Prayer for today

Heavenly Father, I am not worthy to even expect your attention but I know you love me and you do listen to me. Thank you for taking the time to hear my concerns. I know one day, I will stand before you as you rule and judge, and I am so thankful your word says you are fair and just. Because of the sacrifice of your son, I am assured of your acceptance and even seen as perfect in your eyes. Dear Jesus, help me to rely on your guidance.

In Jesus's name. Amen.

Weekend Read

a sisters tribute

Our family ties were very strong after Drew's car accident. Every sibling had an opportunity to share at his memorial service. Our daughter, Robyn, who was very close to her brother, wrote this poem.

My Brother, My Friend

Drew – 1961 – 1998
Robyn Movold

The sibling rivalry within me calls out
"It's not fair"
I want some of what you have, you have to share
You can't be the only one free from this pain
Why is it you, who receives all the gain?
You have to share, my brother, my kin.
And then I cry out and ask again
Why God? Why did he hear your call?
Oh Holy Father, make him share with us all
And then I realize, my brother, my friend
You are sharing even at your life's end
We still feel pain and tears overflowing
But you shared with us a love that was growing
You get to party and dance and sing in God's glory
And for my jealousy, Drew, I am sorry
For a time will come when we will all share
In worship and song in God's loving care
So rejoice my dear brother and please party on
We will see you again when our struggle is gone.

I Love You Drew

WEEK 30

Monday
waiting period

...But Jesus gave her no reply, not even a word...

Matthew 15:23

This is part of a scripture verse regarding a woman who asked Jesus to heal her demon-possessed daughter. I'm sure we have all felt like this woman, we pray and pray and ask and ask and there does not seem to be a reply.

We have a grandson who was born with cystic fibrosis, a genetic disease that only allows recipients a short life expectancy. We have prayed for him since he was diagnosed and there is no reply...at least the reply is silence at this time.

I have prayed for loved ones who are unbelievers for many years, and often the reply seems to be silence. We don't know or understand why the response is such as it is.

Perhaps a silent answer gave the woman an opportunity to think about her life and her situation. We are not told much about her but I wonder what her life was like. Was she a single mom? It does not say anything about her husband. As the story continues, there seems to be a turn of events – at the persistence of the woman we see that Jesus has compassion and ultimately heals her daughter.

I believe we need to be more like this woman, and continue to trust and ask, even though we think there is no hope. In the silence there are benefits to gain and lessons to learn. We can take advantage of the lull and learn important values like perseverance and patience, and it gives us an opportunity to look at ourselves objectively.

Adena H. Paget †

Ultimately, God is in control and as we believe in His promises and learn to trust Him more and more, our lives become less stressful and more joyous.

Prayer for today

Dear Heavenly Father, thank you for hearing my requests and even though your answer is silence, I know you are taking care of my concerns. Help me, Lord to use the waiting time to grow and gain wisdom. I am so glad you are ultimately in control and as I learn to trust you more, let me be patient and wait for your answer because your timing is perfect.

In Jesus's name. Amen.

Tuesday
touching Jesus

"Who touched me?" Jesus asked.

Luke 8:45

A woman, who had been afflicted for many years, knew if she could just touch the hem of his garment, she would be healed. She had suffered for years with an illness that could not be cured by doctors. The crowds were large and it was questionable as to whether or not she could even get near Jesus. The masses were not interested in allowing her access to Him, but she determined in her heart not to give up. As she shoved and pushed, she finally managed to squeeze through the crowd to crawl near him, close enough to touch the hem of his garment.

How often have I longed for the same thing? "If I could just touch him, everything would be okay." I tell myself.

Have you touched Jesus lately?

Have you felt his healing power?

How much time do you give to Jesus, daily, weekly, monthly?

I have learned, there are no better moments in my life than the moments I spend alone with Jesus. He is a friend, a Saviour, a loving father, a comforter, a peace giver, a joy filler, and a loving companion. He not only gives but he takes as well. He takes my heartaches, my loneliness, my fears, and my tears and replaces them with songs of victory and assurance of freedom from depression and anxiety. He provides healing for me each day from hurts, concerns and maladies that befall me. Praise His name.

It is in the quiet time with God, we hear his voice and receive his touch. Reach out and touch him today.

Prayer for today

Heavenly Father, I want to touch you. Hear my prayer of praise right now as I come into your presence. When I am in your presence, I have assurance that all is well but often I get so busy and forget to include you in my daily life. Even though I neglect you, I know you are still with me and I am so thankful for that.

In Jesus's name. Amen.

Adena H. Paget †

Wednesday

choosing the right master

Don't you realize that whatever you choose to obey becomes your master?

Romans 6:16

Who is your master? Every day I am tempted by:

- invitations and requests to participate in activities
- obligations to friends and family
- visitations to the elderly and sick.
- golfing with friends
- being more actively involved in the church.
- catching up with my reading
- cleaning and dusting and laundry
- entertaining and returning dinner invitations
- returning phone calls
- several half-finished craft projects to complete
- spending time to practice music and keeping my voice tuned for entertaining.

It looks like I am making the clock and busy tasks my master.

The above list confirms I have opted for the spirit of busyness instead of the Spirit of God to fill my life. Unless we choose to put God first, our lives will never be what they could be. When we choose to remove Him from the number one position, we interfere with His plan for our lives.

There are many opportunities for us to neglect our relationship with Christ but when we realize the importance of our choices, we can take steps to ensure our master is our Creator. Take a look at your calendar and start reorganizing your daily tasks to make God number one.

Prayer for today

Dear Heavenly Father, I want to be obedient to you and yet I put other things before you every day. Help me to prioritize my life so that you always come first. Help me not to get caught up in the busyness of this life. I don't have to do it all. Let me be willing to say "no" when I need to and make you my Master.

In Jesus's name. Amen

Thursday

giving thanks

I said to the Lord, "You are my Master.
All the good things I have are from you."

Psalm 16:2

Today is a good day to give thanks for all the things we take for granted.

Some days my heart overflows with thanksgiving for the wondrous blessings God provides me with.

I encourage you to look around and be thankful. When we wake up with a thankful heart, it is difficult to feel sorry for ourselves or dwell on our troubles.

Join me in making a blessing list today. These are some things that bless me every day: A warm safe place to live; hot water to take a shower whenever I want; a free country where I can voice my opinion without fear; created beauty with colourful blossoms and lush greenery or pure white snow, depending on where I am; children who love me; a loving, caring husband; friends who accept me; a healthy body and sound mind; food to eat; literature of any genre to read and learn from; and the list goes on and on...

In this psalm, David gives glory to God for providing all the good things in his life. We know David had many trials and temptations, as we also experience, but he also realized his blessings.

Even though we experience sad times, with Jesus, there is never utter despair and we find the peace and courage to dwell on the good things.

We cannot evade confusion or chaos at times, but we have the ability to concentrate on the blessings and good things that the Master provides. When we do this it's amazing how the turmoil often changes to peace and even joy.

Prayer for today

Heavenly Father, you never promised a life without sadness or trouble, and I am so thankful you walk with us through all our experiences. When I am saddened by circumstances, let me dwell on my blessings and realize you are still with me and that alone will bring me peace. I am so blessed in so many ways and often take my blessings for granted. Forgive me for neglecting to thank you.

In Jesus's name. Amen

Friday

joy, joy, joy

His anger lasts for a moment but his favour lasts a lifetime.
Weeping may go on all night, but joy comes with the morning.

Psalm 30:5

When I was a child, I vividly remember being scolded and punished for being disobedient to my parents. My father's lectures and reprimands often led me to see my errors quickly and I remember feeling sorry when I realized his disappointment in my behaviour.

The following morning or even that same evening, my father always surprised me with a special little treat and tenderness, which confirmed that his love for me was intact and would never disappear. I was always assured of forgiveness and unconditional love.

I liken this to being a child of God. Our lives seem to be paths of troubles and trials with consequences or lessons to be learned, but when that has been accomplished, we have joy that is full of glory.

The realization of error brings tears of remorse accompanied by a need to be forgiven, and with the assurance of forgiveness comes joy. As often as we err, Jesus waits for us to come to him and repent because he delights in our joy, which is the product of the process.

Prayer for today

Dear Jesus, how can I say, thank you, for all the times you have forgiven me and the joy you filled me with because of this action. Help me to dwell on the good things and especially the joy that comes from repenting. To know you love me so much you will always forgive me, is peace in itself. Thank you for your unconditional love.

In Jesus's name. Amen.

Adena H. Paget †

Weekend Read

quiet visitor

Christmas was a little less festive the year Drew was killed. On Christmas Eve we were standing by the front window waiting for the festivities to begin and the children to start arriving, when right in front of our eyes, under the huge spruce tree in our yard we saw him.

The Pheasant Visit

I had a visitor today
before Christmas day
What a wonderful blessing sent by God
To say
"He loves me"
To confirm his presence
To bring peace
joy
contentment
But most of all – beauty
What an awesome privilege to behold
the beauty of this wonderful creature.
There he sat
Under the branches
Protected by the canopy of green
Brilliant colors,
blue, green, red, and brown
Long, flowing tail feathers
Gentle as a lamb
Just sitting there
in all his splendour

For so long a time
So I could watch and appreciate
The beauty of what God gave
On December 24, 1998.
Is it a confirmation of the beauty
Of our precious son, Drew?

WEEK 31

Monday

following God's plan

"I know the plans I have for you," says the Lord. "They are plans for good and not for disaster, to give you a future and a hope."

Jeremiah 29:11

Parents usually have plans for their children. I remember our plans. Our child would always listen to us, do as we ask, and never complain because we were going to be perfect parents.

I was never going to lose my temper and always give reasonable explanations to everything. Our children were going to finish school, attend university, go on to careers they would love, and eventually marry and have children, who would then be perfect as well.

It wasn't long before I realized my visualized plans were not coming to fruition. Many times we were frustrated parents because our children would not heed our advice or they would do things that made us unhappy and angry.

Adena H. Paget †

Through all of it we never stopped loving them and kept on believing they would return to the basic moral and right truths they were taught.

Our children are now adults and despite the detours they took, we are proud of each one and they have grown into beautiful people. If we instil the basics in our children and take time to teach them right and wrong and implement the consequences needed, most times our parenting will be successful.

God is our Heavenly Father and also has plans for us, His children. God's plan is always in place and we need to trust Him fully, to lead us and direct us in the path He has chosen for our journey. Even though we detour from time to time, the way to the planned road is always available. This is the path filled with hope for a blessed future. Ask the Lord to direct you to His plan for your life.

Prayer for today

Heavenly Father, I am so thankful you have a plan for my life. So often, I try to do things my way only to realize my way is neither the best nor the way to success. I realize you have given me the freedom to choose, and I want to choose your way. Help me to hear your voice and heed your direction in my life.

In Jesus's name. Amen.

Tuesday
gift of peace

I am leaving you with a gift – peace of mind and heart. And the peace that I give you isn't like the peace the world gives. So don't be troubled or afraid.

John 14:27

God's plan involves the gift of peace, a peace that passes all understanding.

During the times in my life when trials seemed to loom over me, I never experienced hopelessness with my eyes on God.

In sickness or loss, God gives peace. After the loss of our son, many people commented on how strong I was, and yet I knew in my heart it was not my strength that brought evident peace but Christ the Solid Rock. Christ became stronger in my weakness.

How blessed we are to be able to lean on Him in our time of need and rely on His perfect plan for our lives. He waits for us to rely on Him for the peace that he offers for our benefit.

Prayer for today

Dear Heavenly Father, thank you for being the provider of a peace that passes all understanding. Even when we are under siege from the enemy, you help us to overcome all adversity with the peace only you can give. Thank you for the promises in your Word. Today, Father, I ask for a special measure of the peace you provide.

In Jesus's name. Amen.

Adena H. Paget

†

Wednesday

following

You chart the path ahead of me and tell me where to stop and rest. Every moment you know where I am.

Psalm 139:3

How often I have worried and fretted about things that never happened. It all seems to come down to total trust in our Maker.

I have heard individuals say, "God does not care about the little things in my life." His word tells us He cares about all our actions and here David tells us God is even concerned about our time of resting. This indicates to me, we are to take the time to rest. So many of us are too busy to rest and reflect on His will.

God has a perfect plan for our lives but we need to seek Him in order to know what it is and then we need to follow His desire.

He always allows us to choose our action but He is aware of our choices because He knows where we are every moment.

Prayer for today

Heavenly Father, thank you for being concerned about me every moment of each day. I want to do your will and I need your help to know what your will is for me. Help me to take the time to rest and reflect on your word and to listen for your voice to guide and direct me.

In Jesus's name. Amen

Thursday

God knows from beginning to end...

You saw me before I was born. Every day my life was recorded in your book. Every moment was laid out before a single day had passed

Psalm 139:16

What a mighty God we serve. Our human minds cannot begin to comprehend the magnificent and awesome greatness of God.

How foolish we are to follow our own decisions and try to change God's perfect plan for our lives. In our ignorance we follow worldly pleasures, which can only provide satisfaction for a short time.

We are born to follow God's plan for our lives. He ordained our very being. He cares about us and loves us more than our earthly parents are capable of.

He has a plan for our lives and if we seek Him and desire His pathway, we find true and lasting fulfillment. His perfect plan requires devotion and sacrifices and brings total satisfaction and peace.

Prayer for today

Dear Lord, Today, I want to pray this scripture:

Point out anything in me that offends you and lead me along the path of everlasting life.

Psalm 139:24

Help me to be sensitive to your direction today.

In Jesus's name. Amen.

Friday

know and trust

Trust in the Lord with all your heart; do not depend on your own understanding. Seek His will in all you do and He will direct your paths.

Proverbs 3: 5&6

Our responsibility is to seek and trust. God created us for His glory. He is the Creator, all-knowing, all-powerful.

Often the ways of the Lord are strange to us and we don't understand but we only see a small narrow scope of the picture whereas God sees all. Our small window inhibits our view of the panoramic picture God sees.

We are part of His vast plan and when we realize His ways are best and we learn to trust Him in everything, life becomes enjoyable and worry-free.

This freedom enables us to use our time praising God and giving thanks, which is why we were created in the first place.

Prayer for today

Heavenly Father, thank you for your grace and faithfulness. I want to trust you more and know your will so help me to listen and to trust you in everything that happens in my life. I love you Lord.

In Jesus's name. Amen.

Weekend Read

a mothers lament

I hope you will indulge me with one last entry for our son. I trust it may speak to your heart. Searching for unconditional love, to give and to receive, is the essence of the following poem.

To Drew and Others – searching for love

Oh, my son, my son!
You who loved until it overflowed,
You, who felt, who hurt, beyond words.
The sensitivity that you displayed was beautiful
and vivid in my memory as we spent many hours in conversation.
I know you tried to understand me and many others
And yet, you struggled with your feelings.
They got in your way, blurred your vision.
You were trying to understand
Unconditional love!

Adena H. Paget †

What is it, became the question.
It is the love that keeps on loving when it's difficult.
It is the love that keeps on giving when others give up.
It is the love that loves through hurts and destruction.
It is the love that continues when you don't like very much.
It is the belief that you "can."
The faith to pursue
The hope in the dark.
The desire to give of yourself
And the patience to endure.
It is much more than these words can say.
Words cannot do it justice nor can it be articulated,
For unconditional love is perfect and we cannot attain perfection.
We in ourselves, are incapable.
We are creatures who harbour bitterness and shame.
We are not equipped to show perfect love in ourselves,
For our human frailties get in the way.
How then, why do we struggle to envelope it?
Why do we press on to attain it?
Because it is the epitome of all.
It is the grace and mercy of the Redeemer,
And only in him and with him can we even come close.
You are now in a place of perfect love,
My son, my joy and pride.

WEEK 32

Monday
three important points

> *O People, the Lord has already told you what is good and this is what he requires: to do what is right, to love mercy and to walk with your God.*
>
> Micah 6:8

This is the message God gave to Micah regarding the Israelites. This is still what God requires of his children today. If we live by these three simple instructions our lives are pleasing to our Creator.

1. To do what is right – if we strive to do what is right, we aspire to follow the Ten Commandments. Doing what is right is inherent for obedience to all God desires of us. His instructions are very clearly described in His Word.

2. To love mercy – the word mercy is defined as withholding punishment or judgment our sins deserve. God showed mercy to us by sacrificing His only son, Jesus Christ, for our sins. He withholds judgment against us for our sins because the blood of Jesus has washed us clean. God expects us to show mercy to others as He showed mercy to us. The absence of judging others reflects mercy.

3. To walk humbly with God – the greatness and majesty of God is humbling indeed. We take our blessings for

granted, we forget where they come from. We become knowledgeable in secular society and neglect to rely on God. When I become confident in myself and smug in my ways, God allows something totally unexpected to happen, ultimately teaching me a worthwhile truth. To walk humbly with God means acknowledging him in everything, always giving thanks to him, and always trusting him.

When we walk humbly with God our attitude is one of meekness in submission to his perfect will.

Prayer for today

Oh Lord, sometimes my attitude is not what it's supposed to be, I often think of myself first and feel sorry for myself. Help me to show mercy to others as you have shown mercy to me. Help me to do what is right and to walk humbly with you. Let me be all that I can be.

In Jesus's name. Amen.

Tuesday

meaningful prayers

The earnest prayer of a righteous person has great power and wonderful results.

James 5:16

The dictionary defines **earnest** as ardent, fervent, to have zeal.

Often our prayers are general or obligatory. We pray because we know we should. James says we are to pray earnestly, with fervency and zeal. This leads to wonderful results.

Our prayers are not always answered the way we would like them to be answered, but God always answers them in a way that will mature and equip us for the work He has for us and ultimately to prepare us for eternity.

God always has our best interests at heart even though it doesn't seem like it sometimes. We need to trust Him.

If we have confessed our sins and have a personal relationship with Christ, we are considered righteous in God's eyes and we are told our earnest prayers have great power and wonderful results.

How can we neglect our prayer time with a promise such as this? Resolve to spend some quality time with your Creator and through Christ, He will hear and grant results.

Prayer for today

Heavenly Father... (Talk to your Heavenly Father, ask Him to help you free up time to talk with Him each day with earnestness, don't forget to thank Him for your blessings.)

In Jesus's name. Amen

Adena H. Paget †

Wednesday

God sees me as...

*...don't let anyone deceive you about this;
when people do what is right, it is because they
are righteous, even as Christ is righteous.*

1 John 3:7

When we walk with Jesus in a personal relationship, we are considered righteous in God's eyes. It is because Jesus pleads on our behalf, to God the Father, and God sees us as righteous.

As Christians we have the power of the Holy Spirit dwelling in us to keep us holy and do what is right. It is difficult or impossible to do what is right by ourselves.

Paul says, "I do what I don't want to do and don't do what I should do." Even Paul the Apostle struggled with this dilemma, but in this scripture in the book of John, we are assured what we do is right because we become righteous even as Christ is righteous.

It is only through Christ's sacrifice that we are considered righteous in God's eyes. If you are in a relationship with Jesus, don't let anyone instil doubt in you about your righteousness. You are a child of God, seen as righteous by God.

Prayer for today

Heavenly Father, I am so thank full you see me as righteous. Thank you for taking my sins and removing them as far as the east is from the west. Thank you for sending Jesus to shed His perfect blood to save me and make me righteous in your sight. I am in awe of you seeing me as clean and saved from all unrighteousness. Thank you for the glorious promise of one day being with you for all eternity. Help me to let the Holy Spirit guide me and direct me.

In Jesus's name. Amen.

Thursday
the source

...the Lord is the source of all my righteousness and strength.

Isaiah 45:24

My husband and I were on a breathtaking hike in the Alberta Rockies. We were marvelling at the magnificence of the Bow River. It serves many communities; Calgary being the largest consumer.

I am always concerned about the possibility of a shortage of water and I wondered how this river could provide so many people with water and never run out. Soon we came to the source of the flowing water and realized the potential of the glacier that enabled the river to flow so abundantly. Although scientists say it is frightening how rapidly the glacier is melting, it is a majestic thing to behold. It reminded me how our Heavenly Father is the source of our strength and righteousness.

Unlike the glacier, He never runs short of living water and there is no danger of a slow melt. His water is freely given to us as we need it and it is this water, this Holy Spirit infilling that enables us to be righteous and strong.

In order to enter Heaven, we must be righteous. Can we obtain righteousness on our own? Perhaps by good works or by clean living? No, definitely not. Where then or how can we become righteous? Only through the source, Jesus Christ who became our source of righteousness.

When we confess our sins, He is faithful and just to forgive our sins and to cleanse us from all unrighteousness.

1 John 1:9

Our righteousness comes from the Lord, who sent Jesus to die for our sins and therefore we can stand before God as righteous people. This enables us to be strong in faith and bold for Christ.

Prayer for today

Heavenly Father, I'm so thankful that you are a never-ending source of living water. I am thankful I can draw from this living water to fill me with the strength I need each day. You never change or waver and you long to fill me daily.

In Jesus's name. Amen.

Friday

on the topic of righteousness....

Genesis 15:6 And Abraham believed the Lord and the Lord declared him righteous because of his faith.

Romans 5:21. So just as sin ruled over all nations and brought them to death, now God's wonderful kindness rules instead, giving us right standing with God and resulting in eternal life through Jesus Christ our Lord.

Romans 5:18. Adam's one sin brought condemnation upon everyone, but Christ's one act of righteousness makes all people right in God's sight and gives them life.

Romans 6:18. Now you are free from sin, your old master, and you have become slaves to your new master, righteousness.

Psalm 85:11. Truth springs up from the earth and righteousness smiles down from Heaven.

13. Righteousness goes as a herald before him/her preparing the way for his/her steps.

There are numerous passages in scripture pertaining to the righteousness of a believer, declaring that we are made right or righteous by faith, as Abraham was.

Even though one man's sin, Adam, brought condemnation upon everyone, Christ's shed blood is able to make everyone righteous in God's sight. Our righteousness through Christ enables us to delete our desire to sin and become instead, a slave to righteousness. A slave to righteousness is not being a legalistic slave or bound by a law, instead, it includes a desire to please. It asks, "What can I do to please you, Lord?"

Prayer for today

Dear Lord, I am in awe of your love and ability to make me righteous, even as you did for your servant, Abraham. I am so thankful to be your servant, even your slave. I want to please you Lord and continue to be righteous in your sight. Thank you Lord for saving my soul. Thank you

Lord for making me whole, Thank you Lord for giving to me, thy great salvation so rich and free.

In Jesus's name. Amen.

Weekend Read

journal entry

My mother-in-law

My mother-in-law was a generous person but never learned how to display love to her family. As a result it was difficult to openly show affection toward her. In her later years, I visited her often in the nursing home. This is an entry from my diary.

> *1996*
>
> *Through the love of Christ, I am gaining compassion for Bob's mom. I'm remembering her generosity to me many years ago.*
>
> *She gave monetarily – it was the only way she knew how to show her love. She expressed her love seldom, if ever, but I probably never told her that I loved her either. Perhaps it was because of the many hurts she caused my husband when he was growing up.*
>
> *I realized the deep wounds that were inflicted and the healing process took many years. I thank God, He has*

granted me patience and the ability to show grace and mercy during the healing time.

After many years, my caring husband is no longer afraid to display tenderness and allow his emotions to show. What a wonderful blessing.

Through God's grace, I can now say, "I love you," to his mom and mean it. I know how important it is to hear those words and I pray that I will be able to concentrate on her good points. May my love be able to drown out the negative things that have occurred during my forty years of knowing her. She is very frail and her wish is to die.

I pray that the Lord will take her soon. I can't even imagine being in her place. She feels unloved and unneeded. Not many relatives or friends or grandchildren visit, and I know this hurts her deeply.

I realize she did not try very hard at developing a relationship with them, but I still feel sorry for her loss. I must remember to pray for her more.

I pray that our children will not suffer guilt feelings for their absence in her last years, their lives are truly busy and in a different place right now.

Update – Mom Paget passed on to her eternal abode, May 14th 1999. I had the privilege of leading her to Jesus shortly before her death. I am so grateful for that experience. I have the assurance of seeing her again in a place of perfection. May she rest in peace.

Adena H. Paget †

WEEK 33

Monday

good efforts are never wasted

So my dear brothers and sisters, be strong and steady,

always enthusiastic about the Lord's work,

for you know that nothing you do for the Lord is ever useless.

1 Corinthians 15:56

Sometimes we feel our efforts to serve the Lord are insignificant. It is easy to become despondent and allow negative and selfish thoughts to overtake us. We may be experiencing a time when our production of fruit is meagre and we wonder if we are even capable of any type of ministry that furthers the Kingdom of God.

Paul is telling us to be strong and enthusiastic in our efforts. Whether we make muffins for someone, give to the Lord monetarily, visit the sick or lonely, or take a moment to comfort a small, hurting child, if it is done to honour the Lord, it is never wasted.

Never give up because God sees what is done in His name even if no one else knows about it or sees it. No matter how great or how small, our work for the Lord is never in vain.

Prayer for today

Heavenly Father, I am so thankful for the promises in your Word. Forgive me for being discouraged, when I know everything is in your hands and all things work together for good because I love you. I am so glad you see what I do for you even if no one else does. Help me to continue to do good for others and thank you for loving me just as I am.

In Jesus's name. Amen.

Tuesday
sensitivity and discretion

Live wisely among those who are not Christians, and make the most of every opportunity. Let your conversation be gracious and effective so that you will have the right answer for everyone.

Colossians 4:5-6

I was taken out to brunch the other morning. As we sat in the booth waiting for our food, my companion, who is not a believer, overheard two men who were sitting across from us. It sounded like two pastors discussing other denominations. In their conversation they proceeded to bad-mouth faiths that they were apparently not part of. The volume of their conversation was distinctly audible and my companion was immediately negative towards Christianity and especially these two men.

I believe they were Christians, but in their zeal to defend their chosen faith, they neglected to be sensitive to those around them. I believe the careless conversation of these two individuals had a negative impact on my non-Christian friend and affirmed his decision to remain a non-believer.

It taught me a valuable lesson in sensitivity toward those around me whether I know them or not. I'm sure when we disagree with other Christians, we voice our opinions, but our conversation for strangers to hear should be gracious and effective and generate positive attitudes towards others who are following a Bible-believing faith.

The people who don't agree with biblical teaching should be respected as fellow human beings and shown sensitivity. God created them and loves them and we need to show God's love to everyone.

Prayer for today

Dear Jesus, Help me keep my conversation gracious and uplifting no matter where I am. I want to be more like you, Jesus. When you spoke to the woman at the well, you did not put her down or bad-mouth her for her lifestyle. You simply told her where to find peace and forgiveness. Help me to show more Christian love to the friends and neighbours you have blessed me with.

In Jesus's name. Amen.

Wednesday

chosen

How thankful I am to Christ Jesus our Lord for considering me trustworthy and appointing me to serve him.

1 Timothy 1:12

God chooses us to be ambassadors for Him. We cannot make this happen by our own power. It is the Holy Spirit working in us and through us.

There have been times in my life when I was strongly prompted to speak to someone or make a call or approach certain ones with an idea or message. As I look back on those times and remember the results, I realize God was directing me. Many times, the recipient told me my call was exactly what they needed, or I learned that a friend was lonely for someone to talk to, or similar reactions.

God used these instances for His glory. Our job is to be close to God so we can know His will for our lives and increase our sensitivity to hearing His voice and know His directives.

By reading His Word and spending time with Christ, we increase our awareness of Him thereby making it easier to know where He is leading us, which enables us to serve Him more and love Him more and know Him more.

Prayer for today

Heavenly Father, I praise and thank you for choosing me to be your child. I am so blessed to be part of your family. I agree with the author of this verse, who is also grateful to be your child. Help me to acknowledge you in every situation and never forget who I am.

In Jesus's name. Amen.

Thursday

things get in the way

Dear Children, keep away from anything that might take God's place in your hearts.

1 John 5:21

We have a little motor home where we spend our winters. We travel to Vancouver Island for five or six months each year where the flowers bloom and the grass stays green.

About the third year of our arrangement, I really wanted a bigger rig. I had all kinds of excuses for needing one, from being able to invite friends for dinner to carrying more necessary stuff with us.

After listening to my nagging, my generous husband finally agreed to look. As we spent time viewing bigger and newer rigs, God brought to mind this verse and I realized why I was so adamant in purchasing something larger. It was partly to satiate my worldly desires, partly pride, and partly the fact that I knew my husband would sacrifice our savings just to keep me happy.

This selfish desire consumed me until he gave in and agreed to buy a new rig.

When God helped me see my selfish attitude, I realized that the idea of a bigger and newer motor home had consumed places in my heart that belonged to God.

I learned how easy it is to get wrapped up in worldly goods and activities and desires that take the place of God's presence in our hearts.

We need to guard our hearts against allowing these desires and activities to become too important. Put God first in your life and keep your hearts free from things that may crowd Him.

For the world offers only the lust for physical pleasure, the lust for everything we see, and the pride in our possessions. These are not from the Father. They are from this evil world.

1 John 1:16.

Friday
reflecting God's presence

Go out! Prepare the highway for my people to return! Smooth out the road! Pull out the boulders; raise a flag for all the nations to see.

Isaiah 62:10

Every year when we make our autumn trip to Vancouver Island and when we return in the spring, we study maps and talk to others who have experienced the same destination, then we weigh the pros and cons and also take the scenery into consideration, and then, we contemplate which road we will travel on.

We both enjoy traveling and seeing new sights but we also want to make sure our road choice is not undergoing major construction which might hold us up or make it impassable for us in our motor home. There are many factors to consider.

In the margin of my Bible I have written, "Am I building a highway that people will want to travel on?"

How are we portraying our walk with the Lord? Are we making the road inviting? Do we preach or live the joy and fulfillment of His presence? Do others say, "I want to travel on the road you're on" or, "If that's Christianity, I don't want any part of it"?

I encourage you to use this day to evaluate your portrayal of Christ and ask Him to help you model His fullness.

Prayer for today

Dear Lord, forgive me for the times I forget to show the joy you fill me with. Sometimes life gets hard and I dwell on the problems instead of trusting you. I know you will take care of my burdens. Would you help me to reflect your joy and peace to others today?

In Jesus's name. Amen.

Weekend Read

life is a song

As we struggle to sing
the song of perfection
We practice and think,
"I have the solution!"
Perfect pitch is the goal
we try to maintain,
The song comes together
but alas, all in vain.
Perfect pitch on our own
cannot be attained,
downright impossible,
gives us a pain.
To accomplish this task
may take us years,
for efforts too flat
or too sharp for the ears.
We muster the courage
to continue to sing
And strive for perfection
with a prayer and a wing.
Sometimes we achieve

a song with a lilt,
and others will say
what a great thing we built.
That makes us feel good,
and we strive for perfection
Only to realize
The dissatisfaction.
We forget to rely
on the master musician,
Our notes then deny
any chance of affection.
Start again with the coach
he directs and he leads,
With him we will conquer
the aria He feeds.
His marvellous patience,
His grace bids us come,
The joy and the essence,
the perfect pitch sung.
If we should stop singing
or stray off the key,
His love keeps on blessing
on you and on me.
Encouraging our spirit
with patience and prayer,
providing the ticket,
teaching with care.
When we join that great choir
of Heavenly saints,
it is then we'll aspire
no more flats or constraints.
We still have a mission
while here on this earth,
to continue the action

and fill it with mirth.
For without song and music
and the effort to write,
To sing clever limericks
that raise to new heights.
There won't be a sweet
or a new perfect song,
When we join with the Father
And the Heavenly throng.

WEEK 34

Monday
developing character

Until the time came to fulfill His word, the Lord tested Joseph's character.

Psalm 105:19

Are you waiting for something to happen in your life? Is God testing your character as He did with Joseph? How are you handling the wait?

It has been years since I started praying for loved ones to embrace the grace and forgiveness of the Lord Jesus Christ. During the wait, I have learned much. At the beginning, I was impatient and tried to change them on my own until I realized I was only hindering God's work by interfering with Him.

I finally started praying for God to give me the heart He wanted me to have and an evident Christ-like love.

As I waited, I was blessed with a peace I had never known before. I am not in a perfect place yet because I still get frustrated and impatient at times, but God grants the grace I need each day as I learn to lay my concerns at His feet and allow Him to carry my burdens.

My character is being developed while I wait for His perfect timing and I know one day God will fulfill His promise as I allow Him to work in the lives of loved ones.

It is not easy to give up all the worries but it is important to learn to wait for God's timing just as Joseph did many years ago. We know, in the end, God fulfilled His purpose in Joseph's life.

Prayer for today

Dear Lord, I know I get impatient at times and I also know your timing is best. Help me to be patient and wait for you to fulfill your plans in my life and those around me. My desire is to please you and accept your plan for my life.

In Jesus's name. Amen.

Tuesday

getting to know Him

Instead we will hold to the truth in love,
becoming more and more,
in every way like Christ.

Ephesians 4:15

Adena H. Paget

†

My husband and I are celebrating over fifty years of marriage this week.

We have spent many frustrating times learning how to be compatible. We have learned much about each other, and although our differences have become less, our personalities are still very individualistic and independent.

As time goes on and we continue to grow in our relationship, I find our similarities growing and our differences diminishing. It doesn't just happen, it takes determination, perseverance, communication, consistency, and a shared love.

I believe this is how we can achieve Christ-likeness, we need to spend more time with God. We need to read His Word and spend time in prayer and listen to Him when He speaks to us. We need to praise and worship Him and become more sensitive to His leading and His guidance.

Our desire needs to be a longing to draw near to our Heavenly Father, through Christ Jesus and this is achieved by knowing Him more.

Prayer for today

Heavenly Father, as I live day to day in this busy world, I want to become more and more like you. Help me to be able to spend the time to get to know you more and even to become more like you. Let our differences become less and our similarities become more and more alike.

In Jesus's name. Amen.

Wednesday

suffering to learn

So even though Jesus was God's son,
He learned obedience from the things He suffered.

Hebrews 5:8

Many times I have asked God, "Why?" as I'm sure you have. When we find ourselves in a valley of sickness, frustration, hurt, or any other suffering, we are not alone. Why would we think we might be exempt from suffering when we see here that even Jesus, God's own son had to learn obedience.

When we were children we often learned by natural or unnatural consequences. Many times our parents exercised their mature wisdom to teach us obedience.

As adults we still need to be taught and reminded what obedience to God really is. Therefore, God allows suffering in our lives. It is not a punishment, it is allowed to happen to teach us wisdom and maturity.

God uses our suffering to teach us and train us for our future life with Him. It is our responsibility to learn obedience, thereby causing us to grow spiritually. We are in "training" and sometimes the training process is difficult. There is always a purpose even though we can't see it at the time.

If you are in a valley, be thankful because it is enabling you to ultimately grow to become all you can be.

Prayer for today

Heavenly Father, forgive me for griping and complaining when things do not go my way. I know the trials and frustrations in my life are there for a

Adena H. Paget †

reason. Help me to see the trials in my life as stepping-stones to becoming what you want me to be.

In Jesus's name. Amen.

Thursday

virtue of patience

Then Abraham waited patiently and he received what God had promised.

Hebrews 6:15

When I think about God's promise to Abraham, I have admiration and great respect for Abraham. He was already an older man when he was told he would be a father to as many people as there are grains of sand. Abraham, in his "blind" faith, accepted God's promise even though he had no children. As we read the outcome, we know God's promise came to pass.

When I grow impatient, which is often, I think of Abraham who waited patiently until he was an old man, to see the promise of God become reality.

If you have been waiting long, don't give up. Through this wait you are displaying patience, which builds strong character. This life is a training ground for our Heavenly home so it is a time of learning and becoming.

Do not fear but rest in the assurance that God is answering your prayer and has your best interest at heart. God always fulfils His promise.

Prayer for today

Dear Heavenly Father, thank you for being a Father that I can rely on. I know you love me more than I can conceive and therefore you have my best interest at heart. Let me live in your perfect will and always trust you because you know what is best for me. Help me not to become impatient when things don't go my way because your way is the best.

In Jesus's name. Amen.

Friday

sustaining love

May the Lord bring you into an ever-deeper understanding of the love of God and the endurance that comes from Christ.

2 Thessalonians 3:5

When my only sister passed on to her Heavenly home, I wasn't sure how I would be able to cope without her love, prayers, and friendship.

After my mom's death when I was eleven years old, my sister became my care- giver. She took me shopping for clothes and taught me how to take care of myself. When I married, it was her instruction I listened to. She became my listening ear and shoulder to cry on. She was my confidante and comfort.

I had the privilege to be with her the last five weeks of her life and sat by her bedside as she raised her arms in anticipation of being lifted in the arms of Jesus to her Heavenly home.

As I look back to that time, I know it was one experience that brought me into a deeper understanding of God's love. We cannot understand

Adena H. Paget †

when we are in the eye of the situation, but when we look back it becomes clear how God's love sustains us while we are in the trial.

Be patient and take comfort that this trial will generate a deeper understanding of God's love and one day you will look back and say, "I understand."

Prayer for today

Heavenly Father, I praise you and thank you for taking care of me. When I experience trials and wonder where you are, I know you are right here with me and you care for me. Help me to look at the valleys with joy because I am moving into a deeper understanding of your love. Thank you, Lord for having patience with me.

In Jesus's name. Amen.

Weekend Read

a tribute

The following poem was written by our daughter, Robyn, following the death of my dad, her grandfather. She read it at his memorial for the first time. It was a blessing to all and my hope is you might be blessed by her offering.

In Memory of Grampa

January 23 1910 - August 7, 2003

With gospel songs and meal time grace,
My heart will always see his face.
His deep bass voice in prayer or song,
We knew his blessings would be long.
When Grandpa prayed to start the day,
All was well as we went our way.
Precious memories, flood my soul,
His steadfast faith, helped make me whole.
No matter his faults or his unbending ways,
No matter his errors or some sinful days,
No matter the wrong he may have done,
My grandpa was tops. The very best one.
The sadness, it seeps deep down in my heart,
For the fact does remain, that now we must part.
Many will miss his particular ways,
Many remember his long lived out days.
Many will cherish the memories we hold,
As love for my grandpa, is more precious than gold.
Today as I bid him farewell from this place,
I imagine him standing before Jesus's face.
His rewards waiting there and his mansion prepared,
Not a gift left ungiven, not a treasure be spared.
As he walks with his Saviour discussing God's gifts,
Our hearts can be lightened as our sorrows lift.

WEEK 35

Monday
good thoughts

Fix your thoughts on what is true and honourable and right. Think about things that are pure and lovely and admirable. Think about things that are excellent and worthy of praise.

Philippians 4:8

We sure could dwell on the negative aspects of our world these days. Wars are raging and evil people are oppressing good people. Many are angry, many are sad, some are in agreement with one side while others are in agreement with the other side. Emotions are mixed but strong.

It seems to be an accepted way of life to be critical about leaders and the decisions that are being made. It becomes habitual to argue and be negative and call down the people in power who have to make the ultimate decisions.

Paul says we should fix our thoughts; that means "adhere" to what is honourable, pure, lovely, and admirable.

Even in trying and unknown times we need to look for the good. We need to keep our eyes on Jesus. Every day our responsibility is to dwell on good and lovely things, to think about excellent and lovely attributes of others.

Pray for those in power, pray for our leaders, and keep your eyes on Jesus. It is difficult to speak harshly about people when you are praying for them. Life becomes easier and the world becomes a better place.

Prayer for today

Heavenly Father, thank you for reminding me to look for the good things. You created a wonderful world for us to enjoy and instead of counting our blessings, we tend to dwell on the negative things. Forgive me Lord and help me to remember your teaching and your love and your beauty. Also, Lord, I lift up our leaders to you and pray you will give them wisdom in making decisions. Give them the courage they need to follow the convictions of their hearts.

In Jesus's name. Amen.

Tuesday

producing good fruit

The way to identify a tree or a person is by the kind of fruit that is produced.

Matthew 7:20

We bought a beautiful new portable printer the other day. It was expensive with a sleek appearance. The size was what attracted us to this particular model because it was exactly the right size for our RV lifestyle.

Since we had already purchased a new digital camera, we wanted to print our own photographs. We were amazed at the quality of the pictures it produced; realistic skin tones, vivid color, and sharp lines.

We discovered very shortly afterwards that it did not have the power to feed the heavy photograph paper through the cogs. We had to apply extra pressure to enable the paper to catch and it often got caught, which caused the ink to blot in the workings and then we had black liquid blotches on the next few copies.

Finally, in exasperation, we called the manufacturer to ask what we were doing wrong. The conclusion was this particular printer was not designed to feed photograph paper or card stock through the print process. We returned our purchase and exchanged it for a cumbersome printer that doesn't look as nice or as sleek but does a great job.

I asked myself, what kind of fruit am I producing? Am I a good ambassador for Jesus? Are people attracted to God by my life? Do I do the job required of me or do I just try to look good doing what I do? Is my attitude right to perform the job expected?

Prayer for today

Heavenly Father, thank you for your grace and mercy. Help me to do a better job of portraying your love and forgiveness. Forgive me for hastily dismissing some people on their appearance alone. Thank you Jesus for being our example and accepting all who come to you. Would you help me produce fruit for your kingdom?

In Jesus's name. Amen.

Wednesday
give it up

In everything you do, stay away from complaining and arguing.

Philippians 2:12

I remember as a small child, listening to my dad and aunt argue about scripture. It often became a fist slamming, table banging, and door slamming battle. The combat consisted of a bantering of scripture verses tossed back and forth like a ping-pong ball.

It left a bad taste in my spirit and in the rest of my family's as well. After leaving the scene, often in a huff, we would be subjected to days of listening to my father defend himself to us. I vowed never to argue about scripture with anyone for my entire life. Although I have had tempting moments, I find it a valuable exercise to stick by my convictions. I know it fosters harmony with others.

Our winter lifestyle of living in a motor home six months of the year, has taught me to weigh what is truly important enough to complain or argue about.

In the years of our adventure, my husband and I have engaged in only a few arguments. I believe a large part of the credit is due to the marvellous grace of God and the indwelling of the Holy Spirit, peppered with a good portion of self control.

When we let go of the small stuff, the victory of harmony between a married couple and others can be accomplished. Life becomes more enjoyable if we make this scripture a daily reminder of how to live.

Take your complaints to the Lord and leave them at the foot of the cross.

Prayer for today

Dear Heavenly Father, thank you for your forgiveness and thank you for not remembering my faults or sins. I know I am forgiven by your grace and my repentance. Help me not to dwell on the faults of others, especially those close to me. Keep me from making a big deal of things that don't matter in the big picture of life. I love you, Lord, enable me to love with a Christ-like love and be forgiving like you.

In Jesus's name. Amen.

Adena H. Paget †

Thursday

clothing and robes

I am overwhelmed with joy in the Lord my God. For He has dressed me with the clothing of salvation and draped me in a robe of righteousness.

Isaiah 61:10

I was a retailer in a ladies wear store for several years before I returned to university to complete my degree in education.

Working in this environment increased my desire to wear the latest fashions and build my wardrobe beyond reason. I also enjoyed a substantial discount and seldom wore the same outfit more than two or three times. My clothing became very important to me.

I'm not saying that we should not or cannot dress well but when our clothes become the most important part of our lives, we need to reassess our priorities.

When I rededicated my life to Christ, I realized that my earthly coverings were not even comparable to the covering of salvation and the robe of righteousness that the Lord was covering me with. What an undeniable feeling of worth encircles us when we accept the covering freely given to us by the Lord.

When my sister was very ill she spent many hours in prayer. Before her passing she related a vision she experienced. While kneeling by her bed, she was asking God to make her righteous. She then saw herself kneeling before Jesus who was approaching her with a large beautiful robe. As He draped the robe over her kneeling body, He even took the time to tuck in the edges and corners so that not one part of her was exposed.

I believe this is how God sees us, completely wrapped in a beautiful robe of righteousness.

Prayer for today

Dear Heavenly Father, help me to keep my priorities in order and to trust you more. Help me to let the riches of this world become a shadow and to make you the center of my life. Thank you for providing your cover of righteousness and dressing me with clothing salvation.

In Jesus's name. Amen.

Friday

let it be

A home divided against itself is doomed.

Mark 3:25

I had a very dear uncle, who was one of my spiritual mentors and heroes for as long as I can remember. I remember when he returned from the Second World War, the most handsome man I had ever seen, especially in his uniform. I think I was about five or six years old and very impressionable.

Being from a Mennonite family, he was regarded as a rebel to the faith. He served in the medical corps and so he was able to justify his service by saving lives instead of destroying them.

We loved and admired him because he was a legend and hero in our family. He was not afraid to do what he thought was right and he was not bound by the rules and regulations of religious encumbrances and legalities.

When he matured and aged, he wore a huge cowboy hat and played the dobro and guitar and sang country-flavoured songs. He was also gifted with a generous heart that never stopped giving.

Several years ago he was diagnosed with a brain tumour that became inoperable. His last word of advice to me on his dying bed was, "Don't be afraid to be wrong when you're right." In other words agree to disagree and move on.

Life becomes easier as I attempt to follow this gem of wisdom. I wish I had realized this many years ago. Even when we don't agree, if it doesn't compromise our beliefs or convictions, it is really quite painless to be quiet and stop the process of creating distress.

Prayer for today

Heavenly Father, I am so thankful for your acceptance of me even with all my faults. Help me to let the unimportant things become just that – unimportant. Let me be more humble and less argumentative. Help me not to dwell on having my own way but being more empathetic towards others. Let me be someone who displays positive thoughts and words of encouragement so that others may see your love through me.

In Jesus's name. Amen.

Weekend Read

a letter

The following writing was presented to me by my daughter on Mother's Day 2001. May it bless you as a mother, as well.

Dear Mom;

Being a woman has brought many trials and many blessings and as I walk this walk of motherhood, my thoughts often turn toward my mentor in mothering.

I put myself in her shoes at various times in her life and I reflect...

Doing so has helped me realize that she too is all human. She has other roles in life - other than being a mother.

She too has struggled, cried, laughed and rejoiced. She too has had moments of defeat as well as celebration.

My mentor, my mother heroine, knows what it feels like to be pregnant before marriage, understands what it means to have a disease-stricken child, has wept many tears for wayward children, has experienced the huge disappointment of her offspring quitting school and walking away from responsibilities.

She has felt the cutting hurt of unspoken and verbalized cruelty that comes from the mouths and actions of selfish children.

She has felt sorrow, grief, anger, rejection, fear, and jealousy.

When I reflect over the past forty years, I realize my mentor has taught me these mothering pains are natural, a part of life and reproduction.

She has taught me through her perfect example through the pain comes joyous celebration.

Celebrating a first step, a first word, a first passed test, first dollar earned, first car, first date, first love, and a first home.

Adena H. Paget †

She has shown me that mothering is a celebration of blessings, the
blessings of unconditional love, warm hellos and genuine hugs.

The exploding pride that a child can bring into your life
far outweighs the imploding strife that is inevitable.

My mentor has walked the walk, and has always
talked the talk of perfect mothering.

Thank you, Mom for your example of what a mother should be.

Thank you for your unconditional, unself-
ish, and ever present love and belief in me.

Thank you for being my mentor, not only in moth-
ering, but also a perfect example of a

wife, a friend, and a daughter.

There is no other

Like my mother.

By Robyn

WEEK 36

Monday

short lived troubles

...For the troubles we see will soon be over, but the joys to come will last forever.

2 Corinthians 4:18

When we are waiting for the end of an ordeal, we wonder and ask," Lord, How long? When will this be over?"

There are times in life when troubles seem to last forever. Some people seem to experience more troubles while others seems to be exempt.

I have a friend whose suffering has gone on for many years. She no sooner gets through one affliction and she is into another one. Sometimes it is health related, sometimes financial, and often she hurts for her children, who appear to be victims as well.

Despite this dilemma, her life is an example of the hope of our glorious Lord Jesus Christ. She seldom complains and continues to cherish the promise that "Joy comes in the morning." She longs to go home and be with Jesus but until that time comes, her diligence and perseverance is very evident to anyone who knows her.

She is my inspiration when I encounter troubles and through her example I can face my dilemmas with the glorious hope of being rid of troubles and having everlasting joy. What a glorious day that will be.

Prayer for today

Dear Lord, I am so thankful for the promises in your Word. I am glad this worldly life is just a training ground for our glorious life with you.

Adena H. Paget †

Thank you, Lord that our troubles will soon be over and even when we are experiencing trials you are watching over us and walking with us through them. Thank you that you promise us joy everlasting. What a wonderful hope you give us. Help me not to grumble and complain but to wait and look to that day when we shall see you and be with you.

In Jesus's name. Amen.

Tuesday
communication through sorrow

For God can use sorrow in our lives to help us turn away from sin and seek salvation.

2 Corinthians 7:10

I love to receive calls from our children, especially in the winter when we're on the island. I have noticed when they are experiencing hurts, anguish, or sorrow, the phone calls increase.

Last year our beautiful grand-daughter was experiencing growing pains. As she brought pain upon herself and her family, I was privileged to be kept in the loop of communication.

Her parents called often. They needed reassurance and feedback from us that the discipline measure they were administering for the situation was okay. I am thankful this winter has been easier for them and we haven't received as many phone calls.

I believe we have similarities to our children when troubles come upon us. When we experience hard times we realize our great need for Christ, but when things are going well, we often neglect our prayer life.

By spending more time in communication with the Lord we move toward Him and the closeness gives us peace and assurance of His presence. As we grow closer to our Father, our lives reflect His love and keep us from sinning.

Prayer for Today

Heavenly Father, forgive me for neglecting you. I know you still love me even though I seem to forget about you. Your love is ever present. When I wander from you it is not you who moves but it is I. Help me to communicate and learn to hear your voice. When I am close to you, you keep me from sinning, but when I wander away it becomes easier for me to stray from your will. I love you Lord.

In Jesus's name. Amen.

Wednesday

timely action

Remember, it is sin to know what you ought to do and then not do it.

James 4:17

James tells us to not do something that we know we should is just as serious as doing something you know you should not do. (This is sometimes called the sin of omission.)

My problem is procrastination. I hesitate to do things that I know I should.

Sometimes when I hesitate too long, the thing that should have been done, cannot be accomplished.

I am thankful for the teacher training I experienced because I learned the importance of facing a problem or task and acting upon it as soon as possible.

We all have deadlines to meet and if the process is postponed too long, it becomes an exercise in frustration and futility. Often the opportunity is completely lost.

Procrastination is not a sin in itself but when the Holy Spirit prompts us to act and we choose to ignore the prompt, it is often too late to perform the action and we rob ourselves of the blessing that comes from obedience.

Christ longs to shower us with His blessings but if we do not obey His request, He is deprived of the joy of sending us His blessing and we are deprived of receiving it.

Prayer for today

Heavenly Father, today I want to be obedient to you. Help me not to put things off but to act upon your requests when I need to. Forgive me for putting things off or not even doing the things you would have me do. Help me not to sin by neglecting to act when you have something for me to do.

In Jesus's name. Amen.

Thursday

devouring the Bible

...real life comes by feeding on every word of the Lord.

Deuteronomy 8:3

One translation of the word feed is "to devour." How often have we devoured the word of God or the Bible?

When my brother was studying to earn his degree in theology, one of his many tasks was to write a summary of every chapter in the entire Bible. When I have a question that I cannot find the answer to, pertaining to scripture, I ask him. I am always amazed by his knowledge of biblical content. I am sure his study did not end with that assignment but that is how it began; which in turn spurned his interest and thirst for more knowledge, motivating him to pursue God's Word further.

As He studied, God opened new revelations and blessed him by directing him to a further and deeper understanding of spiritual truths.

To delve into God's Word reinforces our relationship with Christ thereby allowing us to experience real life. To feed on the Word of God enables us to fully abide, to become all that God intended us to be, not on our own strength but by His power bringing us to the peace that leads to real life.

Prayer for today

Heavenly Father, I long for a deep thirst for your Word. Give me an unquenchable thirst that motivates me to study and search. Your Word has the answers to all of life's difficult questions and the real meaning of life. Thank you, Lord, for giving us the Bible. Help me to be a child of God who knows Christ on a personal basis and understands "real life."

In Jesus's name. Amen.

Adena H. Paget

†

Friday

safety

He led me to a place of safety; He rescued me because He delights in me.

2 Samuel 22:20

This is part of David's song to the Lord after the he was rescued from Saul and all his enemies.

Do you sense the Lord has led you to a place of safety? Is He in the process of leading you, even now?

Are you following or are you continuing to follow the path of destruction? If we do not follow the path the Lord prepares for us, we will never reach that beautiful place of safety. That place where we know we are sheltered by Him, sheltered from the enemy who tempts us with worldly pleasures that look appetizing and may even be fun for a time. That wonderful place of safety is where we will find and enjoy the sweet peace, contentment, and joy that only the presence of the Lord provides.

He delights in our need for Him and provides everything we need. When we allow His plan to unfold and follow the path He has chosen for us, we know we are in a safe place where nothing can harm us. This is where we need to be.

Ask the Lord to show you where He would have you walk and listen for His answer.

Prayer for today

Dear Lord, help me to be more like David, who searched for you and longed for a deeper relationship with you. You led him to safe places even though his enemy pursued him day and night. Thank you, Lord for delighting in me and loving me beyond comprehension. Help me to know you more and see where you want me to go. Lead me today, Lord.

In Jesus's name. Amen.

Weekend Read

letter for Blake

My firstborn – written January 1986

Over the years I have kept a personal journal. Perhaps you will be blessed by my ramblings and maybe it will encourage you to write your thoughts, convictions, concerns, prayer requests or feelings, as well.

You are my first-born and always hold a very special place in my heart. God's *hand has been upon you since you were first conceived. You were stubborn and did not want to leave your comfortable, warm place of nurture. Labour was thirty-six hours long and I almost decided to forget the whole thing…and then a miracle happened.*

You were only 6 lbs. 15 oz and such a precious gift from God. You were perfect and Dad and I thought you were the most beautiful baby that ever had been born. In fact you were far more handsome than I ever anticipated a baby could be. Your little head was covered with long dark hair and I loved every inch of your tiny fingers and toes and active little limbs. You were also the smartest little boy in our eyes; very clever and always ready to recite some little poem that Auntie "Edo" or myself taught you. We were so blessed by your arrival.

When you were four or five years old, you started complaining of bad tummy aches. They got so bad Dad and I took you to the emergency hospital one night.

We saw Dr. Watkins who told us you needed an appendectomy. We were willing to do anything to ease your pain so we agreed. We left you at the hospital that night, after you fell asleep.

When we returned the next morning we were shocked by your appearance – as a matter of fact, we did not recognize you. The doctor had to take us to your bed before we realized it was you. You had retained fluid and were bloated beyond recognition. It was a terrible day for Dad and me. We were afraid for you and did not know why this had happened. We were just kids ourselves and hadn't a clue what was going on.

Later we learned it was the filtering system leading to your kidneys that weren't working properly. The doctor assured us it was treatable and told us not to worry.

Just as you were hesitant about entering this world, you also were hesitant about responding to this medication. Your condition worsened, even changing doctors partway through did not help.

Finally the doctor told us they had tried everything and there was nothing else to try. He said you would probably not live to twelve.

Dad and I were devastated and very sad.

There were many people who knew about your sickness and many hours were spent in prayer for you.

One day the doctor called us into his office and informed us of a new drug on the market that he thought might work for you. There were nine children in Canada on this drug and they did not know the side effects yet. Of course we agreed to try it. We did not have medical insurance and this new drug was very expensive, so in order to help out some good-hearted people would slip us money every now and then. We are thankful to them even now and haven't forgotten about their generosity.

After some time, we realized this new drug was working for you. What a blessing and an answer to prayer. When you were twelve years old the medical profession gave you a few more years to live.

Taking you off the drug was a challenge because it was a personality-altering medicine and so we had to wean you off the high dosage you were on. Five years later the doctors decided you were totally cured and gave you a clean bill of health.

It is such a blessing to know God never leaves us alone. Even when I was not walking with the Lord, He never left my family or me. His hand has always been on our family. Your life was a confirmation of His love and faithfulness.

I know, because God spared your life as a little boy. He has plans for you and one day He will use your life as a vessel to bring hope, peace, and unconditional love to others who are in need of it.

There were a few years when you seemed discontented, which goes hand in hand with being a youth. You decided to take your life into your own hands and moved out of your childhood home saying you did not want to follow our rules anymore.

Your little brother decided to go with you and you both went to make your own fortune in the world. This was not a fun time for our family and many tears were shed.

At this point in a child's life, parents can just hope and pray that they have instilled a firm foundation in their children's lives and trust God to guard them and let them go.

I am so thankful that even when our relationship was tested, the love we tried to show towards you was always evident in your attitude to us. You seemed to be able to accept it as well as give it.

There are several years in your life I am not familiar with. Those were your dating years. You must have had your heart broken several times and probably broke a few also, but that is all part of growing up and necessary.

One day you met a lovely young lady and fell in love and became a husband. What a blessing that was and what a wonderful wedding.

You are such a beautiful couple. I am so thankful for Bonnie and the love you share. Please don't ever take each other for granted or become complacent with each other.

Then: a father of a beautiful daughter. What a wonderful miracle. Love her always and remember that fair discipline is a large part of love.

Now we are selling the house that you grew up in and I know that you find that difficult to accept, but you will adjust to the idea and home, will still be home (Mom and Dad's) no matter where we live because our love will always be wherever we are.

Our memories are always with us also, some good, some not so good but even the not so good I am thankful for, because we learn from them. Thank you, my eldest son, for the love you have given me. I pray that one day you will truly experience a personal relationship with Jesus who has always loved you even more than I ever could and that's a whole bunch.

Blake accepted Christ as a personal Saviour shortly after Sarah, their daughter was born. He and Bonnie have been a huge blessing to my husband and me. They are parents of two additional sons, Tyler and Isaac, and grandparents to a beautiful little granddaughter, Layla.

They are actively involved in a Bible teaching church.

WEEK 37

Monday

carry your cross

..if any of you wants to be my follower, you must put aside your selfish ambition, shoulder your cross daily and follow me.

Luke 9:23

The translation from the Message is: *Anyone who intends to come with me has to let me lead. You're not in the driver's seat - I am. Don't run from suffering: embrace it. Follow me and I'll show you how. Self-help is no help at all. Self-sacrifice is the way, my way, to finding yourself, your true self.*

Even in the pre-Christian era, the cross was often compared to the cares and troubles of life. Jesus tells us to embrace our troubles.

Adversity develops character and maturity and causes us to grow. Is that why Jesus tells us to shoulder our cross and continue to follow Him?

Sometimes it is difficult and we find ourselves in self-pity mode but no matter what happens, keep your focus on Jesus. He is ultimately in control and allows these circumstances in your life for a higher purpose than we can see.

Prayer for today

Dear Lord Jesus, thank you for being in control because often I am not. Help me to shoulder my cares and not drown in self-pity. Help me to keep my eyes on you.

In Jesus's name. Amen.

Tuesday
meaningless sacrifice

The sacrifice you want is a broken spirit. A broken and repentant heart, O God, you will not despise.

Psalm 51:17

When was the last time you cried out to God? Was your spirit broken and your heart repentant before God?

We often offer sacrifices to the Lord; giving to the church, serving on committees, teaching Sunday School, or volunteering in many other capacities.

I know wonderful people who generously give to good causes or open their homes to others at all times and have little time to enjoy life. These are all good things but we need to be cautious and diligent to schedule time with God. His desire is to abide with us. To come before Him with a need to be cleansed with a repentant heart so He can fill us with His spirit, is His desire.

That is the only way we can achieve the work He has for us to do. In this there is true joy and fulfillment. When our spirit is truly broken before God and we give up trying to control our own lives, He can fill us with His spirit and make us all we can be; filled with His presence and Holy Spirit.

I encourage you to take stock of your life today and question your daily actions. Are you offering yourself to God or are you just going through the motions of being generous with burnt offerings?

Prayer for today

Dear Lord; take my life and let it be consecrated, Lord, to thee. Help me to make this my prayer today. I want to be in your will. I want you to be able to use me in any way that you want, Lord. If my spirit needs to be broken, let it be, Lord.

In Jesus's name. Amen.

Wednesday

a way out

Trust me in your time of trouble, and I will rescue you and you will give me glory.

Psalm 50:15

It is not easy to trust God when trouble is nagging us from every direction, yet God tells us to do just that.

The story of Elijah in 1 Kings 17 & 18, is a vivid lesson in trusting God when trouble surrounds us.

During the drought, God places Elijah by a spring where ravens bring his food. Elijah is thankful for his God-given provision but shortly after, the spring dries up. Does Elijah panic and blame God? No. He continues to listen for God's instruction. His faith is strengthened by trusting. God provides a way out of his dilemma.

God is still the same today as He was then. Even though we seem to be in an impossible situation, Jehovah Jirah (God will provide) is here. He will and does rescue His children.

Look back in your life when the situation seemed impossible and you trusted and things worked out for good.

We need to give God glory for all the times He has been with us, through every trial that befalls us. Our job is to trust Him as His loved and cherished children.

Prayer for today

Lord Jesus, thank you for all the times you carried me when I was unable to make it on my own. I know you will see me through all my trials. Help me to trust you and to give you all the glory and honour for being there.

In Jesus's name. Amen.

Thursday

water and health

The Lord will guide you continually, watering your life when you are dry and keeping you healthy too.

Isaiah 58:11

During my years as a public school teacher, I was very aware of this promise.

Each year God blessed me with two, three, or four students who were from Christian homes and openly professed their faith. This enabled us to bring Christ into the classroom.

I started my personal day with a prayer, sometimes alone, and sometimes with other teachers. Each day I lifted my classroom and each child to God. Although my prayers were often uttered in silence, depending who was in my classroom, the Lord blessed us abundantly. There were many interesting spiritual discussions in our classroom from time to time.

At that time, in Alberta, Provincial exams were a requirement for grades three, six, nine, and twelve, so this was a particularly stressful time for teachers as well as students. Several years in succession the students asked me to start the day with a verbal prayer for them to do their best in the test we were writing that day. What a wonderful blessing to be able to do that at their request.

As I reflect on those years I am still astounded that there were no repercussions from the higher echelon or parents, because of the spiritual freedoms we enjoyed.

I know it was the watering of the Lord in a dry area. I believe some of those children needed the knowledge of Christ and His love.

If you are in fear or timid about expressing your faith, turn it over to God and ask Him to grant you wisdom and boldness in the opportunities He sends your way.

Prayer for today

Dear Lord, I am so thankful for the opportunities you send me to show your love. Help me to be all that I can be and not to abuse the privileges you put before me or to ignore them. I want to be sensitive to the leading of your Holy Spirit.

In Jesus's name. Amen.

Adena H. Paget †

Friday

strength in weakness

My gracious favour is all you need. My power works best in your weakness.

2 Corinthians 12:8.

In Romans, Paul says, "When I am weak then I am strong."

One summer I was asked to share in a ladies retreat by teaching a class and leading worship. The morning of the Sunday service, I awoke with my first full-blown migraine headache. I couldn't stand up and every time I moved, I heaved from stomach turns. I didn't know what to do. This was a new experience for me.

Some helpful souls gave me all kinds of medication, but nothing seemed to work.

In attendance was a dear pastor's wife who gathered some prayer warriors to lay hands on me and pray for strength and relief so that I could continue with leading the worship service.

As I made my way to the platform, I felt another source of strength holding me up. I cannot remember the songs or what I said, but many women came up to me after and informed me it was the best worship service they had attended.

It was not my strength but the Holy Spirit whom God sent to lead through me. This was a great lesson for me not to rely on my own strength but to allow the Holy Spirit to lead no matter what the circumstance. That is not to say we shouldn't be prepared, but once we have done our work it is time to give it to the Lord and let Him do His work.

Prayer for today

I praise you Lord for who you are. I am so thankful I don't have to rely on my own wisdom or strength to do your work. Thank you God for sending

Jesus and thank you Jesus that you came and thank you for giving us the Comforter who helps us in every situation.

In Jesus's name. Amen.

Weekend Read

letter for Darren

Our second-born son, 1959

Taken from my personal journal:1986

Dear Darren, I am now very experienced at birthing babies, after all I was a whole seventeen years old when you came along.

You were very different from your older brother. You could not wait to bounce into this big world. Labour was only four hours long. I barely made it to the hospital when; bang; there you were.

What a perfect baby you were, 7lbs. 4oz. another miraculous happening in our young lives, your dad's and mine.

Your older brother christened you Kai, because every time you cried, which wasn't very often, he would tell me, "Baby cy, Mommy," so everyone started calling you Kai.

You were the most cuddly baby I ever had. You were a picture of health and very nice to cuddle. You used to play with your little plastic cars and trucks for hours while I sometimes stole a little nap. What a good and wonderful little boy you were. You did everything quickly. You were walking around by the time you were only nine and a half months old.

When you were about seven months old, you caught a bad cold. After listening to you cough a lot, I took you to our doctor. He said your ears were infected as well as your bad cough so he gave me some drops to give you. I put the drops into your ears and wondered why you didn't get any better. After a week, I took you back again announcing that the drops had not helped. The doctor then informed me that the drops were for you to ingest into your mouth. I was very embarrassed and walked out of his office with a very red face.

Once when you had croup, you had to stay in the hospital for a couple of days. When you got better and I could take you home, you looked so cute that the nurses didn't want to let you go. You were my first cute, cuddly, teddy-bear baby. You were very affectionate, always ready for a hug.

Your personality, however, was very serious and you never tolerated anyone laughing at you, even when you did cute and funny things. Your favourite expression was, "Don't laugh." We learned to be very careful of your feelings when you were little and I believe you still have sensitive feelings but sometimes you work very hard at concealing them.

My son, please don't ever be afraid to show your tender side, it makes you loveable and vulnerable but that is a beautiful quality in a human being and should be shown without fear.

I like to think I know what you are often feeling even when many others don't and I love you more for those feelings. Don't ever be afraid of emotions, for without them we are just a shell, a robot.

You grew up very fast; as a matter of fact, too fast. I don't think I had enough time to cuddle you as much as I should have.

You were always afraid of being embarrassed. When you were in grade two, I spent hours making you a clown costume for a Halloween party. When Halloween came, you put it on and when you saw yourself in the mirror, you refused to leave the house with the costume on. I forced you to wear it because I knew you would be okay when you arrived at school. You did have a good time.

For many years you appeared to have inherited similar personality traits to your dad's; quiet and somewhat withdrawn. When you became the age to date girls, I remember standing beside you urging you to call this special girl for a date. I think I even had to dial the phone for you. When she answered you stammered and stuttered, but you managed to ask her out.

One year, I realized you were growing out of you timidness when you announced you were going to Yakima to visit a girlfriend.

You were also quite an adventurer; from bike trips, the first time it was all the way to Scott Hill when we had to come to get you, to wilderness camps. One that I remember vividly was with the YMCA wilderness camp. You had to spend twenty-four or thirty-six hours all by yourself in the woods, day and night. I will always admire you for doing that and you learned what a determined survivor you were and still are today. That is a precious and cherished quality.

You were always a hard worker and earned enough money to be able to do many things. From Dickie Dee ice cream to changing tires for the city of Calgary.

One day while you were working at the Bay, you met a girl who captured your heart. I remember you came home and wondered how you could ever muster enough courage to ask her out. One day, much to my surprise, you did. You fell in love and soon after that, the two of you ran off and got married. Dad and I were happy for you both. Noni has many beautiful qualities, which are not found in many. Don't be afraid to show her how special she is.

You have made your dad and me very proud. It wouldn't matter what you did as a career, we would always love you and be proud.

We were so very proud when you joined the Calgary Fire Department and worked your way up to being a captain.

I know it took perseverance to stick to the fire department because you were born with an adventurous spirit and there are times it is difficult to muster the stick-to-it-ivness that is required, but in the end it will be worth it all.

You don't profess to be at all religious. I guess I really don't know what you believe philosophically about destiny and life after death and I know we don't always agree. I also know that one day you will understand the peace and contentment that can be experienced by having a strong faith in a higher power. I pray for you almost every day and I know God answers prayers every day.

You will always be very special to me as you have been since the day you entered my life. I want more than anything for you to find contentment and peace and then you will know that the dream you have been searching for has finally come true and is fulfilled. I love you, Darren.

Darren is the father of three beautiful offspring, Steve, Kelli, and Donovan. He is an exceptionally loving and caring father. We are very proud of him.

Darren is married to Rhonda, a caring loving person who has encouraged him to be himself. He has evolved from his "shyness" to being a confident, retired Fire Captain who enjoys many activities and continues to learn new and wonderful things. I just learned he will become a Grampa in October 2016.

WEEK 38

Monday
fulfillment

The world offers only the lust for physical pleasure, the lust for everything we see, and pride in our possessions. These are not from the Father. They are from this evil world.

1 John 2:16.

We downsized last summer.

Our new home is a small townhouse with much less space than we previously had, but it is brighter and sunnier and newer so in my estimation it is nicer.

People didn't think I could be content in a smaller home but it is not the things of this world that bring us happiness just as John tells us in this scripture.

That is not to say that God does not delight in the happiness of His children, but it is not our surroundings or the things we have that fulfill us.

I know people who have everything their hearts desire and they are the most miserable I have met. It seems the more we have the more we want. There is only one thing that totally fills our need and that is a relationship with Jesus Christ. When He fills us up, everything else is "icing on the cake." If you are not happy or fulfilled, try Jesus.

Today, be thankful for the blessings God has given you and stop lusting after physical pleasures, take pride in the relationship you have with Christ and your family and not in your earthly possessions. Don't let circumstances dictate your attitude or mood. Let the Son of God fill you with true joy and lasting contentment.

Adena H. Paget †

Prayer for today

Heavenly Father, I thank you for my happiness and not my possessions. Your love is all encompassing and you are my source of joy. You fill my life with blessings and in those I have joy unspeakable and am full of glory. Thank you for taking care of me.

In Jesus's name. Amen.

Tuesday

being faithful

In this fellowship we enjoy the eternal life He promised us.

1 John 2:25

John speaks here of being faithful to what has been taught, i.e. to deny the world and cling to the truth which consists of the presence of the Holy Spirit, enabling us to discern right from wrong (vs.27).

Living in fellowship with Christ gives us courage and boldness to profess our faith and not shrink back in shame.

For a close fellowship, the communication between God and me becomes of utmost importance. Any flaw that hinders this sweet relationship creates a crack, which increases as time between prayer and repentance grows.

I have discovered the sooner I ask for a clean heart and forgiveness, the deeper my joy and fellowship grows. We are created to praise our Creator but when sin stands in the way, it becomes difficult to be thankful, to rejoice or give praise.

Prayer for today.

Heavenly Father, I am so grateful for the promises you give to me and especially the promise of an eternal life with you. Forgive me for neglecting to come to you when I have done wrong. If I have any sins that I am not aware of bring them to my mind so that I might ask your forgiveness and be in a closer relationship and fellowship with you.

In Jesus's name I pray. Amen.

Wednesday

be nice

Let us not become conceited or irritate one another or be jealous of one another.

Ephesians 5:26

A well-known adage goes something like this,

"You can't control anyone else's attitude, you only have control of your own."

In light of this, it is our responsibility to choose the reaction to an action or word within ourselves making it beneficial to the situation at hand.

If we succeed in taking control of our attitudes, we can also be somewhat in control of how others perceive us.

Paul has been talking about how to live our daily lives but he does not expect us to live our daily lives this way on our own strength. He advocates living by the Holy Spirit. It is only with the help and power of the indwelling Holy Spirit that we have the strength to endure and live the recommended life as a believer and follower of Christ.

Let us not envy others or feel we are better than them because these feelings hinder our relationship with Jesus. Ask the Holy Spirit to guide your thoughts and deeds and give you strength to live as a true Christian.

Prayer for today

Heavenly Father, I am so thankful today for the Holy Spirit, to help me, give me strength and courage and make me all that I can be. Because of this, help me not to covet what others have or envy what they are, instead, may I be thankful to you for creating me just the way I am and may I be willing and able to hear you when you need to get my attention.

In Jesus's name. Amen.

Thursday

obedience to God's requests

...Oh Lord, you have sent this storm upon him for your own good reason.

Jonah 1:14

This was the cry of one of the sailors on the boat that carried Jonah.

When the storm grew violent and the seamen felt they had lost control, they realized it was Jonah who was responsible for the dilemma. Jonah was trying to run away from God and in his attempt he was causing great havoc and danger, not only to himself but to others as well.

This an excellent illustration of the consequences we often suffer when we disobey the requests of the Lord. How often have ignored the voice of God and continued going our own way only to find dire consequences waiting for us?

God will not be ignored and He will not accept disobedience from His children. Sometimes it is our own conscience that causes our grief but usually it is the Holy Spirit that pricks our conscience and causes us to change our situation.

I have experienced the voice of God urging me to do something when I made excuses like: inconvenience, or no time, or I am not equipped for that, and later I realized if I had obeyed I would have experienced success because God wanted me to do it. But we usually realize it too late and live to regret our disobedience just as a child regrets disobedience to an earthly father.

Let us be sensitive to God's direction and obedient to His cause because it is then it becomes easier to sail through life. We will still experience storms but God will be with us through each one of them and perhaps we can avoid the deep dark ones that bring us to the depths of where Jonah ended up for three days.

Prayer for today:

Dear Lord, I am so thankful you give us second chances and even when we disobey you, your grace and love reach out and hold us close to you. Help me today to hear your voice and be obedient to your requests and directions.

In Jesus's name. Amen.

Friday

God's gifts

"God has given gifts to each of you from His great variety of spiritual gifts. Manage them well so that God's generosity can flow through you.

1 Peter 4:10

Do you know what gift or gifts God has given you? Are you using them for His glory?

As a child, I loved to sing in front of an audience. I was sure my gift was singing. When I married, I forgot about singing because I thought I was too busy with my family, although I always sang to the children and still had a burning desire to sing for others.

Years later I began leading worship in a small church, which I found very satisfying and enjoyable, but after five years this situation came to an unpleasant end. I felt abandoned and useless as a singer and stopped singing.

My brother, who is a professional musician, encouraged me to sing, just to sing, even if only for myself. I began singing and the Lord opened several venues for me to use my gift. Now I sing unto the Lord and He blesses me.

For a time I placed my God-given talent under a bush but when I began to exercise it again, God started using it for His glory. I believe He will continue to bless me as I use the gift He entrusted me with.

Prayer for today

Dear Lord, thank you for giving us gifts we can use for you. Help me to recognize my gifts and use them for your honour and glory. Help me not to push them down and bury them but to be blatant and look for opportunities to use them. May you be blessed by seeing me use your creation to its fullest.

In Jesus's name. Amen.

Weekend Read
song in my heart

One day during my quiet time with the Lord, I was overcome with His great love for me. I was awed by His mercy and His faithfulness, not only for me but for others as well. As I meditated on this wonderful blessing, the Lord gave me a song that reflected my feelings somewhat. It began with the story of the woman in the Bible who was healed by touching the hem of Christ's garment.

The Hem of His Robe
2004

I'm not worthy to kneel at your feet, Lord.
I'm not worthy to look on your face.
But I know you have made me complete, Lord.
Praise your name, I am saved by your grace.
Cho
Oh, draw me close enough to kneel at your feet, Lord
Let me come and touch the hem of your robe.
I can never walk the steps that Jesus walked for me
But let me be worthy to touch the hem of the robe.

There's a story in the Bible of a woman
With a sickness that could not be cured.
She was humbled by the love of the Saviour
And found healing in the touch of His robe.
I'm just a lowly sinner on this planet
But in the eyes of the Lord I can stand.
He's forgotten and removed my transgressions
And I have felt the healing touch of His hand.
I am humbled by the love of my Saviour
And I know that He is mine eternally.
I can never repay His awesome favour
Yet, He tells me of this debt I am free.

WEEK 39

Monday

give them all to Jesus

Give all your worries and cares to God, for He cares about what happens to you.

1 Peter 5:7

I struggle with this scripture, do you?

As a wife for many years, mother of five children, grandmother of eleven, and retired teacher, life has been good but I can't deny the troubles and worries I have experienced.

I have always been aware of this promise and have tried to apply it in my life. With good intentions, I give my worries to the Lord and I know He willingly accepts them. All too soon I start feeling guilty because I'm not worrying anymore. Soon I find myself taking back the problem and worry takes over.

I know this is the work of the enemy telling me I should not really give up the problem. I take it back feeling that I am too important to really submit the worry.

I have discovered many people do the same thing about the cares of today but Peter tells us to give them to God. Oh that we could be so strong in faith and mature enough to realize it is against scripture to worry and fuss.

Let us practice His advice today and see what a wonderful peace is ours. Perhaps we can also carry it into tomorrow and the next day until it becomes a spiritual automatic reflex. What a glorious God we serve and how much He must love us to take all our cares.

Prayer for today

Dear Heavenly Father, I am so thankful that you care about my worries and you tell me to give them all to you. Help me, Lord to realize life is much easier when I do what you expect me to do. You are the great I Am and everything is possible with you. I am not able to solve the problems so Lord, help me to give them and continue to give them to you. My life will be less cumbersome when I truly trust you with my whole life, even my troubles and worries.

In Jesus's name. Amen.

Adena H. Paget

†

Tuesday

virtue of integrity

..I will lead a life of integrity in my own home.

Psalm 101:2

Are you considered a "Sunday Christian"? Are you a, "What I want people to think of me, Christian"?

I fear many of us may fall into this category of worrying too much about what others think, and we put on a positive face in the eyes of the people.

I have to confess, at times, my husband is the only one who knows how I really feel. I tend to put on a company or visitor face and when we are alone, my real face or attitude returns.

At this time in our lives, we only impact ourselves and each other, but I have witnessed several church couples who profess to be Christians when it suits them, yet in their everyday lives they gossip, use bad language, cheat on their taxes, cuss at their children, and speed in their vehicles. I believe this is what David means when he promises God he will live a life of integrity.

God sees all and hears all and it is Him we strive to please. On Judgment Day what we do for Jesus will count, not what other people think of us.

Let us go forward and please Jesus and the result will be living the lives we were meant to live. The good thing will be our peace in knowing we are living a life of integrity.

Prayer for today

Heavenly Father, thank you for loving me and giving me your Word as an instruction manual for my life. Help me to be able to say with David that I will live a life of integrity. Help me to be what you want me to be each day of my life, not only when others are around or when I attend church but to my family and in everyday circumstances. Give me patience with an open heart so that I can hold my tongue when I need to and speak after considering what I should say.

In Jesus's name. Amen.

Wednesday
Godliness

Light shines on the Godly, and joy on those who do right.

Psalm 97:11

My strongest spiritual desire is to reflect Godliness. I had a friend tell me once her desire was to be a Godly woman and I thought, "What a goal and hope to have."

Imagine what an honour it would be to have the "Light of the World" reflect off you or through you. What a marvellous blessing to hear Jesus say, "My light will shine on you because you are Godly."

With the Holy Spirit dwelling in you, you are equipped to be that person. Even when we don't feel Godly or joyful we can still reflect our desire to be a Godly person because it is the presence of Jesus that enables us to be perceived as Godly.

What a wondrous God we serve, who makes us appear better than we are in ourselves. We are not able to do this on our own but Jesus says in our weakness, He is made strong. Let God do His miracle in you today.

Adena H. Paget †

Prayer for today

Heavenly Father, Oh. that I could be perceived as a Godly woman. I know this is only possible with you and not on my own. You are such a merciful God, full of grace and forgiveness, and you can use me to be what you want me to be if I allow you to be in control. Help me to let my defenses down and yield to you in every way.

In Jesus's name. Amen.

Thursday

He will take care of you

Choose to love the Lord your God and to obey Him and commit yourself to Him, for He is your life.

Deuteronomy 30:20.

This is part of the message Moses gave to the Children of Israel before he announced his retirement as their leader. It implies we have a choice; to follow God or not. It also tells us if we choose to obey the Lord God, we will experience life.

So many people today, are existing and missing out on the way life was meant to be enjoyed. They scurry about trying to earn enough money to buy, buy, buy, and in the end, they miss out on true peace and inner joy.

A commitment to live a Godly life is what brings a full life. To be fully alive in God's presence is the ultimate. It is then, we can give our burdens and concerns to Him and trust Him to resolve whatever the problem is.

At times, we are often amazed and surprised how God really helps us despite His Word telling us He will take care of us.

Prayer for today

Heavenly Father, I am so grateful you are a mighty God and promise to give me life and give it to me more abundantly. All I need to do is choose to be your follower and your grace and mercy will enable me to live a fuller life. Without you, Lord I am nothing, so today I ask you to give me a deep desire to follow you in all my ways. Thank you for being my Lord and loving me.

In Jesus's name. Amen.

Friday

promise to help

Do not be afraid or discouraged, for the Lord is the one who goes before you; He will neither fail you nor forsake you.

Deuteronomy 31:8

Do you have unsurpassable concerns looming ahead of you?

Joshua had just inherited the leadership position in taking the Children of Israel into the Promised Land. It would seem feasible for Joshua to be concerned and perhaps quivering in his sandals at this huge responsibility considering whose sandals he was filling.

God, however, confirmed Joshua's position and gave him assurance he would not be alone in his quest. All Joshua needed to do was be obedient and allow God to lead him.

This promise is in God's word for us as well as for Joshua. The Lord will go before us and with us through all the trials that we encounter.

We are not promised an easy life, free from strife, but God promises to walk through the trials and flames before us and with us. He never leaves us alone to flounder on our own.

Prayer for today

Heavenly Father, I know you are with me no matter what and I want to thank you for your presence and your guidance every day that I live. I cannot imagine how difficult life would be without you. You are my strength when I am weak. My hope is built on you and I am so thankful to be your child. Thank you for your promises to Joshua and to me even today because you are the same yesterday, today, and forever.

In Jesus's name. Amen.

Weekend Read

last days

In April 1991, I was privileged to be at my sister's bedside for the last four weeks of her life.

She suffered for years with a disease called scleroderma, a terrible disease that causes the organs of the body to solidify. It is disfiguring and it becomes very difficult to move. It attacks the organs of the body, and the skin, being the largest organ, becomes solidified with no elasticity or give, and slowly it attacks the other organs in the same way.

Sometime before her death she also suffered from ovarian cancer. Although she underwent many chemo treatments and a variety of drugs, she never experienced release from this disease.

Esther's daughter, Nancy was also there with me. Together we managed to care for Esther in her last weeks of life on earth. Esther had suffered for several years and had a strong desire to go home to be with Jesus.

Death seemed to take a long time. Even though she wanted to die, we learned, life and death are in God's hands.

He is the giver and taker of life but the wait is often difficult to endure. She passed peacefully on April 9, 1991.

The following is a poem I wrote March 28 while we were waiting.

My heart is tired, I am lonely
I am longing for laughter, for joy
There is none of that here
It is not a good thing to wait for death
And yet..that is what we are doing
We are consumed by the wait
We think every breath is the last
We have put our lives on hold
It is amazing how one can be done without
We think we are all important
But when I am out of the picture
Life will still go on
People will still laugh, play, and work
I am in another world
Where all this is on hold
We do what we have to
Our minds do not take a break
They are ever conscious of the waiting
When will it end?
Would I want to be somewhere else?

No. I am needed here
Thank God, He is in control
Sometimes I feel abandoned
But ultimately, I know He is here
I do have peace
An awesome peace that passes all understanding.

WEEK 40

Monday

God is present in losses

The righteous pass away; the godly often die before their time. And no one seems to care or wonder why. No one seems to understand that God is protecting them from the evil to come. 2. For the godly who die, rest in peace.

Isaiah 57:1-2

When our son was taken from us in an accident, it was devastating to our family. His siblings mourned the loss because he was often the glue that made a positive difference.

A short time after, the Lord showed me this verse. My heart leapt for joy because I knew Drew had found rest. As the years progress, I realize he is at perfect peace.

When my mom passed away after suffering for years in terrible pain, I was a child who desperately needed a mother. My life took a different turn and the things that transpired made me what I am today and led me on my journey that has been an enjoyable ride and exciting adventure.

This verse helped me understand and realize our losses and grief are also ordained by God. It also tells me the Bible addresses any issues we experience.

I understand the wonderful promise of this short passage in Isaiah. Thank God, He knows what is to come and gives us an escape from future heart-breaks.

Prayer for today

Heavenly Father, I am so glad you know everything. Even when I think something is too much to bear, you know exactly what is happening and you always have a reason. Forgive me for jumping to conclusions and giving up or feeling exasperated when things don't go as I think they should and help me to trust you more in everything.

I pray In Jesus's name. Amen.

Tuesday

speak with caution

Honour the Lord in everything you do,
and don't follow your own desires or talk idly.

Isaiah 58:13b

To honour the Lord in everything we do seems impossible at times. We ask, "Everything, Lord?"

Adena H. Paget †

When my sister was still on this earth she used to greet strangers with the phrase, "Hasn't the Lord provided us with a glorious day?"

In her last years, I sensed her closeness to the Lord by her acknowledging remarks in everyday situations. Even though I vowed to do this myself, I often fail miserably.

His Word tells us to honour Him in everything we do and make our conversation meaningful. How often have I caught myself speaking foolishly and saying meaningless things just to fill a lull in a conversation?

This world would be a better place and we would be more in tune with God if we followed this command to acknowledge Him in everything and strive to keep our conversation positively meaningful.

Many words are spoken in haste and are often harmful to others and ourselves

Prayer for today

Heavenly Father, I know I often disappoint you in my speech and I don't acknowledge you in my everyday language. I also know without you I am nothing. Help me to say and do the things that bring glory to your holy name. Help me not to waste time in idle talk or to follow my own desires but to reflect on your Word and your direction. I want to be what you want me to be.

In Jesus's name. Amen.

Wednesday
get on with it

If any of you wants to be my follower, you must put aside your selfish ambition, shoulder your cross daily and follow me.

Luke 9:23

The cross was often compared to the cares and troubles in life, even in the pre-Christian era.

Circumstances sometimes cause us to feel sorry for ourselves, to crave sympathy and attention. We want others to know we are suffering and to dwell on our problems in thought and conversation. Jesus is telling us we need to shoulder our cross – don't dwell on it but carry it.

When the shepherd carried the sheep on his shoulder his hands were free to accomplish other tasks.

When our family was young, my husband often carried our youngest daughter, Shona, on his shoulders, which enabled him to carry on with other duties, especially when we were camping.

Let us shoulder our "cross" and get on with the task at hand.

The translation from the, Message translation says,

> Anyone who intends to come with me has to let go and let me lead. You're not in the driver's seat – I am. Don't run from your suffering, embrace it. Follow me and I'll show you how. Self-help is no help at all. Self-sacrifice is the way, my way to finding yourself, your true self.

Prayer for today

Heavenly Father, sometimes I am caught in self-pity instead of carrying my cross and getting on with the task at hand. When I think of what you

Adena H. Paget †

suffered at Calvary for me I feel ashamed and embarrassed. Please forgive me and help me to do better. I know only by your spirit can I accomplish the things you require of me and even if I fail, I know you still love me and forgive me when I ask.

In Jesus's name. Amen.

Thursday
praying blessings

When David returned home to bless his family…

2 Samuel 6:20

Have you taken the time to bless your family today?

I heard a pastor, a while back, speak on this passage. He referred to a terrible event he'd experienced in his family and confessed to a lack of praying blessings on them.

As I listened, I found myself searching my heart and remembering the many times I had entered our home with accusing questions.

I regret the times I lashed out to my children for not having completed a chore, instead of taking a few moments to establish a positive and respectful attitude.

It occurred to me, as I listened to the speaker, I had missed many opportunities to bless my family. I regret the loss of precious teaching and modeling moments I missed while our children were young and impressionable.

Today, even if you have had a bad day or you're tired when you arrive home, take the first few moments to consciously bless your family.

Often it takes only a short phone call or a little prayer lifting them up to Jesus. Make sure you bless your spouse as well, sometimes they need it more than your children.

Prayer for today

Heavenly Father, I praise you for your Word and the lessons in it. Today, help me to take the time to bless my family. Let me set a positive note in my home and compliment them on their good points. Help me to be an encourager to them first and then teach wisdom.

In Jesus's name. Amen.

Friday

blessing of giving

It is more blessed to give than to receive.

Acts 20:35

As a grade six teacher, I vividly remember the Christmas parties we enjoyed in the classroom. I received many precious gifts from my students at Christmas time.

It was not an expectation to give a gift to the teacher but many students did. I was always sensitive to the students who could not afford to give. I used to take my gifts home and open them there, thinking I was protecting the feelings of the students who could not give.

One year a fellow teacher reminded me of the joy of giving and I realized I was depriving joy to the givers. They felt disappointed not being able to witness my reaction to their gift.

I realized I was interfering with their joy of giving. I also realized what a precious moment it is when you give a gift to someone you respect who joyfully receives it. It surpasses any gift I have ever received.

Although I enjoy receiving gifts, to give is a bigger thrill.

I believe our gifts, whether material, emotional, or time consuming are true joy and fulfillment. When we give of ourselves, it brings numerous benefits.

Prayer for today

Heavenly Father, thank you for being a giver. You have given so much to me, even your Son's life and I can never repay you for all you have done but I know you still love me even if my debt was paid by you. Help me to be a gracious giver like you and through this, experience the joy of being a giver.

In Jesus's name. Amen.

Weekend Read

A tribute to our son, Drew Robert William

February 22 1961-October 6 1998.

April 28, 1986

The following letter was written to Drew, our third son. Little did I know that Drew would never read these words. He was only twenty-five years old at this time and looking for peace and contentment. I Praise God that he is now at perfect peace with his Heavenly Father.

My advice is to allow yourself to enjoy each moment with your children because none of us ever knows how long we have here on this earth. May you be blessed by the words I wrote out of love.

Dear Drew:

My precious baby boy, what will I say to you besides I love you very much and pray for your happiness. No, that's not all: I could write many things because I also have many memories of your years so far.

You did not want to enter this big world, I was in labour for twenty-two hours and then the doctor needed forceps to deliver you, face down, I might add. You started out being a free spirit and have been a unique individual ever since. One day I hope you find your illusive dream.

Your free personality was very humorous when you were a toddler, everyone loved you and laughed a lot at your funny antics. Your goal in life became to make people laugh.

Somewhere you acquired an old cowboy hat and when it fell down over your eyes, you would come out with the funniest lines. One classic that many people mimicked for a long time was, "Hello deah."

From the time you were about eighteen months old, you tried very hard to make the world a happy place. I regret the times I did not spend enjoying and appreciating your wonderful sense of humour. I was more concerned with your behaviour than your personality.

In all fairness, you were not a piece of cake to raise. Your free-spirited personality always craved complete freedom to do whatever was fun and even crazy. At times your behaviour became very difficult to curtail at an acceptable level.

Though these were stressful times, our love for you never diminished. We always loved you very much, but discipline often brings a sense of being unloved or disrespected. Dad and I could see the mistakes you were making and we tried to teach you how to be a better person by conducting your life in a more successful way.

When a child chooses not to conform to the wishes of the parents, or establishment, it can be exasperating and create tension for a loving and congenial relationship.

Thank you, my son, for forgiving us for our mistakes – we were learning as well as you. When we are learning, we all make mistakes.

I will never forget the sad day when you decided to move out with your big brother and truly exercise your freedom. As a parent, I had high hopes for your future and this was not in my plans.

Somehow, between God and Blake you were protected and survived without too many scars. I was very thankful you and Blake were together.

I am also very thankful that you reformed for your sister's wedding. You made her feel special when you sacrificed your long hair and comfortable casual clothes for conservatism. Dad and I were very proud of you that day. That day was also a good day for Dad and yourself because you mended much of the dissension that was gnawing at both of you.

You have many beautiful qualities; the love you have for your family and friends is so very precious. When you take the time to call Granny or myself or your sisters, it is very meaningful to us all.

We all love you very much and appreciate your tender moments. I know your feelings run deep and you sometimes have trouble being open about your emotions. Don't be afraid. I know you are afraid of being hurt because you have suffered many hurts, and I hurt for you when you are experiencing these things. I hope you know you can always come and talk to me no matter what.

Another quality you display is that you are a hustler, a hard worker. We are proud of you for what you have accomplished. Your efforts are impressive. Not only are you a hard worker but also your intelligence is so very evident. In simple terms, Drew, you are a smart guy. And you know how to use your brains. I am thankful that God gave you a level head to direct your path. I pray that you will one day experience perfect peace and happiness because you are deserving of the BEST there is.

Know that I love you very much: Love Mom. x o x o x o

Drew and Terri were joined in marriage for several years and became proud parents of two beautiful children, Dylan and Adena.

Drew became a successful insurance agent with London Life in a few short years.

WEEK 41

Monday

attending church

And let us not neglect our meeting together, as some people do, but encourage and warn each other, especially now that the day of His coming back again is drawing near.

Hebrews 10:25

After being involved in the same church for many years, God impressed upon me to change and move on to another congregation. I searched for a church to fulfill my expectations. Every church I attended did not seem to be the right one for me to become part of. I had many excuses; the music wasn't what I liked, the pastor wasn't friendly or I didn't care for his messages, or the people weren't welcoming enough, and on and on went the excuses.

One day, God showed me people were not perfect and churches were filled with people, therefore church congregations could not be perfect.

In Hebrews, the writer tells us not to neglect meeting together. I realized it was my attitude that was keeping me from the joy of becoming a part of a fellowship.

Christ loves us and accepts us as we are and we must do the same for others. Churches may not fill our entire criteria, perhaps we need to work at being more tolerant and acceptable of the efforts of those in the church. The important thing is to hear the Bible being taught.

God created each one of us as unique human beings; our differences form the tapestry known as humanity. We need to accept each other as we are and concentrate on the positive aspects of our fellow human beings, always setting an example as a child of God with love in our hearts for others.

Prayer for today

Heavenly Father, thank you for accepting me just as I am, even with all my flaws. I pray I can be used by you to show your love to others. Help me to be a positive influence to those at my church, displaying love and acceptance even to those whom I don't like very much. I pray that I will be a faithful attendee and an encourager.

In Jesus's name. Amen.

Tuesday
who is the judge

And why worry about the speck in your friend's eye when you have a log in your own?

Matthew 7:3

This is how my mother-in-law used to say, "It's like the pot calling the kettle black," an original adage from the days when cooking was done on an open fire which turned the pans black. Anyone who has camped and cooked on an open fire can testify to this.

I'm sure there are other adages that parallel this scripture. What Jesus meant when He declared this was, you and I are not eligible to judge anyone else because we are likely to be guilty of the same sin we are accusing someone else of.

I am guilty of this transgression myself. I have often caught myself accusing someone of something negative and later find myself doing exactly the same thing. It is usually quite difficult for us to see our own faults and yet we quickly observe similar shortcomings in others.

Today would be a good day to think introspectively. Challenge yourself to look inwardly with honest eyes asking the Lord to show you any areas in your life that you need to work on or get rid of.

Jesus says it is His job to judge others, not ours. One day we will have to answer to our Creator for our own actions or log in our eye.

Prayer for today

Heavenly Father, thank you for being the judge in our lives, so we need not concern ourselves with the faults of others. Help me to be forgiving and accepting, not judgmental and condemning.

I pray in Jesus's name. Amen.

Wednesday

what's in the heart

People judge by outward appearances but the Lord looks at a person's thoughts and intentions.

1 Samuel 16:7

Aren't you thankful the Lord does not judge us by our looks, what we wear, or how overweight, underweight, puny, or large we appear, or whether we have stylish coiffures or straggly hair? Whether we wear expensive outfits or hand-me-downs?

I recently heard about a study being researched regarding employer hiring. Through various means, it was established that people who were attractive were often preferred and hired before people who were better qualified but not as attractive.

We are appalled by this statistic, and yet I fear many of us are guilty of the same thing. When I managed a ladies-wear retail store, I often hired salesgirls for their attractiveness instead of their qualifications. I'm sure this truly happens often in many companies.

Aren't you glad God sees the inside of us and does not judge us by our outward appearances? Could we be more Christ-like in this area and perceive others for who they are instead of what they look like?

Prayer for today

Heavenly Father, I am so thankful you see my thoughts and intentions instead of my outward appearance and outward actions. Help me become what you created me to be so my heart is beautiful to you.

In Jesus's name. Amen.

Thursday

timing

This is what the Lord says, "At just the right time I will respond to you."

Isaiah 49:8

This response was given to Israel regarding the restoration of Israel, but it is relevant for us today as well.

We often tend to forget that God's timing is perfect. We get impatient, and like the person who prayed for patience saying, "Lord give me patience and give it to me now," we want instant results.

God will not be rushed by our timing or our demands. His timing is perfect. The scripture says, "A thousand years to us is like a day to God." Who are we to imply we know better than Him?

When I reflect on my past, I can vividly see where God's timing was far better than mine would have been. He sees the big picture and knows what lies ahead.

Today let us ask the Lord to help us put our trust in Him and rely on His perfect timing for our needs and requests.

Prayer for today

Heavenly Father, thank you for knowing what is best for me. I realize I can only see with my earthly eyes and I do not know what lies ahead but I'm so thankful you know. Help me to trust you more for everything in my life, especially to trust you when I get impatient and discouraged.

I pray In Jesus's name. Amen.

Friday

memorizing scripture

I have hidden your word in my heart;
that I might not sin against you.

Psalm 119:11

I memorized this verse when I was a child. Most of the Bible verses I remember today are the ones I memorized as a little girl in Sunday school.

My dad was my Sunday school teacher for many years and he impressed upon me to learn and memorize the scriptures. I am ever thankful to him for insisting on that. I regret that I didn't continue after I became an adult.

This winter, I was challenged by the pastor of the church I attended to memorize the Book of James. My first reaction was, "I'm too old to memorize now." I questioned the reasoning behind memorizing when I could look it up and read it. In spite of my apprehensions, I started the task of memorizing the scripture.

There are actually many scriptures instructing us to hide God's Word in our hearts.

I did not succeed in memorizing the entire book but I have memorized three chapters, and am working on the rest. I am discovering the usefulness of being able to recite these meaningful verses from time to time, when I don't have my Bible with me.

It has been a rewarding experience for me to hide God's Word in my heart. I challenge you today to start memorizing a portion of scripture. You will be blessed for doing it, and you will be surprised how often the opportunity to use arises.

Prayer for today

Heavenly Father, I am so thankful for your Word. It is my roadmap for life and it tells me how to live. When I have a question, the answer can always be found in the Bible. Forgive me for taking it for granted and for not taking the time to memorize new scriptures; to hide them in my heart. Help me to remember more verses from your Word.

In Jesus's name. Amen.

Adena H. Paget †

Weekend Read

to love

There's the love we have for our offspring
And the love we share with our siblings,
There's the love we have for our Mom and Dad
Our friends, our God, and our blessings.
All of this love is so very real
The word is simple and yet we're confused.
Most times it's evident how we feel
But many differences in how it is used.
In the ancient Greek language the meaning was clear
With filio, eros, agape
But in our English tongue it's rolled into one
And it causes our words to get sloppy.
And yet in our lives there is nothing that's greater
It makes our life worth living
And when it's mature has been nurtured and sweeter
The pleasure is all in the giving.
For unless you are willing to be generous and giving
And not hold on too tight,
The love that was meant to make life worth living
It just won't be quite right.
I guess we can say as we give it away
I'm so glad to be part of the chain.
We receive it on one hand and give on the other
It often eases the pain.
Love unconditional is never positional
It shouldn't matter, who.
For with Christ at the head in His Word, He has said
My love I give unto you.
As we journey through life with our worries and strife

Let the love of God reflect,
Off of you unto others our sisters and brothers
Just wait and enjoy the effect.

WEEK 42

Monday
good deeds

So you see, it isn't enough just to have faith.
Faith that does not show itself by good deeds
is no faith at all - it is dead and useless.

James 2:17

My father quoted the Apostle Paul in many situations. He was definitely a Paulian adherent, to the extent of neglecting other parts of God's inspired Word.

I recall discussions about speaking your faith or living it by deeds and actions. Dad would say faith is enough, in and of itself. I would advocate good deeds are necessary to show our faith to others. I believe he did not fully understand what James is telling us in this scripture.

James does not deny the importance of a belief but confirms that only believing does not model our faith. How can others see our faith if it is not accompanied by good deeds? James does not say that good deeds will save us but that they become a necessity in order to display faith. James tells us that faith without good deeds is dead and useless.

Adena H. Paget †

In our walk with God, in faith, we develop a desire to do good and it is a joy to follow through.

I have discovered, if I want real joy, carrying out a kindness to someone always brings joy. To do good anonymously brings greater joy and results in a deep peace and joy. When we make an effort to bring happiness to someone else, it returns to us in abundance.

Prayer for today

Heavenly Father, I praise you today for who you are and for what you did for me. You gave your life for me and shed your blood so I can have eternal life and spend it with you. While I am here on earth, help me to be what you want me to be. Help me to have willing hands to do your work and perform good deeds. I pray others will see you through me because of my good deeds. Thank you for being my guide and Saviour.

In Jesus's name. Amen.

Tuesday

honesty and deceit

And the person who keeps all of the laws except one is as guilty as the person who has broken all of God's laws.

James 2:10

Have you ever told a white lie? I guess we are all guilty of doing that at one time or another.

Most of us have, at one time or another, cheated on our taxes, paid the wrong price for something we purchased, sped along a highway or in the city, or made some excuse for something we knew was not right.

We think these are harmless little mistakes at the time, but James tells us if we break one law, it is like breaking all God's laws. According to this, we should never be deceitful in anything.

We know it is impossible to be perfect but we need to become aware of the little mistakes we make and try to keep from repeating them.

Every time we neglect to tell the truth or do anything deceitful, we are hindering our relationship with Christ. We think it does not matter but each time we are deceitful, we become a little more independent and move towards self-rule. We stray a little with each deceitful act until it does not seem to matter.

Our thoughts are in danger of straying from the Lord with each deceitful act.

Prayer for today

Heavenly Father, I know your laws are put in place for us to use as a guideline so I'm asking you today, to help me be honest in all the things I do. I want to be transparent so you can work through me and others will see you in me. Forgive me for the times I have been deceitful in anything I've done or said. Thank you for being my Father.

In Jesus's name. Amen.

Adena H. Paget †

Wednesday
controlling the tongue

We all make many mistakes, but those who control their tongues can also control themselves in every other way.

James 3:2

Why do we say things about someone we know to another friend? The trouble our tongues get us into is astounding. We blame the tongue but it is really our own minds that control the tongue.

I remember an incident of being told something by a friend, in confidence, and then repeating the story to someone else. Of course it returned to my friend via another friend. Our friendship was damaged and it took a long time for my friend to confide in me again.

Why do we do this? Is it because we want to tell the world that someone likes us and trusts us, or do we just want to know the secrets of someone else?

The tongue is a little organ that gets us into more and deeper trouble than any other part of our body. It is so small and yet so mighty. As I become more mature with the years, I am learning to keep my tongue in control and life becomes less stressful.

James tells us if we learn to control the tongue, we are able to control all other parts of ourselves.

Let's accept the challenge of keeping our tongues in control. We will become more sensitive to the feelings of our friends and soon others will realize we really are safe to confide in.

Prayer for today

Heavenly Father, I am so thankful for the friends you have blessed me with. I cherish them and never mean to hurt anyone but at times, Lord, I get carried away with telling stories that I shouldn't be sharing. Please forgive me for saying the wrong things and repeating things that have been shared with me in confidence. Help me to become a better friend and keep confidences to myself. Help me Lord, to control my tongue.

In Jesus's name. Amen.

Thursday
sin of gossip

As surely as the wind from the north brings rain,
so a gossiping tongue causes anger.

Proverbs 25:23

Gossip is a wicked sin that only brings destruction and harm to another person.

Why do we do it? Is it because we dislike the person we are gossiping about? Is it to prove we know something about someone that another may not know, and we want to be the first to tell them? Is it to let someone know we have been taken into confidence by someone else? Whatever the reason, be assured, it is not a valid one.

I cannot and do not respect nor trust anyone who comes to me and says, "Have you heard..?" or proceeds to tell me some secret about someone else's faults, sins, or actions. I always find myself wondering what that person is saying about me when I am not around.

I'm sorry to confess, I have been in prayer meetings where some have used the situation to relay imperfections and faults about someone else. I am not advocating the absence of realizing another friend's sins, but to broadcast these in a public meeting is not right.

If we are guilty of committing this sin, we lose respect and credibility with friends and acquaintances. It causes a gap in the relationships we have strived to form with others and it causes a wedge in our relationship with Christ.

Prayer for today

Heavenly Father, I praise you today for who you are, the Great Creator who made Heaven and earth and all the things upon it for our benefit. Thank you for being my personal Saviour and sending Jesus down to make this possible. Help me be more like Jesus and give me the willpower to remain faithful and true to Christ and to my friends. I know I have imperfections that I don't even know about and many I do know about and yet I make blunders every day. I am as vulnerable and sinful as the next person and I know you forgive me every day. Help me to be an encourager not a discourager, and not to tell tales that do not benefit others. Help my tongue to stay clean and pure.

In Jesus's name. Amen.

Friday

spiritual clothing

Since God chose you to be the holy people whom He loves, you must clothe yourselves with tender-hearted mercy, kindness, humility, gentleness, and patience.

Colossians 3:12

God is our Heavenly Father and deserves to be loved and adored. Paul gives us lofty requests here and, by ourselves, this would be impossible.

When we receive Christ as our Saviour, He gifts us with an indwelling Holy Spirit who enables us to be clothed with the attributes Paul tells us to have.

I have noticed, when I wander from the closeness of my relationship with Christ, it becomes more difficult to be clothed with these fruits of the spirit.

As long as I rely on the Lord and welcome the presence of the Holy Spirit, He leads and guides me in the path that brings peace and contentment and clothes me with these attributes.

If we desire these attributes, we must let the Holy Spirit lead, thereby confirming we are in line with God's plan for our lives.

Prayer for today

Heavenly Father, I am grateful to be loved by you, and yet I know I don't have to do anything to receive your love, you give it freely. Thank you Father, for making me your child. Help me not to take you for granted but to desire the attributes that give you pleasure. Fill me with your Spirit so I may be empowered to be all I can be. Make me more like Jesus, your Son.

In Jesus's name. Amen.

Adena H. Paget †

Weekend Read
a story in three parts:

The Scrambler

Once there was a magnificent gander who fathered a near-perfect family of goslings. There were five to be precise.

He was such a proud papa and his beautiful bride and partner for some time now, had diligently sat on those five little eggs and kept them warm and safe for the time required to incubate and hatch them. It had seemed like forever, waiting in anticipation for the shells to begin cracking open to reveal the wonderful offspring.

Everyone in the entire gaggle came to ogle and admire the new offspring. Of course there were several other families who also had new families, but none were as handsome or clever as his own dear family of five; three males and two females.

When the happy pair first observed the fascinating miracle of each special creation appear, wet feathers and eyes that could not focus yet and little spindly legs that were wobbly, they wondered if they would ever be able to walk, never mind fly.

They were especially taken with the last little gosling who broke out with such determination that it brought a giggle from both parents as they watched in anticipation. Even before he was out of his shell he was scrambling to go. Ever after he was always called, The Scrambler.

The papa gander walked around with his head held high and his chest puffed out because he was so proud of his wonderful family.

One day papa decided it was time to start teaching the goslings how to learn to live and survive on their own should they ever need to. He started slowly and carefully, first teaching them how to line up one behind the other, with Mama at the end of the line to watch and make sure everyone fell in line and obeyed what their proud papa was modeling for them.

As he puffed out his chest and stretched his neck high, the little goslings all did the same: all that is, except The Scrambler who loved to trail behind and gawk at everything on the grass and in the sky.

It seemed he was born to dawdle and often forgot the purpose of these exercises was to teach him valuable lessons that might save his life one day.

Among other interesting sights, Scrambler had become intrigued with those small white balls that often flew through the sky above him. Actually they weren't all white, sometimes he saw bright pink or orange balls and once or twice he even saw blue ones.

He was definitely one who longed to do his own thing and was scolded again and again for not being attentive or listening to his elders.

This day in particular Father warned the offspring to dive into the deep grass for cover, just in time to protect them from one of those flying balls that the humans seemed to love to hit with a long stick they called a club.

The Scrambler was much too interested in what was happening around him to hear the warning and just managed to escape the danger in the nick of time.

Sometimes these objects soared through the air at extremely high speeds but he could never tell where they were going to land. Other times they would just skitter along the ground, bouncing in or over or through the creek where the Canada goose-family had settled and built their home.

Papa had repeatedly cautioned his little ones to watch and follow every movement and step he made but of course Scrambler was so interested in the attempts the humans made to hit the balls that he forgot to watch his papa.

It was his brave mama that ran up and brushed him out of the way just in time.

He heard it bounce where he had been standing and if Mama hadn't pushed him swiftly away, he would have been badly hurt or never even lived to discover the marvellous things life had in store for him. He was vehemently reprimanded and had to promise to be obedient in the future before he was allowed to continue to join his siblings.

He hadn't meant to be disobedient or thoughtless, but he really was intrigued by the humans that kept walking by his home on the short grass aisles that were everywhere, and wondered why they kept hitting these little balls with those sticks.

End of Part 1 – Part 2, next weekend.

Monday

let go and let God

...And as the Spirit of the Lord works within us, we become more and more like Him and reflect His glory."

2 Corinthians 3:18

We sing, "Make me more like You Jesus," "Take my Life and Let it Be," "Lord Make me an Instrument for You." All these wonderful worship songs asking to be more like Jesus. With the power of the Holy Spirit, this is possible.

I am aware I was created with a strong and somewhat stubborn mind. I used to wonder and ask God why He created me this way and I came to the realization, as I grow spiritually, I am learning to give up my stubborn nature and let it go. As I continue to work at this I sense progress, I sense the glory of the Lord becoming stronger in me. As I let go, God takes over.

I am aware of my stubborn nature and selfishness becoming fainter. I realize this is a process that needs to evolve. Were it not for the actual process, I would never experience the struggle of letting go. Yes, it is a struggle at times but the product at the end is worth it all.

If I continue barging ahead on my own path without allowing God to control, I will never become what God intended me to be. As I allow more and more of myself to go, I can become more and more like Christ. This is the goal of my life.

How about you? Are you willing to let go and let God take control?

Prayer for today

Heavenly Father, I am so thankful I am your child and you are my Father. You are the potter and I am the clay and even though it has taken me many years to allow you to be Lord of my life, I have experienced much learning through the process. I thank and praise you for having patience with me and loving me through it all. I want to become more like you, Jesus.

I pray in Jesus's name. Amen.

Tuesday

helping the needy

No one has ever seen God, but if we love each other, God lives in us and His love has been brought to full expression through us.

1 John 4:12

I feel so blessed for the privilege of living on the west coast during the winter months where the temperature is considerably warmer than the prairies.

The warmer temperatures exacerbate the number of homeless people who live on the streets. As I walk by them downtown, I often whisper the prayer, "God help them." But if that is all I do, who will actually physically help them? It is only through us and by us that the poor and needy can be helped. I need to do more than pray for them.

I have a dear friend, eighty-six years old, who is my spiritual mentor. She has much wisdom for the things of God. Last winter, she initiated a program that enables organized groups to collect food at regular intervals from neighbourhood homes and deliver it to a community food bank so the needy can come and collect the necessary food for their family.

This program is considered a huge success. She said it occurred to her that people are willing to give but don't have the time to deliver the food to the food banks, so she is providing the means to obtain the needed food.

Perhaps there is something similar or something totally different, but needed, to become involved in.

We can become the hands that God needs, or the eyes, or the mouth and feet.

Heavenly Father, I'm so thankful that you care about the homeless and the poor and needy. I pray for a right attitude toward them. Help me not to belittle or look down on them. I want to remember them with love and I want to be used by you for them. Help me to seek your will and be ready to help in any way I can. Help me show your love to everyone and do what I need to.

In Jesus's name. Amen.

Wednesday

accepting others as they are

So accept each other just as Christ has accepted you; then God will be glorified.

Romans 15:7

Christ accepts us just as we are, whatever our faults, or where we are, or who we are.

Even though I came to faith as a child, I became a rebellious teenager and strayed from my Christian upbringing.

Before I re-committed my life to Christ and made the decision to live a life that is pleasing to Him, I spent many years sinking in the miry clay of sin. I justified living a sinful life by telling myself I deserved fun and happiness. Many times I neglected my husband and family to pursue the things of the world.

I am so thankful that Christ still loved me even when I lived a selfish life.

When I finally realized the things of the world offered no satisfaction and lasting joy, I cried out to God to deliver me out of the pit I had dug myself into. He did not judge or belittle me, He gently lifted me out, and set my feet on the Rock (Jesus). How wonderful for Him to welcome me back home without question.

We are to accept others just as Christ accepts us. Through this, God will be glorified. So often we judge other Christians and find fault with them, even to the extent of spreading gossip instead of loving them back into the Kingdom.

We need to work on accepting others just as they are and leave the judging to the Holy Spirit who will do the convicting and bring them to repentance.

Adena H. Paget †

Prayer for today

Heavenly Father, I am so thankful for your grace, which accepts me just as I am even though I have not done anything to earn it. Your grace is free and liberally handed out each day. Help me to be accepting of others and love them into your Kingdom without being judgmental. I pray for wisdom to know when I need to be quiet and when I need to speak the truth to others. I know my job is to love them and I pray you will help me do this.

In Jesus's name. Amen.

Thursday

a caring God

And you saw how the Lord your God cared for you again and again here in the wilderness, just as a father cares for his child. Now He has brought you to this place.

Deuteronomy 1:31

Where has the Lord brought you from? What has He led you through?

As I reflect on my life, I can see the evidence of God's hand in many circumstances.

When I wandered away, He was still with me.

When I traveled through the valleys He led me through.

When I lost precious loved ones, He walked by my side.

When I didn't know where to turn, He opened doors for me to walk through.

He enabled me to put one foot in front of the other, to keep going forward.

He gave me the strength I needed,
The courage to pursue
The encouragement I craved to reach the goal.
I learned:
If we trust Him and allow Him to lead, He does.
If we listen to His voice and are willing to follow where He leads.
He will do it.

Prayer for today

Heavenly Father, I am so thankful for your hand of mercy in my life. You care for me every day no matter what my circumstances are. You are my Father, my Daddy, who loves me and you take me through each wilderness that life has to offer. Thank you for loving and caring for me.

In Jesus's name. Amen.

Friday

hands and feet in action

If you are wise and know the ways of God,
live a life of steady goodness so that only
good deeds will pour forth.

James 3:13

James emphasizes the concept of acting out our faith. The instruction to believe and accept Jesus, to be saved, is true. But to live a fulfilled Christian life, it is important to act out our faith.

If we just sit around and utter the words of faith and salvation how will others know the love of God? We cannot convey the love, grace, and mercy of our Lord by only preaching and praying. We must show our faith by doing good deeds and helping others in need or some similar action. Our goodness needs to be evident for the unbeliever to witness.

I have often heard unbelievers bad-mouth Christians by accusing them of being self righteous and pious, and indeed, many believers think of themselves as being better than non-believers.

We are all sinners and Christ died for all, there are just some who have not accepted this joy yet.

One day we will all stand before God and every knee will bow and every tongue confess that Jesus Christ is Lord. Each one of us was an unforgiven sinner before we confessed our sins to God. God loves the sinner and waits for them to ask.

Prayer for today

Heavenly Father, thank you for other Christians who have enabled me to become a better person and those who have helped me along the way materially and spiritually. Help me to show your love by being helpful to those who need it. Help me to be sensitive to the leading of your Holy Spirit to go to those in need whom you have put in place for me to help. I pray that my hands will be helpful when they need to be.

In Jesus's name. Amen.

Weekend Read

the scrambler

-Part 2-

On the day Papa Gander decided to give the lesson on swimming and diving, everyone followed instructions very well. If Papa dived, they all dived exactly the same way. When Papa flapped his wings as if he was going to take off, they all flapped their wings too.

It was great fun splashing each other and trying to emulate Papa to see which one could flap the most like him.

They all tried very hard, except for Scrambler. He seemed to be more interested in a strange, four-legged animal chasing birds and other geese in the water. That looked like more fun to Scrambler so he tried to get into the game but just as he felt like he was making friends and able to participate, Papa was at his side lecturing on the importance of listening and paying attention.

"Oh dear," Scrambler thought, "Papa is angry again."

Sometimes Scrambler felt like all the instructions his parents valued were a drag. He really didn't want to be bothered with the details and specific strategies on what to do in case you found yourself in a dangerous situation or accept the responsibility of learning this stuff.

One day Papa announced it was time for a flying lesson. This excited the Scrambler because he had tried to fly on his own but he had found it difficult to manoeuvre his wings and catch the correct wind current that seemed to lift the elders off the ground effortlessly.

He decided, today he would really pay attention and listen. He had such a deep desire to fly. To him this truly was freedom and independence.

It was quite a day. The Scrambler and his siblings lined up and intently observed Papa's instructions. Scrambler was trying very hard to concentrate and started flapping his wings just as Papa instructed him

Adena H. Paget †

to. It wasn't too long before he successfully left the ground and realized he was actually rising above it and the green grass and pond were beneath him.

What a wonderful sensation. He knew he had been born to fly. He never wanted to stop or land. He loved it up here and felt he was capable of conquering the world.

He just kept flapping his wings and soaring in the breeze. Before long he discovered a new level of confidence and independence in his ability.

In his quest to be free from responsibility he forgot about his family and the leadership and training he had received from his parents. He quickly gained a high level of confidence and knew he was ready to fly on his own.

Being a team member and belonging to a family became trivial and listening to authority was boring. He wanted to experience living life to the fullest and he knew his parents would not allow him to become who he really was. Listening and learning had become such a chore for the Scrambler that his longing for independence overcame any responsibility towards his family.

- Part 3 -

It was a sad time for the rest of the family the day Scrambler realized his ability to take off and soar through the air on his own. Not long after, he left his loving family to experience the world in his way.

It wasn't that he didn't love or respect his parents, but adventure was calling and it seemed like his family and the establishment didn't understand his longing or share his desire to explore new adventures.

After a time of being on his own he discovered many wonderful and wild experiences. He met interesting characters; some just like himself with free spirits, some snobs who turned up their noses at him and his lifestyle; and others who were searching for satisfaction.

One day as he was soaring and experimenting with new dips and dives in the air, enjoying himself and his freedom, he met a very beautiful female who greatly attracted him.

She was a shy little goose standing by some tall bulrushes. As he approached her, she quickly moved behind some thick grass clumps in order to hide but he slowly continued to pursue her. Soon she became comfortable with him and even enjoyed the attention. As they became involved in conversation they realized they were both lonely and attracted to each other.

She related how her family had disappeared when she was very young and how she had survived by staying hidden and being cautious. She had taught herself to fly but always with extreme caution, even being fearful to venture out into unknown territory.

Scrambler was surprised at how small her world was. He realized he was quite attracted to this shy female and his feelings for her grew as he spent time with her. He took it upon himself to show her the world.

Before very long her confidence increased as she improved in her skills. It wasn't much longer before they realized their feelings had grown into love and they decided to become partners for life.

She was happy to be part of his life and knew that if it wasn't for him her abilities would have remained small compared to what he encouraged her to be.

As her skills increased, she often wondered why they weren't part of the magnificent flocks of birds that soared overhead in perfect V formations. When she tried to discuss this with Scrambler, he would always reply that he was a free spirit and had no interest in conforming to what everyone else did. She learned to accept his answer but deep down she wished she could be part of the families who flew overhead so beautifully.

Part 4 – The Scrambler

After some time she thought it would be wonderful to have a family of their own. Scrambler wasn't at all sure this was what he wanted but when he realized how important it was to his lovely bride, he agreed.

It seemed like forever before the eggs were incubated and another forever before they hatched. She knew she must endure and be patient. For him it was difficult and often he left to seek adventure while she diligently remained on the eggs, keeping them warm until the very end.

The day finally came when the shells started cracking; first one, then two, then three perfect little goslings appeared. Scrambler was indeed very proud of his new family and his beautiful partner. He walked around with his head held high and his chest puffed out. He loved the attention of being a new father and this elation lasted for quite a while.

Mama was excellent at her new job and all too soon Scrambler thought she was spending too much time with the little ones and he was being neglected.

Every day he would leave and continue his quest for adventure but he tried to return every night.

As time went on, Mama realized the need to start teaching the offspring how to survive and prepare for their future. When she approached the subject with Scrambler, he seemed to completely ignore her and his responsibility as a father.

The truth of the matter was that he didn't know how or what to teach his little goslings because his training in these areas were a part of his life that he'd missed. Instead of admitting his lack of knowledge, he just flew away and looked for further adventure.

One evening when he returned home there was no one around. He was quite concerned and started searching in all the favourite places. Despite his irresponsible attitude towards his partner's concerns for teaching the goslings, he still loved her and his offspring very much.

As he proceeded to search he thought he heard his little ones laughing and playing. He tried to sneak up on them but much to his surprise and disappointment, as he was about to jump in on them, he could see they were not alone.

There on the pond he loved was another gander, patiently teaching his offspring to swim with precision and dive for cover. They were having so much fun laughing and splashing water on each other, that Scrambler sadly walked away to his hideout and escape.

After several weeks of being alone, he looked up and heard a familiar honking. High above him, flying in a perfect V formation were his young goslings led by the other gander and his beautiful bride following close behind.

Pangs of hurt filled his entire being and he mustered enough energy to fly the opposite way, out of sight. He knew he had lost his beautiful family to another gander, who obviously knew how to teach and instruct the goslings.

It was then he realized all his life he had wanted to be free and do his own thing.

He never wanted to listen to lessons that his father had tried to teach him and he didn't think his siblings were important. He had shown very little respect towards his parents and now he had lost everything he really cared for.

He realized the loss he was experiencing was because of his irresponsible attitude. He had been a rebel and now he was paying for being a selfish goose, putting himself first at all costs and never thinking about how it affected others.

He knew he was too late to win back his first love and wonderful family but perhaps he could change himself.

He decided to change his attitude that very minute and become what he should have been a long time ago.

Upon making this important decision, he already felt better about life and himself. He knew his life was going to be difficult but at least he would try his best to be the responsible goose he was meant to be.

There was hope for Scrambler because he was still young enough to start over but he regretted the time he had wasted and the wonderful family he knew he had lost forever.

Adena H. Paget †

The End

WEEK 43

Monday

acceptance

Finally, all of you should be of one mind, full of sympathy toward each other, loving one another with tender hearts and humble minds.

1 Peter 3:8

I visit churches frequently and while I enjoy celebrating the differences and similarities in different denominations, the thing that is most disturbing to me is the unrest and negativity that exists among many adherents.

Sometimes it starts in the music department. Some say the songs are too new and contemporary, and others say the hymns are too old and can't be understood by the new Christians. There are complaints about the musicians and singers that range from, too impersonal, too loud, too soft, too fast, or too slow.

There are also murmurs complaining about everything from the pastor's wife's wardrobe, to her hairdos, or the way she communicates. There seems to be evident jealousy and selfish ambition in many situations. It must grieve the Holy Spirit to see the misuse of his people in this way.

Peter is reminding us how our attitude should line up with the will of God. Surely it is not God's will for us to whine and find fault in the people He has put in our sanctuaries to worship with us.

Changes for improvement can only start in our own personal attitude towards others. We can only change ourselves. Today, let us check our conversation and ask the Lord to direct our thoughts and conversation.

Prayer for today

Heavenly Father, forgive me for finding fault in your children, especially those who are giving their time to lead congregations in worship and are desiring to do your will. Help me to be in harmony with your children and to be tender-hearted and humble towards them. Thank you for the people in my church who are willing to give of their time and talent so I might enjoy you more fully.

In Jesus's name. Amen.

Tuesday

freedom and protection

For you are my hiding place: you protect me from trouble.
You surround me with songs of victory.

Psalm 32:7

What a glorious comfort to live a victorious life. Only in God can we truly experience the freedom of victory.

This Psalm confirms the freedom and protection available to us when we confess our innermost secrets and seek forgiveness for our rebellion against the honesty that God desires.

Allow the Holy Spirit to surround you with songs of victory so that nothing can interfere with your relationship with God.

When we allow deceit to be a part of our lives the gap begins and as we allow this to continue the gap becomes wider until we find ourselves wandering further and further away from God and the protection of His hiding place.

Prayer for today

Heavenly Father, thank you for your protective hand upon me and for surrounding me with songs of victory. When I am surrounded with your victorious music, I know I am safe from the evils that are ever present. Help me to be transparent with you and my loved ones and friends so that you may be glorified. Thank you for allowing me to be in your hiding place, a place of safety. I want our relationship to grow, so I ask you to keep me close to you.

In Jesus's name. Amen.

Wednesday
grumbling

Don't grumble about each other, my brothers and sisters, or God will judge you.

James 5:9

The temptation to grumble about some people is fierce and happens often. It makes us feel superior and better than them but it is wrong. Instead of grumbling, we are to build others up, and speak only good to them and about them.

I have attended prayer meetings and witnessed gossip sessions in the name of prayer for a particular person.

We know it is not necessary to be detailed about someone else's problems. God already knows about their problems and all the details.

A simple request for strength or courage or health or wisdom, whatever the area is, is all that's required.

James tells us we also must not grumble to one another about someone else or we will be judged by God. Keep our complaints about someone else to ourselves or just be available for that person to come and talk if they desire to do so.

Prayer for today

Heavenly Father, I thank you for being a God of judgment as well as merciful and gracious and forgiving. We are to reverence you and fear you in a reverent way. Help me to obey your precepts and listen to your inspired Word. Help me to speak only good about others and not to grumble about anyone else.

In Jesus's name. Amen.

Thursday

malicious behaviour

So get rid of all malicious behaviour and deceit. Don't just pretend to be good. Be done with hypocrisy and jealousy and back stabbing.

1 Peter 2:1

Do you know any Christians who religiously attend church, give their tithes every week, and say all the right things on Sunday to others and the pastor?

Then when it comes to Monday, Tuesday, Wednesday, Thursday, Friday, or Saturday their faith is difficult to see or non-existent.

If we try to live a Christian life by our own power, we can become hypocritical very easily. To live a true life as a believer all the time requires change from the inside. It is impossible to fool all the people all the time and it is impossible to fool God.

To get rid of hypocrisy and jealousy we need the presence of the Holy Spirit. We need to pray for an increased desire to be closer to God.

Only He can make it possible for us to live a life pleasing to Him, without the presence of jealousy, back stabbing, or hypocrisy.

Prayer for today

Heavenly Father, I want you to fill me with a hunger for you and a desire to be close to you, and to be rid of anything that might hinder our relationship, like jealousy or deceitfulness. Help me to love others just as you do and see their good qualities. I love you Lord and want your will in my life.

In Jesus's name. Amen.

Friday

in obedience

..for God is working in you, giving you the desire to obey Him and the power to do what pleases Him.

Philippians 2:13

True peace and joy comes from doing what God desires of us but before we can do what God desires, we must have the desire to be that person and live that life.

As a believer, obedience to God in every way is the epitome of life. Just as a child who obeys the parent is in a continual state of happiness and peace so are we when we are obedient to our Heavenly Father. But also, as a child suffers the consequences of disobedience, we must also suffer consequences for disobedience.

Just as this dilemma occurs in our earthly relationships, it serves as an illustration of what happens in our relationship with Jesus Christ.

In my personal experience, acts of disobedience have caused friction in my relationship with Christ, which in turn, led to more disobedience, followed by a defiant attitude. The relationship suffers separation as communication comes to a halt.

On the other hand, when we are right with God and honest with Him, and ourselves, the Holy Spirit gives us the desire to be obedient which nurtures

a closeness with Christ.

Adena H. Paget

†

Prayer for today

Heavenly Father, I'm so thankful you are still working on me. I have learned obedience to you results in peace and contentment. Help my desire to be obedient to you in everything.

In Jesus's name. Amen.

Weekend Read

a tribute to our grandson, Jarvis

1985 - 2007

In April 1985, our second grandchild was born to our daughter and son-in-law, Robyn and Randy; a beautiful baby with a personality that melted your heart.

At the age of nine weeks, he was diagnosed with cystic fibrosis, a disease that affects the lungs, pancreas, and digestive system.

Children born with this disease are not expected to have a very long lifespan. They are not able to breathe easily because of the build up of mucous in their lungs. In order for them to digest food properly they need to ingest enzymes before eating. To keep the lungs clear enough to breathe, requires physiotherapy several times a day and breathing exercises constantly.

A child with a disability such as this often nurtures a closer relationship with the caregiver than a physically healthy child.

At a very young age, Jarvis accepted Jesus as his personal Saviour at his daddy's knee. This was a huge blessing and enabled him to live in hopes of a Heavenly home even though he knew he might not live on this earth for a long time.

Jarvis never complained even though he spent many months in the hospital hooked up to intravenous and in never ending physio and other inconvenient treatments.

He finished high school and started working and became one of the healthiest CF patients in Canada, we were told. We were so thankful for his diligence in taking care of himself. He became a popular kid in his town of Cochrane, Alberta, much loved by anyone who knew him. He developed a great sense of understanding of others, as well as integrity, character, honesty, and many wonderful qualities that made him special.

As a CF patient, he could never run quite as fast as other guys, even though he was an amazing basketball team member, or keep up with his older brother.

When he was twenty-two years old, he bought himself a beautiful, red racing motorcycle. Some people called it an "organ-donor." It went very fast.

He was learning to control it one day on a country road and missed a turn, flew off the bike and hit his head on a signpost. He was instantly killed.

His death was felt by the entire town, but it was his family who suffered most.

It was one of the most difficult trials I have ever been through, and yet my faith, again, brought me through this devastating time.

Our daughter was crushed and pretty much gave up on life for many years. Jarvis was the son who worked at relationships and talked freely with his mom. Many sons find this difficult but not Jarvis.

There is nothing more difficult in this life than watching your offspring suffer a huge loss such as this. There was nothing for me to do to make the hurt less severe. All I could do was pray. Nothing anyone said or did was helpful, the grief was all encompassing for Robyn. We could only be available for her if she needed us.

We will be ever indebted to Randy, our son-in-law, who diligently cared for her through years of depression and dysfunctional conditions and to wonderful friends who stood by her side and nursed her through this time of insurmountable sadness.

The most devastating thing for me during that time was her anger with God. It took a number of years for her to realize God still loved her. For several years she rejected the comfort of her Heavenly Father and lived in anger.

The best thing was God took her into his loving arms when she was ready and brought healing and comfort to her hurting heart.

Things are never quite the same after we lose a child, but there is healing available and we learn to go on living accepting the void in our lives.

This is one more account of how comforting it is to know God and allow him to walk beside us during the storms of life. I am grateful for my relationship with him and the knowledge of his hand upon me in all circumstances.

I included this tribute here with the hope it may bring comfort to someone who is experiencing grief from a loss so great you think you can never recuperate or go on.

Robyn and Randy have moved to Vancouver Island where she is once again walking with God close by her side. I am thankful for their steadfast faith.

WEEK 44

Monday

desiring wisdom

But the wisdom that comes from Heaven is first of all pure. It is also peace loving, gentle at all times, and willing to yield to others. It is full of mercy and good deeds. It shows no partiality and is always sincere.

James 3:17

Oh. That I should desire wisdom. Solomon asked God for wisdom and God granted his request. He is known for being the wisest man who ever lived. This is a lofty request. We cannot all be as wise as Solomon but in everyday living, to ask God to give us wisdom in making decisions, is wise in itself.

Did you notice what James deems as wisdom in his review of Chapter three? He includes peace loving, gentleness, mercy, good deeds, and a willingness to yield to others.

These qualities seem to be related to the fruits of the spirit Paul addresses in Philippians. Therefore, if the Spirit dwells in us and we allow God to lead and direct and we ask for wisdom, will we become wise? I believe we will be wiser than if we did none of those things.

We need to constantly guard against making hasty decisions that may be selfish or leave out the prompting of the Holy Spirit. Our lives will be richer and more focused aiming toward the right direction if we wait on the Holy Spirit to guide.

Adena H. Paget †

Prayer for today

Heavenly Father, Oh God, you alone are the great God of all wisdom. I am so thankful to serve you and be your child. Help me to be sensitive to the wisdom you offer and to obey you in all I do. Grant me the power to become peace loving, gentle, and most of all, willing to yield to others. Give me wisdom to know when to speak and when to keep my opinions to myself, for they are, many times, only opinions.

In Jesus's name. Amen.

Tuesday

desire knowledge

Fear of the Lord is the beginning of wisdom. Knowledge of the Holy One results in understanding.

Proverbs 9:10

The kind of fear mentioned here refers to a reverent fear or a sense of awe.

We often trivialize the power of God or God himself. We comprehend Him as numerous different characters. I believe it influences our perception of who God really is. When we stop to think about the greatness of God, we cannot comprehend the vastness or depth or breadth of Him. It is more than we are capable of understanding and so we often shrink Him down to a size or figure that we can conceive or imagine.

God is Creator of Heaven and earth and you and I and the tiny blossoms of the plethora of flowers and the huge dinosaurs and everything else we enjoy and are amazed at. His vastness is beyond our comprehension, and yet He is capable of dwelling in us, of inhabiting our spirit.

A power that great and yet that small is who the Lord is. If we have a desire for wisdom and understanding, we cannot ignore this insight from the Proverbs. Start knowing God today and He will lead you in wisdom.

Prayer for today

Heavenly Father, I want to know you more, and praise you more and thank you more, for you are worthy of all thanksgiving and praise. Help me to know your heart and your ways instead of relying only on myself. I am in awe of your greatness and the knowledge you impart on us if we ask. Grant me the wisdom I need each day in all I do.

In Jesus's name. Amen.

Wednesday

awesome wisdom and knowledge

Oh what a wonderful God we have.
How great are His riches and wisdom and knowledge.

Romans 11:33.

I encourage you to spend time today, reflecting on who God is. How great He must be to form all creation with a breath, a word, or a thought. How rich He is; everything is really His, even though we often take credit for wonderful structures and ecological successes.

He is capable of everything in our realm of thinking, creating, destroying, or sustaining. His wisdom is far beyond what our human frailties can comprehend and yet He is gracious and grants us as much as we need.

In His goodness, He created you and me and gifted us with uniqueness and the ability to decide whether or not to worship Him and believe that He is. He is the one who sustains life and provides the very air we breathe.

One day He will come to earth again and take us to be with Him where we will finally understand His greatness.

Let us praise Him and thank Him for giving us life and giving it more abundantly.

Prayer for today

Heavenly Father, Sometimes I feel so insignificant, especially when I think how great you are and yet I know you love me more than I can comprehend. It is humbling to think how much you love me. You, who have everything in your power, to give and to take. To think you gave your most precious jewel, your Son to die for me so that I can be your child, is overwhelming. Yet I know it is true. You have all riches and wisdom and knowledge and you still care for me. I can never thank you enough and yet you tell me I don't owe you anything for all your grace and mercy and blessings.

In Jesus's name I thank you. Amen.

Thursday

searching for wisdom

"Wisdom will save you from evil people,
from those whose speech is corrupt.

Proverbs 2:12

Oh. How I regret the years I spent listening to corrupt speech and looking for fulfillment in the environments conducive to this kind of lifestyle.

The bar scene was exciting to me at one time. The people who frequented these places seemed to be enjoying themselves and I longed to be a part of this party crowd.

As I spent time in this scene and learned more about the people, I realized their lives were empty and mine was becoming the same way.

When you live in a world such as this, you can never get enough. The nights aren't long enough, and you never feel satisfied because it is unfulfilling.

I believe it was God's gentle hand that guided me away from this empty life. He helped me see the futility of it all.

As I yielded to Him and let go of the worldly ways, I learned to walk on the road that led to God. I began to feel free and content. My desires changed from searching for fun to searching for the root of wisdom, in God.

He has filled me with wondrous peace, joy, wisdom, and total fulfillment since I have turned my eyes and heart to Him. Praise His name.

Prayer for today

Heavenly Father, I am so grateful that you are the answer to life. When I seek your will, you guide me and direct me. You provide wisdom when we

Adena H. Paget †

ask. Thank you for providing everything I need. Help me to show your love and grace to others.

In Jesus's name. Amen.

Friday

wisdom in God's eyes

For the wisdom of this world is foolishness to God.

1 Corinthians 3:19

I've noticed, there are some wealthy people in this world who have achieved much. It seems as though the more they accrue the more they profit. We often think of rich people as wise in making financial decisions.

Paul tells us the kind of wisdom displayed by the world is foolish to God.

Our wisdom comes from God and even though the world may call us foolish, we are anchored on the wisdom of our Creator.

There is nothing wrong with being wealthy but money should not be the first priority on our list.

When we study the scriptures, we realize the world is in the hands of God and we learn to trust Him though the world does not know Him and decisions are made that seem foolish.

Prayer for today

Heavenly Father, I am thankful you care about me and my well-being and you promise to provide for my needs. I often look at others who seem to have much and wonder why they are rich or seem to be exempt from daily worries. Help me to keep my priorities in order and to rely on you for my needs, striving to continue to put you first in my life.

I ask this in Jesus's name. Amen.

Weekend Read
a journal entry

February 2000

On January 16, Robyn had a special birthday dinner in honour of my birthday. Everyone was there. It truly was a wonderful day.

It is such an immense blessing to see our children together and while I know they will never be best of friends, they do pull together under tough circumstances as when Drew was in the fatal car accident. They also practice tolerance with each other when we are present.

They all have their strengths…and weaknesses; we all do and I love each one of them very much.

A mother's heart is difficult to describe when it comes to her children. I realize their differences and their shortcomings and because I have lived longer, experienced more, and prayed much for wisdom, or perhaps because I am now an onlooker at their lives, I see them and watch the growth taking place in their lives.

I can discern the successes and disappointments and my heart hurts for the areas in their lives where there is a need for growth. I know they still have difficult lessons to learn ahead of them.

No matter how much we would like to shelter our children from the pain of life's lessons, we cannot. I understand we all have our individual journeys to travel, over the bumps through the valleys and around the corners of change in order to arrive at our destination.

Thank God there are plateaus and yes, even mountaintops when we feel like we are on top of the world but these times do not linger and then we are faced with another valley.

The good thing about being in the valleys, is we learn to accept what we cannot change, where our very souls are being refined, and where we really become familiar with who we are. Each valley brings us closer to the epoch of where we strive to be…where there is truth, love, joy, and peace of mind. This is when we are able to see and understand what really matters.

Are we there yet? I don't think so but we keep pressing on, forgetting what is behind and pushing on toward the goal…the destiny of our journey. And we hope our children find the peace and contentment that we, as ageing parents, know is attainable.

WEEK 45

Monday

marvellous grace

For the Lord God is our light and protector. He gives us grace and glory. No good thing will the Lord withhold from those who do what is right.

Psalm 84:11

Grace: God's free and unmerited favour towards sinful humanity.

Unmerited favour means receiving favours we have not earned.

God, in His goodness, gives us a plethora of good things that we have not earned.

If we worked day and night all our lives, it would be impossible for us to pay for the gifts God offers. It is only by His grace that we have hope of living eternally in a place where there is only goodness.

While we are on this earth, in training for our Heavenly dwelling, He is our light, our protector and giver of all good things. When we walk with Him and serve Him and trust Him we enjoy the fullness of His grace and glory.

What an amazing God we have. Take time today to thank Him for His marvellous grace.

Prayer for today

Heavenly Father, I just want to thank you for your gifts. I know I could never pay for the joy of your salvation or the peace that passes all understanding, but by the grace you give it is mine. All I have to do is accept and acknowledge you as my personal Saviour. You are the forgiver and Saviour and I know one day I will stand before you and realize the wondrous gifts from your hand. Help me to always give thanks and never take your gifts for granted. Help me to freely give grace to others like you give to me.

In Jesus's name. Amen.

Adena H. Paget †

Tuesday

first martyr for Jesus

Stephen, a man full of God's grace and power, performed amazing miracles among the people.

Acts 6:8

Stephen is one of the first martyrs for Jesus. The evil forces became very strong during Stephen's life and caused the people to stone him to death because of his teaching.

Jealousy and lies of the higher echelon incited the people to accuse Stephen of lying. They were reacting to the wisdom and grace and glory that Stephen displayed. They knew the crowds were listening and accepting the teachings of Stephen instead of the priests of the day and this infuriated them.

I fear the times we are in now are becoming as they were then. I read about incidents that prohibit Christians from freely worshipping or displaying their faith openly. Schools are omitting prayer, teaching creationism as an alternative is forbidden, and our politicians are fearful of acknowledging God publicly.

I pray that we would be filled with God's grace and power like Stephen and have the courage to speak out for the purpose Jesus came into the world. He came so that man might have life and have it more abundantly and yet, it seems to be forbidden at times.

Prayer for today

Heavenly Father, I thank you for being with me and enabling me to live a life filled with your grace and glory. I enjoy your presence each day and see the beauty of your creation around me. Help me to acknowledge you in all I do and give you the glory that you deserve.

In Jesus's name. Amen

Wednesday
strength by grace

By God's grace remain faithful.

Acts 13:45

As God gives us grace, we become stronger and more courageous for Him.

In my life, it seems, each time I step out in faith and follow the prompting of the Holy Spirit, I gain strength. I liken it to a teenager experiencing a growth spurt. They eat like every morsel might be the last bit of food they will ever receive and soon after, they shoot up another two or more inches.

When we feed on the spiritual food that God provides, the Bible, we become more mature, thereby gaining strength to do more.

As God gives us grace we can, in turn, offer it to others and truly become workers for our Lord.

To be consistent and faithful in obedience is the key to steady growth and a closer relationship with Christ. Without God's marvellous grace, we fail miserably.

Prayer for today

Heavenly Father, I am so thankful for your free grace and I pray you will help me to be bold for you. I ask for wisdom and strength to say what you would have me say and may the timing be yours. My desire is to remain faithful to you and your teaching.

In Jesus's name. Amen.

Thursday

blessings of rain

Rejoice, you people of Jerusalem. Rejoice in the Lord your God
For the rains He sends are an expression of His grace.

Joel 2:23

Withholding rain was considered the most severe punishment in the Old Testament and conversely the abundance of rain denotes the rich blessing of the Lord upon His people.

The term rain is used both figuratively and literally in the Bible. We have evidence of the rains of blessing in abundance occurring in several significant revivals. To name a few:

- - John Edwards in the 17th-century,
- -his grandson, Timothy Dwight at Yale College, circa 1790s.
- -Charles Finney in the 18th century.
- -Billy Graham in the 20th century

Many were brought to a new and glorious relationship to Christ after hearing these great men preach.

Great revivals seem to happen after much time in prayer by many people.

We are witnesses to the beauty of rain in the literal sense all around us. Our prayer should be that the rains would fall upon us, in abundance again so His grace can be experienced in new and glorious manifestations that astound and awe all.

Prayer for today

Oh Lord. send your rains.

In Jesus's name. Amen.

Friday
finding mercy

So let us come boldly to the throne of our gracious God. There we will receive His mercy, and we will find grace to help us when we need it.

Hebrews 4:16

During my teaching years, I experienced many children who came to me in confidence with questions or concerns, while others would hesitate or use someone else to ask questions. The questions were often regarding marks from a test, or an assignment, or a complaint about another student.

The students that approached me were usually confident students with whom I had a positive relationship. We trusted each other and that trust was evident from their actions.

The students who were hesitant to ask the questions were often the ones who caused dissension or disruption in the classroom and they did not trust enough to speak openly to anyone.

I did not always know the reason neither could I ask but sometimes after a few months, they would tell me and that was a breakthrough and a joyous occasion.

I believe our relationship with Christ is similar. If we have a trusting relationship with Him, we do not hesitate to come to Him in honesty and openness but if we let sin come between our relationship with Jesus, it causes a wedge and a division between us.

When the relationship is not right between us we hesitate to be honest in our communion and conversation with Christ. To come to Christ with openness and honesty and receive mercy and grace is where our relationship needs to be.

Prayer for today

Heavenly Father, thank you, again, for your grace to me. I know I desperately need it because I fall so short of your glory and it is only through you and from you that I can walk upright and stand before you and ask forgiveness from you each day and sometimes more often. I want to be an open book for you because you see me at my most vulnerable times and you still love me. Thank you for your mercy and grace.

In Jesus's name. Amen.

Weekend Read

the lady with the big blue car

A true story

It started with a lady sitting on a curb - Bag Lady, they called her.

She was older. She was lonely. She lived in a little one-room shack.

One cold day as she was sitting on the curb begging and trying to keep warm by wrapping her old worn sweater around her shoulders a little tighter, a big blue car slowed down and stopped right beside her.

A tall, lovely lady got out. She stooped to ask the bag lady what she could do to help her. The bag lady looked up, her dimming eyes reflecting sadness and dejection, answered, "Everything."

Then the tall lady from the big car asked her if she would consider going for a drive with her. She took the bag lady to her home and asked her to choose some things that she would like to have.

There were many things in the tall lady's house that the bag lady had not seen for many years and she looked longingly at many of them.

The tall lady started putting household items and clothing and small furniture in her big blue car and before long, the bag lady was driven back home, accompanied by a warm quilt, two woollen blankets, two pillows, some fancy dishes, an almost-new winter coat, two warm sweaters, various small furniture items, and a box of food.

The bag lady couldn't quite believe what was happening. She was most grateful and overwhelmed by it all.

As she sat in her little shack and realized all that she had gained that day, her eyes filled with tears of joy and thankfulness.

After that, the lady with the big car made several more trips to the bag lady's little house.

There were no names exchanged but there were several street people and many new refugees who were helped by her. She didn't want to bring attention to herself.

Adena H. Paget †

It didn't matter that they didn't know her name or that no one else realized who was diligently bringing treats, necessities, and happiness to these forgotten people.

She would load her car with linens, furniture, and food for Vietnam refugees, and the children watched for her and they would jump up and down and announce that "The lady with the big car is coming." Parents would come out of their dwelling places in anticipation and excitement with ready hugs and loving looks. Everyone in the area knew what the announcement meant and it brought them joy and hope.

The lady with the big car was my sister. After our mom died, just before my eleventh birthday, she became my caregiver. She taught me many things at that precarious time in my life. She loved me much.

She spent many years helping others, specifically those who were in need.

She had spent many years in poverty herself as a single mother, trying to raise two boys until she married a generous man who loved her and bought her a big blue Lincoln.

Not many people knew about the hours she spent with needy refugees and street people.

Several years ago she died after a lengthy battle with scleroderma and cancer. She was my hero and I just thought someone else might like to meet my hero, my sister, Esther.

WEEK 46

Monday

mercy and forgiveness

Mercy: 1. Forgiving, compassionate, withholding of the punishment or judgment our sins deserve.

2.The compassion that causes one to help the weak, the sick or the poor.

I am the Lord, I am the Lord, the merciful and gracious God. I am slow to anger and rich in unfailing love and faithfulness. I show this unfailing love to many thousands by forgiving every kind of sin and rebellion.

Exodus 34:6 &7

We serve a merciful God who forgives our sins because we ask Him to.

In turn, it is our responsibility to be merciful to others.

When God created humans, He gave us a free will and by doing this, He knew we would disappoint Him many times in our lifetime by making bad choices.

I am thankful God is merciful and waits to forgive my numerous sins thereby showing me His tender mercies.

Prayer for today

Heavenly Father, let me be merciful to those who sin against me. Let me show mercy to the ones who hurt me or do me wrong. I want to be forgiving as God is forgiving unto me. Hear my prayer, oh God.

In Jesus's name. Amen.

Tuesday
mercy & judgement

For there will be no mercy for you if you have not been merciful to others.

But if you have been merciful then God's mercy toward you will win out over His judgment against you.

James 2:13

When I was a child, I heard many sermons emphasizing the judgment of God. I heard about hellfire and damnation and I believe it was fear that prompted me to accept Christ as a small child.

While God's judgment and wrath are meant to be feared, His love and mercy must be given equal, if not more, emphasis.

James tells us God's mercy toward us will win out over His judgment against us. Did you notice the positive and negative connotations in the vocabulary?

-mercy towards - judgment against.

Does this imply emphasis on God's judgment? If His mercy toward us is strong enough to overcome His judgment and forgive any sin, then it is only fitting and natural for us to reciprocate by showing mercy to others.

Prayer for today

Heavenly Father, I come to you today asking for mercy. You know I am in need of it every day. The more mercy I receive from you the more I can give and also the more I give to others, the more you give. You never run out and I know there is a never-ending supply, so let me be that way with the people you put in my life each day.

In Jesus's name. Amen.

Wednesday

never changing God

His mercy goes on from generation to generation.

Luke 1:50

It is a comfort to serve a God who is faithful and never changing.

These changing times often create stress for us, we become comfortable in our own world only to find the familiar slipping away more and more.

Our environment seems to be eroding. Morals are weakening, laws are favouring criminals while victims are looked upon as perpetrators, fashions show little modesty, music accepts lyrics that are blasphemous, movies and other entertainment exercises filthy language that becomes acceptable, and the list goes on.

As we grow older, we witness more and more changes in the world, and yet our Lord never changes. We can always rely on His unchanging love, faithfulness, forgiveness, grace, gentleness, peacefulness, and mercy that is unending from generation to generation until that glorious day when we will hear Him say, "Well done, my good and faithful servant, come on in."

No matter what happens in this old world, we have the comfort of knowing we can rely on our Lord who is the Rock that never moves. It is on this Rock we stand.

Prayer for today

Heavenly Father, I come before you in thanksgiving. Thank you for showing mercy to me even when I don't deserve it. Your mercy is unchanging and faithful. Help me to show mercy to others as you have shown to me.

In Jesus's name. Amen.

Thursday

comfort

All praise to God the Father of our Lord Jesus Christ. God is our merciful Father and the source of all comfort. He comforts us in all our troubles so that we can comfort others. When they are troubled, we will be able to give them the same comfort God has given us.

For the more we suffer for Christ, the more God will shower us with His comfort through Christ.

2 Corinthians 1:3-7

Many times we don't understand the trials we are in but God has everything in control even when we lose it completely.

His mercy endures forever and when we are in a trial, it is then God teaches us and shows us His tender mercies. Often we do not know or see the benefits until later when the storm has passed and sometimes we never see the benefits but God knows. That is when our trust in Him is tested.

Sometimes we suffer in order to be able to empathize with others who may be suffering the same afflictions we have experienced.

Trust Him, no matter what you are experiencing today. The morning brings new hope and new mercies.

Prayer for today

Heavenly Father, help me to endure this trial and continue trusting you because I know you have everything in control. Even though I cannot feel you right now I know you are with me. You have promised to walk with me through all the storms and I know you are with me. Make me a comforter to someone else. Thank you, Lord for your mercy.

In Jesus's name. Amen.

Adena H. Paget †

Friday

faithfulness

For the Lord your God is merciful - He will not abandon you or destroy you or forget the solemn covenant He made with your ancestors.

Deuteronomy 4:3

As believers, our ancestors are also the great prophets of old like Moses and Abraham.

Generations ago, God made this promise to them and it is still valid for us today because God is an unchanging God.

The popular trend today is to change in order to keep pace with the times, for fear of appearing out-dated. The fact is, we do need to change some things and ideas in order to live successfully in this world.

It is a great comfort to know God remains the stable, merciful anchor in our lives; the constant variable that is always present and always reliable.

People have and always will make promises only to break them when we expect them to be consistent, but our faith is built on our creator, the solid Rock, Jesus Christ. When He makes a promise, He never forgets or breaks it. His mercy is refreshing and a constant comfort to us, always.

Prayer for today

Heavenly Father, I am so glad you are an unchanging God and I can worship you freely without fear. I thank you for the promises you made to my ancestors generations ago and I know you are still the same God today as you were then. Thank you for your unchanging love and mercy. I pray for consistency in my life so that others may be able to rely on me too.

In Jesus's name. Amen.

Weekend Read

a wayward son

October 2000

Soon after our first grandson turned seventeen years old, he decided to seek his independence. The parting was not easy. As our daughter, Robyn, spent time in prayer, she wrote these words: I trust they will be a source of comfort and blessing to you.

Why does it hurt so
To let my treasure go?
A gift in youth, a gift of love
Sent to us from our Father above
A treasure to cherish for a short while
One that often brought a smile
The while is over, the smile, a tear
The heartache is great this 17th year.
No more can I help or nurture along
No more can I mend with a hug or a song
The treasure God gave me, alone on the street
Keep away from him Satan, God keep him sweet
Protect him and help him as he finds his way
Broken and humble, returning one day
To the Father who gave him a purposeful life
Into your arms, away from strife
Ministering, healing comfort, forgiving
Once again Dear Jesus, for you he'll be living
In this world of darkness, may he not find pleasure
Your gift, my son, my beautiful treasure.

Adena H. Paget †

WEEK 47

Monday

the Holy Spirit

The earth was empty, a formless mass cloaked in darkness. And the Spirit of God was hovering over its surface.

Genesis 1:2

The Spirit of God has always been; just as God is, so is the Spirit.

He is the third person of the Triune Godhead (Matt. 28:19)

The Old Testament richly alludes or prepares us for the revelation of the Holy Spirit in the New Testament. (Judges 3:10, is one example)

The Spirit was active in creating life as we know it on earth.

We can embrace the Holy Spirit and invite His presence into our life to indwell us and equip us with the strength, wisdom, and courage we need so that we can be all that God desires us to be. (Ephesians 1:13)

Prayer for today

Heavenly Father, Thank you for sending The Comforter, The Holy Spirit to be with us while Christ is with you. I am so glad that you, in your wisdom, knew we would need someone to enable and equip us to have the courage to be witnesses for you and spread your gospel to those who are in need of it. I invite you, Holy Spirit, to fill my heart with fullness so that I can be all God intended me to be.

In Jesus's name. Amen.

Tuesday

spirit in us

And I will put my spirit in you so you will obey my laws and do whatever I command.

Ezekiel 36:27

This is part of God's revelation to Ezekiel when He promises restoration to Israel.

The endowment of the Holy Spirit enabled the people to be obedient followers of God's plan. It renewed their desire to obey and quenched the desire for corruption.

We often look at the Israelites and wonder how they could have been so fickle and shallow in the journey but we neglect to look at ourselves and our society today or at least look at it honestly.

The same grumblings and discontent exist in modern-day Christians. We wander and lust after worldly pleasures. We are duped by the ways of this world and corrupted by the smooth talkers and devices of the enemy.

I encourage you to ask for a refreshing of the Holy Spirit in your life, in order to give you wisdom and strength to remain true to the convictions, which were put into your heart when you first came to know the Lord. To have the wisdom to see through the deception the world offers and reject anything not from God.

Prayer for today

Heavenly Father, I need a touch from you today to renew my convictions and give me a new strength to face the battles the world puts before me. Help me to allow you to do in me, whatever your perfect will is. Let me be open to whatever you speak to me in your still, small voice, and help me to have the eyes and ears to hear and see you in all circumstances.

In Jesus's name. Amen.

Wednesday
anointing of the Spirit

And everyone present was filled with the Holy Spirit and began speaking in other languages as the Holy Spirit gave them this ability.

Acts 2:4

To speak in other languages in this way is sometimes called a manifestation of the Holy Spirit.

Some churches are witness to several different kinds of manifestations. Some will go to extremes and use it as a way to obtain attention from media or other sources. Some churches discourage any manifestations of the Holy Spirit.

My own experience was quite specific, giving me a feeling of being showered with warm oil. The feelings of love and emotions were so powerful, I could not contain them in my being. I felt like the joy inside me bubbled over in joyous emotions. I remember longing for this feeling to remain.

I was accompanying a class of high school students from a Christian School on a short-term mission experience in Mexico. I was feeling superfluous and wondering why I'd actually come. One day after we finished lunch, the power of the Holy Spirit came upon me so strongly that I could not do anything to suppress it or control it. The only three people in the room were the cook, a dear friend, and myself and the Holy Spirit.

It was a positive and memorable experience that enabled me to gain strength with a new and wondrous peace that enveloped me for some time after. I long for another touch like that but I know there is nothing I can do to have it repeated, it must come from the hand of God or it will not be real. I feel it was a gift from God to comfort and confirm that He was taking care of me while enabling me to become closer to Him with a new understanding of who God is.

Prayer for today

Heavenly Father, I just want to thank you today for your faithfulness. I know you are with me, for anything that is not real could never touch me as you have. Your promises are evident and you deserve all honour and glory for you are the one and only God.

In Jesus's name. Amen.

Thursday

allowing the spirit to fill us

> *And I will ask the Father, and He will give you another Counsellor who will never leave you.*
>
> John 14:16

I fear, there are many Christians who find it difficult to receive the fullness of the Holy Spirit. They repent and know they are forgiven and they think it is enough.

Without the empowerment of the Holy Spirit, it is very difficult to do the work of the Lord.

Through the Spirit, we receive courage, wisdom and a new boldness to be all that we were meant to be. If we reject the Holy Spirit, we are depriving ourselves of a wonderful blessing.

It is the act of allowing the Holy Spirit to have His way in us that brings the strength and freedom to be obedient to God's plan in our lives.

I encourage you to invite and receive the blessing of the fullness of the presence of the Holy Spirit.

Prayer for today

Heavenly Father, I am thankful that you gave us your Comforter, the Holy Spirit to be with us and in us. Help me to be open to the will and leading of the Counsellor you provide for my well being. Let me hear the voice that leads me into your perfect will.

In Jesus's name. Amen.

Friday

the counsellor

But when the Father sends the Counsellor as my representative - and by the Counsellor I mean the Holy Spirit - He will teach you everything and will remind you of everything I myself have told you.

John 14:26

Do you find it difficult to understand the scriptures sometimes?

There were times when I read the Bible just because I knew I should and often it was just a futile exercise.

Since I have experienced the touch of the Holy Spirit upon my life, physically and spiritually, I see new meaning and experience a deeper understanding of the anointed Word of God.

It now speaks personally to me. I now invite the presence of the Holy Spirit to give me understanding and help me see the message that God wants me to learn.

I have also initiated some simple methods to help me. Sometimes I study one book at a time or I study one particular topic until I've exhausted it.

I find, often, God directs my reading through the still, small voice of the Holy Spirit and gives me insight to use the information in a productive way for ministry to others or enables me to remember content when necessary.

Prayer for today

Heavenly Father, I am so thankful for the Holy Spirit. How wonderful it is to know that I don't have to shoulder the responsibility of being everything I can be by myself. With the help of the Holy Spirit, I can be all you created me to be. I ask you Lord to give me sensitive ears so that I can hear the urging and advice of your Holy Spirit.

In Jesus's name. Amen.

Weekend Read

how to pray

Devote your selves to prayer with an alert mind and a thankful heart.

Colossians 4:2

It's just a little verse hidden away like other little gems found in the Bible. They are all filled with wisdom and meaning. This one speaks to me about my prayer life and tells me how to proceed when I pray. After taking it apart, I summed it up this way.

1. Devote: What is the meaning of this word? To me, it means to give with generosity, totally, withholding nothing, consecrated or dedicated.
   The dictionary defines it as: To give or apply (one's time, attention, or self) entirely to a particular activity.

Do we spend time in communion with God in this way? Do we devote ourselves to Him in prayer?

2. Alert Mind: Vigilantly attentive, watchful, mentally responsive, and perceptive, brisk or lively in action.

An alert mind is indicative of knowing exactly why you are there; why you are praying; why you are communicating with God at this particular time. It is a concentration of the act – an alert mind is aware of the action being displayed. It is not a half-hearted attempt of saying a few words as a request while thinking of other things or other urgencies. No, an alert mind is having your mind on the task at hand, one goal, one job, at one time. Praying, conversing with our Heavenly Father, not looking past Him to other things.

3. Thankful Heart: A heart filled with thanks, a heart that cannot be or will not be hindered by desires, but one that is truly thankful.

I liken it to being on a dry, desert sand and finding your water supply dry. We know a human being cannot survive long without water. After a time water is the only thing one can think about. Just when you think you are dying of dehydration, someone comes along with a cool drink of clear water or you discover a stream with clear running water. Can we imagine how very thankful one would be to find this immense treasure? That is what our prayers need to reflect, that is what a thankful heart looks like and sounds like.

In this verse in Colossians, we are told to pray with these three components in mind.

Devotion, Alertness, Thankfulness

Prayer for today

Lord, help me to speak to you in this way, exhibiting these three components.

In Jesus's name. Amen

WEEK 48

Monday

the blind leading the blind

What good is it for one blind person to lead another? The first one will fall into a ditch and pull the other one down also.

Luke 6:39

Jesus used this statement, metaphorically, to create an awareness of the dangers of following a leader who may lead us astray. Often we follow others who do not deserve our trust or devotion. I see this happen in young people or those who have low self-esteem. This is where peer pressure is prevalent.

When I was out of fellowship with the Lord, I made several friends who were single and game for anything. Several times they were able to talk me into doing things that were against my moral standards. The action of agreeing to be involved in their actions was like falling into the ditch that Jesus talks about here.

The people I was with had closed eyes to spiritual things and even though I was spiritually astute, my flesh was weak, and as a result I made bad decisions. My goal became to be accepted in groups who appeared to be enjoying themselves.

Many mature people are easily swayed by others, but it is most prevalent in teens who want to be accepted by their peers. When parents are too busy or negligent at working at a relationship with their children, the children search for other groups to be part of.

Parental responsibilities are to guide and teach and model desired behaviour but mostly to love and spend time with their children.

The secret is to be strong in faith, live the faith, and teach that faith to our children.

Prayer for today

Heavenly Father, I am so thankful you have provided your book of truth, the Bible, for our benefit. Help me to live by your laws and teach them to our children and grandchildren. I pray others may see your precepts in my life. Help me to be strong in truth and not to be duped by anyone who wants to me to stray from you.

In Jesus's name. Amen.

Tuesday
the tempter

And don't let us yield to temptation but deliver us from the evil one.

Matthew 6:13

The world offers many temptations today. I believe the enemy knows his time is running out and he is fighting like never before to place temptations before many.

The media bombards us with temptations, some of which are harmful. There are new freedoms to experiment with harmful substances, and television shows and movies encourage sinful living in the name of freedom.

Computers are often tools used to corrupt innocent minds, satiate sexual abusers, and promote pornography. The tempter is everywhere, using every means available.

Jesus gives us this prayer for us to pray. Our plea needs to be for strength to overcome evil desires. A close relationship with Jesus gives us the strength and courage to refuse temptations. Communion with God and the power of the Holy Spirit enables us to live as Jesus modelled when He walked the earth.

Prayer for today

Heavenly Father, I know I'm not always what I should be, and many times I succumb to the things of this world. Help me to be strong in my faith and give me strength to refuse anything that will harm me in any way. I know you want what is best for me and so I pray that you will give me wisdom in staying strong and not be tempted by things that may harm.

In Jesus's name. Amen.

Wednesday
modelling moral behaviour

There will always be temptations to sin, but how terrible it will be for the person who does the tempting.

Luke 17:1

We often blame others for leading us into sinful actions, just as Adam did.

Adam blamed Eve for causing him to sin because she offered him the fruit.

In modern times, we are still doing the same thing. Every day, we hear of more and more people who refuse to take responsibility for their own actions.

Tobacco companies are being sued for ailments caused by smoking, restaurants are being sued for serving coffee that is too hot, schools are being blamed for violence on the playground and the list goes on and on.

These things are individual choices being made by free people who need to accept responsibility for themselves.

We all make choices every day. It is time to take responsibility for our decisions and stop blaming society and public organizations for bad choices.

Our lives need to reflect honesty, thoughtfulness, responsibility, and wisdom in light of being a model to others and to refrain from leading anyone astray.

Prayer for today

Heavenly Father, thank you for the role models you have put in my life. Help me to look to you for strength to reflect the kind of person you want me to be. Help to take responsibility for my actions and always be able to defend whatever I do. Only by your Holy Spirit can I do this.

In Jesus's name. Amen.

Adena H. Paget

†

Thursday

productive time

Be sure to do what you should, for then you will enjoy the personal satisfaction of having done your work well and you won't need to compare yourself to anyone else, for we are each responsible for our own conduct.

Galatians 6:4&5

As I write this, the Calgary Flames are trying to win the Stanley Cup. They have clambered their way to this level and it is an exciting series. I also enjoy watching football. I feel so blessed when the players profess a relationship with Christ on the public podium. However, as I watch these players, I see temper tantrums and adverse actions that are often inexcusable. I realize it is a sign of frustration and usually an impromptu action.

I think about how often we, as Christians, do something or say something in the heat of the moment only to be sorry after. Numerous times, this has happened to me but it is usually too late to do anything about it.

I also have caught myself sloughing off at work, wasting my employer's money by not being as productive as I could be.

If we endeavour to live as Paul instructs, we would not have these moments of regret for bowing to frustration or saying or doing things we regret. We need to take responsibility for our words and actions and work at being the kind of people we want to portray at all times.

Prayer for today

Heavenly Father, help me to accept responsibility for my own actions and not blame anyone else for my shortcomings. Help me to do my work well so I won't be embarrassed or ashamed of anything I do.

In Jesus's name. Amen.

Friday

resisting temptation

Temptation comes from the lure of our own evil desires.

James 1:14

James speaks about the weakness of bowing to evil desires.

I am thankful for God's grace and forgiveness because we all find ourselves giving in to temptation at times.

We display maturity, obedience, courage, and strength when we say "No" to the temptation.

I have discovered, after giving in the first time, it becomes easier the second time, and it becomes easier each time we falter. Soon the senses become dulled to the idea of the act being sinful and we gradually begin to accept it as permissible.

On the other hand, each time I resist temptation, it becomes easier to refuse and soon it becomes an automatic "No." After a few refusals, I notice, temptations stop coming my way.

I believe, with God's help, it is possible to resist temptation, and soon the temptation loses its enticement because our desires turn toward Heavenly things that edify and glorify the Creator.

Adena H. Paget †

Prayer for today

Heavenly Father, I am thankful for your forgiveness when I falter. Your grace is free and I know you love me even when I do things that are wrong. I ask you today to keep me from temptations, give me strength to say "No" to things that are not from you. I pray that the lure of temptation will diminish as my walk with you becomes stronger.

In Jesus's name. Amen.

Weekend Read

a Christmas story

by Randy Movold

This is a story about Emillio Mandou, who lived during the very first Christmas.

Emillio was the son of a shepherd named Aehzad, who had settled near the town of Bethlehem many years ago. Christmas was still in the future during this time. Even though some people knew a special day was coming, they did not know when it would happen or how.

One night Emillio and his two older brothers, Plutuspar and Herkinny, were going to relieve some other shepherds in the fields. As they trekked up the hills they noticed a sharpness in the cloudless starlit sky.

A distant light in the western sky awed Emillio, who was quite a dreamer. It couldn't be the sunrise because he knew the sun rose in the east and it couldn't be the sunset because that had already happened. He wondered why this light was there and what it meant. It was also evident to his brothers and they all stared in awe. Just about that time, three sheep decided to head for another pasture on the far side of the creek, up the hill and on the edge of the forest where wolves hid out

Emillio and his brothers did not notice the three sheep missing until they heard the howl of the wolves and then the sheep crying. The brothers bolted in the direction of the noise, yelling back to Emillio to stay and take care of the rest of the flock.

Emillio had never been alone with the sheep before let alone in the dark on this eerie night. The glow he had seen earlier became a comfort to him and for security he gathered the rest of the sheep around in a huddle nearer to him.

As Emillio gained comfort in this situation, he heard his name being called:

"Emillio, Emillio."

"Yes, my brothers, what is it? Have you returned?"

The voice said, "Emillio, I am not your brother but a Host from Heaven, a servant of the living God, who has made Heaven and earth, indeed who has made all things in the universe. Gird yourself, child, tonight is the night. Let me put it this way, Emillio:

An early rap

"My name is Gabe,
And I'm here to tell you
Of a Babe
He came to earth this day for grace,
He came
for the human race
Now go, my son, and don't be slow,
Grandson of Jo
Go west, young man and follow the glow
I know you's tired and wants to sleep
But grab your staff and drive dem sheep

West, yeah west,
'Cause God knows best.

"Excuse me, Host of Heaven, but are you trying to tell me something?" asked Emillio.

"Yes, Emillio, But I don't think you're ready for Heavenly Rap just yet. One day in the future, kids your age will understand the meaning of that rhyme. What I want to say to you is, "Follow that light in the sky. Take your sheep with you and that special box you have been working on. You will want to give it to the Christ Child as a gift, Emillio. Follow the star, Emillio and the light will lead you to true love. When you arrive, open your heart and whisper your acceptance to this Christ Child. Invite him to come and enter your heart. Go now, Emillio, Christmas is waiting for you."

Emillio grabbed his staff, wooed the sheep to follow him and headed straightway for the light. As he came closer to Bethlehem, he noticed many people in the streets. "How will I ever find the Christ Child, the angel told me about?" Emillio thought.

Just as he wondered how he would do this, he saw the light; it was now a very bright star and he proceeded to follow it. As he made his way, he knew he was getting nearer. Emillio started running and leaping with his sheep following close behind.

As he drew nearer he asked a merchant if he was on the right road. "Yes!" said the merchant, "Around the corner, up the next street, you will come to an inn called the Way-Side Inn, where the star shines the brightest. And son, don't forget your sheep. Also, tell at least one other person along the way about the bright light and the special babe."

Emillio was so excited, he almost knocked a man down at the corner.

"Whoa…boy. What in Prophet's name is this?"

"The star, sir, at the Way-Side Inn."

Looking towards the inn, the stranger saw the brilliant light over it. "What are you waiting for, son, the star awaits us. Is this your box? It must have fallen out of your carry pouch as you were running."

"Yes sir, it is my box, I've been working on it for quite some time and I'm going to give it to the Christ Child when I see him. Inside the box are miniature turtles from Persia. They are precious to me. I've been collecting them for a while, they live a very long time and yet they remain small."

"Tell me your name, boy."

"Emillio Mandou, sir."

"So Emillio, I am sure it is you who is the first one to give a box of turtles as a gift."

"Yes, sir. My grandfather always told me to give only what is precious and you will never be in want of anything."

"Your grandfather was a very wise man, Emillio."

"And good too, sir."

So Emillio and the stranger entered the Way-Side Inn leaving the flock of sheep outside. They inquired about the newborn babe. The manager of the inn looked tired and extremely puzzled.

"I know nothing of this babe and please don't ask me for a room, I have none. I even had to rent out my stable on the west side of the inn. Come to think of it a young couple came in late on a donkey and by Jove, that girl was pregnant. Come follow me to the stable."

Out the door and around to the inn's side they went, and lo, the star, which they had seen, went before them until it came and stood over where the child was.

And they came in haste and found the child as he lay in the manger.

Emillio was honoured to present the child with the gift, which he had lovingly prepared for a very special occasion, and he also felt compelled to give his heart and soul to this babe who he realized was really a King.

That evening, Emillio not only discovered the first Christmas but also was able to share it with the stranger and the innkeeper.

And Emillio was honoured to be the first one ever to give a box of turtles as a gift.

Adena H. Paget †

WEEK 49

Monday

true patience

Wait patiently for the Lord. Be brave and courageous. Yes, wait patiently for the Lord.

Psalm 27:14

How long have you waited for your prayer to be answered? Does it seem like forever? Sometimes it seems as if God is not hearing us and yet, we have his promise that He hears our prayer. In Matthew He says," *Ask anything in my name and it will be given to you."*

Many times, David cries before the Lord asking for mercy or freedom. Often David asks the Lord if he has been forsaken. We see in other passages, when David takes his eyes off himself and begins to praise and give thanks, his requests are answered.

The same is true in our own situations. If we spend all our prayer time asking and requesting and drowning in self-pity with self-ish prayers, we have little time left to count our blessings and be thankful for what we have been given. When the waiting seems to take forever, remember the waiting time makes us strong and develops character and endurance.

Prayer for today

Heavenly Father, I know I need to be thankful for the trials and troubles you allow in my life but at times it feels like you aren't listening to me. Forgive me, Lord for thinking I know better than you. Help me to trust you more, love you more, and praise you more. I know you love me more than I can even comprehend and so help me give all my cares to you.

In Jesus's name. Amen.

Tuesday

wonderful joy in the wings

So be truly glad. There is wonderful joy ahead, even though it is necessary for you to endure many trials for a while.

1 Peter 1:16

Sometimes the darkness seems to last forever and our faith is certainly tested, but it is in the darkness we search for the light.

God tells us if we search for Him, we will be found by Him. If we never experience the darkness we need never look for the light, and then we miss the blessing of finding the true light and seeing with new eyesight that leads to a deeper understanding of His glorious truth.

Keep searching deeper into the truth until His comfort and peace permeate your entire being, and you find the kernel that satiates your desire for Jesus more and more.

He waits to comfort you and hold you when you are ready to accept Him, totally. There is wonderful joy ahead.

Prayer for today

Heavenly Father, I just want to thank you for your promise of joy and even if I don't experience it all the time, I know when I see you I will have joy beyond measure. Help me to live in that hope and learn to endure whatever I need to while waiting. Thank you for your love and grace.

In Jesus's name. Amen.

Wednesday

let God steer the ship

Be glad for all God is planning for you. Be patient in trouble, and always be prayerful.

Romans 12:12

My friend, how difficult it is for us to let go and let God.

Some of us were created with a strong nature and we have great difficulty giving our concerns and worries to God.

As I continue to mature, I am learning that life becomes easier as I let go of the control in every situation.

God, my Creator, has planned my life and when I ease up on the tiller and allow God to steer the ship and be the helmsman, the voyage becomes more enjoyable and much easier. However, this does not give me permission to become lazy in my spiritual quest but enables me to seek the will of the Holy Spirit.

My job is to meditate on His Word and give thanks and praise instead of wasting time worrying and wondering. I love to spend time in prayer and communion with Jesus, my personal friend.

Prayer for today

Heavenly Father, thank you for planning my life. I'm afraid I am not very patient in trouble, but when I remember whose child I am and who is ultimately in control, I can spend my time in praise and thanksgiving and my troubles become smaller and even disappear. Help my unbelief and let me become reliant on you for all things.

In Jesus's name. Amen.

Thursday

true love

Love never gives up, never loses faith, is always hopeful, and endures through every circumstance.

1 Corinthians 13:7

The word love is often bandied around and used frivolously. From time to time, I use the word lightly myself in the context of meaningless banter. We hear people exclaim they love their car, or a particular food, or a piece of furniture, or style of clothing.

When we read the love chapter in 1 Corinthians, we begin to understand the real meaning of love. We realize the greatness of the concept. I fear that the true meaning of love is losing its greatness. Are we truly capable of loving another person as the Bible means it to be?

Paul tells us that love endures through every circumstance – *every* circumstance. Not just when things are in harmony but even when people or things seem impossible and exasperating, love endures. This is the same love Jesus has for us and in turn we must strive to attain the same level of love, even though it may seem impossible. Our job is to try.

With the Holy Spirit dwelling in us, the tasks required become easier to accomplish.

Prayer for today

Heavenly Father, I cannot express how much your love means to me. The only way I can tell you is by my attitude and the things I do. Forgive me for becoming exasperated at others when things don't go as I want them to. Help me to love others as you do. Help me to be forgiving even when I don't receive forgiveness. Make me more like you. I know I cannot attain that level, but with you everything is possible.

In Jesus's name. Amen.

Friday
embracing trouble

Dear brothers and sisters, whenever trouble comes your way, let it be an opportunity for joy. For when your faith is tested, your endurance has a chance to grow. So let it grow, for when endurance is fully developed, you will be strong in character and ready for anything.

James 1:2-4

The pastor challenged the congregation to memorize the book of James. I attempted the challenge and at this time I have accomplished learning four chapters.

After I learned the first chapter, I discovered these three little verses are sometimes all you need to witness effectively, and I wondered how I managed without being able to quote them.

As I listen to others, I realize we all have a need to know the purpose for our suffering and the troubles we experience. I have also learned there are no exemptions from trials and troubles – everyone experiences some.

These verses acknowledge our suffering and confirm the benefit of the experience. They tell us our troubles are not useless or unnecessary because they result in a good thing.

Troubles ultimately lead to strong character. A strong character is a desirable trait in the eyes of the Lord. James proceeds to tell us we should actually be joyful in our troubles because the end result is good and strengthens our endurance. I am trying to look at my troubles from a positive aspect and they don't seem as big as I once thought they were.

Prayer for today

Heavenly Father, often my troubles control my thoughts and my focus becomes selfish when I dwell on trouble. I know the troubles in my life will make me a better person and better able to understand others. Even though I experience trouble, I know you are aware of everything in my life and I thank you for helping me grow in you.

In Jesus's name. Amen.

Adena H. Paget †

Weekend Read

use me, Lord

The long lazy river
runs in an endless line
as if it has no connection with time

Oh what joy to flow so free
and be so strongly led
to twist and turn and laugh with glee
but never lose my head

I've seen the streams that overflow
I've seen where roiling waters go
I want to run in the riverbed
that the Master chose
where I'll be fed

and for evermore my will secedes
in the furrow where He daily leads

I pray, O Lord, that I will not stray
consistently walk on the narrow row
may I be a blessing every day
so your perfect will can flow

Use me Lord to plant your seed
of truth and joy and peace
of love and comfort
your will to heed

where worries and heaviness cease

Let me be the hands to help someone

in my life each day, may thy will be done
Let me be the river that flows each day
touching souls I meet along the way
giving hope to hearts waiting on the banks
as my eyes look up to express my thanks.

WEEK 50

Monday
prayer life

Epaphras from your city, a servant of Christ Jesus, sends you his greetings. He always prays earnestly for you, asking God to make you strong and perfect, fully confident of the whole will of God.

Colossians 4:12

This verse is a small portion of Paul's letter to the church in Colossi. When I read this verse, I long to become like Epaphras. To have a reputation and a legacy like he had with Paul and the Christians in Colossi, is desirable.

We are first introduced to Epaphras in chapter one, verse seven and learn he is the founder of the church.

The first thing we learn from Paul about Epaphras is that he is a servant of Christ Jesus. It makes me wonder…whom do we serve? Can we be called servants of Jesus Christ?

Next we are informed about Epaphras's prayer life. What can be said about my prayer life? We learn Epaphras is detailed in his prayers; asking for specific answers, which indicates an understanding of the needs of the people.

Do we take the time to understand the needs of the people we are praying for or are our prayers general and only for the purpose of being able to say,

"We prayed for you"?

What is your prayer life like?

Prayer for today

Heavenly Father, sometimes my prayers are hurried or general, forgive me for not taking the time to understand the needs of the people I pray for. My desire is to be more like Epaphrus, especially in my prayer life.

In Jesus's name. Amen.

Tuesday

no worries

Don't worry about anything; instead, pray about everything. Tell God what you need and thank Him for all He has done.

Philippians 4:6

Are you a worrier? I have known people who worry about everything. It's as if, by worrying, they feel they show a caring concern. That is actually belittling God.

The Bible tells us to give our needs to God and He promises to take care of them.

When we worry, we are saying, "I know you can't handle this, God so I'll help you by worrying about it."

Theologically speaking, we are disobedient when we worry. We are saying our efforts are more important than God's promises.

Worries can consume us and interfere with our joy in the Lord and the peace He longs for us to accept.

Often, we give our worries to Christ only to keep taking them back. We don't do that with tangible gifts from a friend, why is it we insist on doing this with the gift of peace that Jesus gives?

Do not lack in trust. Give God your worries and do not take them back after you give them.

Prayer for today

Heavenly Father, forgive me for worrying about the things you handle for me. I know you are so capable of taking care of all my worries. Help me to be thankful for your promises and help me to trust you enough to give you all my worries and not take them back.

In Jesus's name. Amen.

Adena H. Paget †

Wednesday

prayer help

...For we don't even know what we should pray for nor how we should pray. But the Holy Spirit prays for us with groanings that cannot be expressed in words.

Romans 8:26

Many times I don't know what to pray, what to say, how to say what I want to say, or how to present my concerns.

Our will does not always line up with God's will and our prayers are sometimes confusing and meaningless in our minds. It is in these moments we rely on the Holy Spirit to interpret what we are trying to say to God.

I have shed tears in the presence of the Holy Spirit during my prayer times and I know He understands my heart because the Holy Spirit listens to me and relays my heart's desires.

Oswald Chambers alludes to the concept of when we stop praying for ourselves and become more aware of our relationship with the Lord, then our prayers will line up with His will and we can truly glorify God in thanksgiving and praise.

"Quit praying about yourself and be spent for others as the bondslave of Jesus."

(My Utmost for His Highest - Oswald Chambers)

Prayer for today

Heavenly Father, sometimes I get frustrated because I don't know how to pray and then I remember your promise that the Holy Spirit will tell you what I'm trying to say. You already know what I'm going to pray even before I do. Please forgive me for doubting you.

In Jesus's name. Amen.

Thursday

grooving

Be thankful in all circumstances, for this is God's will for you who belong to Christ Jesus.

1 Thessalonians 5:17-18

A golf instructor told me once to practice my golf swing until I grooved it. That way it wouldn't require too much thinking while I was on the golf course.

I haven't spent as much time on the practice range to accomplish this, therefore, I still need to concentrate on skills when I'm playing, which interferes with the enjoyment of the game.

As I spend more time practicing, the swing becomes a natural movement successfully sending the ball toward the target.

Our prayer times need to become grooved into our daily routines so deeply that we automatically move into prayer mode at any time.

We always have something to be thankful for and that is what we need to concentrate on in our prayer life. Even when adversity becomes evident we can be assured it will lead to growth. Keep praying.

Adena H. Paget †

Prayer for today

Heavenly Father, I am thankful for your love and the way you teach me each day. Even though I grumble and complain, I know you allow what is best for me. I ask you to help me see the benefits of trusting you in every situation and keep on being thankful. Let my conversation with you become internalized so much I automatically go to you for everything and in everything. I love you, Lord.

In Jesus's name. Amen.

Friday

humble prayers

...When you pray, don't be like the hypocrites who love to pray publicly on street corners and in the synagogues where everyone can see them.

Matthew 6:5-7

My dad was always called upon to pray in public, in church, always before meals at social gatherings, or at get-togethers with others. His prayers were always eloquent and wordy.

As a child, I grew to dislike his long prayers and devotional epics. I heard the words but I also witnessed a dichotomy. His lifestyle sometimes differed from the words in his prayers. His prayers were delivered with precision and a sense of rightness, but his life often spoke to things of the flesh. And so his professed Christian walk was in conflict with his eloquent prayers.

It is wonderful for children to think their parents are perfect and I was no exception. I am thankful for being taught Bible truths because it brought me to a place where I accepted Jesus as my Saviour at a very young age. In later years, I realized my parents had imperfections and were, indeed, not perfect.

My love for them, however, did not dwindle and I believe I learned from realizing their imperfections.

Jesus, on the other hand, is perfect and He tells us to go into our closet and shut the door and speak to our Father in Heaven in humbleness and contriteness of heart. I believe He is saying our prayers are not to be used as a platform for entertainment or accolades.

Prayer for today

Heavenly Father, I am so thankful you hear my prayer even when I whisper. I know my prayers don't have to be a major production because you know what I am going to say even before I say it. I am awed by the greatness of you, oh Lord, thank you for your faithfulness.

In Jesus's name. Amen.

Weekend Read

words from my grandmother

This last Weekend Read is an excerpt from my grandmother's diary

Maria (Geortzen) Vogt. September 1885 – August 1962

This excerpt was taken from a 1951 diary entry.

Her diary spans the years of 1947 to 1962. She was a soldier for Jesus Christ, which is reflected by her words. I loved her very much and missed her terribly when she passed on. She lived with us for a while during my mother's illness and after my mom passed away in 1953.

Translated from the German language with a sprinkling of Plat Duetch or low German (a Mennonite language).

SOME MEMORIES OF MY LIFE

I, Marie Geortzen, grew up in Russia. Ekaterinaslowsken, Guvernu. I was five years old when my parents moved to Alexandrovka.

We had no school the first winter, then the village rented a room from Heinrich Neufield's and that's where I started school. Jacob Penner was our teacher. We learned to read and write.

The second year, Mr. Enns was our teacher and the third year we had David Dreideger. By this time we were in a school.

Mr. Dreideger taught for three years and next we had Deitrich Enns for one year. So I went to school for six years, learnt German and Russian.

After that I went to work, we always had to get up very early, for we were very busy in Russia. My parents were very poor so we all had to work very hard, which was quite stressful at times.

Then I wished I was grown up and suddenly I was grown up.

I learnt to know a dear young man whom I learnt to love very much, but soon he had to go into the army for four long years. But I loved him and stayed true to him until finally the day came when we said our vows to be true to each other for the rest of our lives.

Oh. How blessed we were - it was as if the Heavens were playing violin music. It was like Paradise on earth.

We bought some land in Alexandra after, we lived for two years with my husband's parents. We finally were on our own, we were our own boss. Had a small house where we had thousands of happy times.

Before Hans (John) was born, our first daughter, Tina, was born. She died at two months of age. After Hans we had Agatha, she was the fifth child in the village.

After this we sold everything and moved to Siberia, here, two months later, Mari (Mary) was born. Here we were very happy.

We were both healthy and worked very hard. My nerves were very weak but my devout Christian parents prayed and I was healed.

After a few years war broke out and all the Mennonite men had to go into the Army. This was the first time for them, before that time they could work in the forests.

Most men were in the army for four years but my husband worked for the government for three years. He had to make railroad ties.

The women had no help financially, we were on our own, very hard to make a go of it. But we were young and courageous - the children forgot their father and many homes and marriages were separated.

Thank God my parents carried us on hands of prayer. The Lord kept us safe in body and soul.

We lived 14 years in Siberia, until it became very restless in the land because of the Communists. That's when we moved to America, (Canada) where we have lived for nearly 25 years in quiet peace.

My husband was in the service of the Lord for many years.

This fall (1951) we moved to Nipawin, Saskatchewan, where we bought a house for $650.00. After one week my husband went to the hospital for surgery. Thank God it was successful and we are so happy.

"Not a hair falls from our heads but that the Lord wills it." (without the Lord's will).

Grousma and Grouspa had three more children before immigrating to Canada, Peter, Tina and Heinrich. They were blessed with 25 grandchildren and many great and great great grandchildren

Grampa Vogt went home to be with the Lord August 1952. Gramma traveled when she could, staying with her children and being a friend to her grandchildren. She was a much-loved, Godly woman.

I am extremely thankful for the rich heritage I have. The prayers of my grandparents and parents have kept me walking on the pathway to an abundant life with a wondrous and glorious eternity to look forward to.

WEEK 51

Monday

proof of God

From the time the world was created, people have seen the earth and the sky and all that God made. They can clearly see his invisible qualities - His eternal power and divine nature. So they have no excuse whatsoever for not knowing God.

Romans 1:20

It is amazing to me, when I read accounts of different, well-known evangelists and prolific Christian writers and speakers who started out with the intent of proving God does not exist.

In many instances they arrived at dead ends with lack of proof for the denial of God and were led to an undeniable belief in the truth of the existence of God.

C. S. Lewis is possibly the most famous writer who came to this decision. There are many more examples of such enlightenment in different men and women.

When we are confronted with these testimonies it seems immature and ignorant to deny the existence of a Divine Creator. It is a false belief without proof and many times a lack of desire to know truth.

Paul tells us to look around and see the evidence of God.

Prayer for today

Heavenly Father, I am so thankful your creation is all around us and we cannot deny your existence when we see the wonders of your wonderful qualities. Help us, Lord not to take your beauty for granted but to give thanks to you for the way you prepared this beautiful world for us to enjoy. Help me today, to see and acknowledge you in my surroundings.

In Jesus's name. Amen.

Tuesday

creation

The Heavens tell of the glory of God.
The skies display His marvellous craftsmanship.

Psalm 19:1

To stand and gaze at the Heavens in the darkness, is evidence enough of a Creator. To think everything fell into place by chance is unthinkable.

We know the movement of the planets, the sun, the moon, and other heavenly bodies are cyclical and consistent. There is scientific proof for the wonders of the perfect timing of celestial bodies in synch with the ocean tides and moon phases.

To believe this is a phenomenon of chance is like finding a perfectly timed engine, intricately constructed on a desolate beach and believe it just arrived there by chance…that no one put it there, created it, or invented it.

Astronauts who have returned from traveling in our solar system have been heard to exclaim that there is no way this masterpiece just happened.

There is no doubt in their minds of a Creator, a Master Designer.

Prayer for today

Heavenly Father, I am grateful for the way you created the beauty of the earth and the people on it. You made everything perfect. Help us to care for it like good stewards and not to abuse your creation.

In Jesus's name. Amen.

Wednesday

the beauty of the earth

So they worshipped the things God made
but not the Creator himself,
who is to be praised forever. Amen.

Romans 1:25

The tranquility of a walk in the woods calms me and I marvel at the beauty of it all.

I see the lush greens of the trees, shrubs, and grass. The pool ponds and streams teeming with life, the small rodents scurrying here and there, the magnificence of the larger animals, deer, elk, moose, and I wonder at the intricacy of each living thing, created to live together, each playing its designed part of the food chain; a perfectly constructed system that works together like a fine timepiece.

When we see the wonder of it all, we understand how people could worship all this, but we know this is just a minute sampling of what the Creator is capable of.

He has placed much beauty on the earth for us to enjoy and find pleasure in. It is not here for us to elevate beyond the Creator or ourselves. It is not here to be worshipped and praised.

All the beauty of this earth is nothing without God, the Creator, who made it.

The worship of anything but God is wrong, for it is putting something else in first place when God needs to be first in our lives.

What are you putting before God in your life?

Prayer for today

Heavenly Father, you are the Creator of Heaven and earth and you need to be first in my life. Without you, I am nothing. Help me to prioritize the things in my life, putting you first. Help me not to put so much emphasis on the things you created I forget why they were created and by whom. I want to worship only you, Lord.

In Jesus's name. Amen.

Thursday

love beyond comprehension

Whether we are high above the sky or in the deepest ocean, nothing in all creation will ever be able to separate us from the love of God that is revealed in Christ Jesus, our Lord.

Romans 8:39

We are not capable of understanding the width, breadth, or depth of Christ's love. We only know the realm of human love for our loved ones, spouses, children, parents, siblings, and close friends, but we are still only human.

God's love is indescribable and we receive a full measure of it. He created us for His enjoyment and it gives Him pleasure to be part of our lives.

He is a gentleman and never forces His way into our lives. He only comes when we invite Him. He could barge into our lives but He loves us too much to infringe on the free choice He gave us.

Isn't it great to know that whatever we do will not alter the fact that God loves us? He forgives and buries our sins deeply, never to be seen again.

This is a mystery but one day we will understand it better.

Prayer for today

Heavenly Father, I just want to thank you for your love. I cannot conceive how great your love is but your word says it will never be altered. Nothing can come between your love and myself. You sent your Son to reveal this to all mankind and it is awesome. Help me to put you first in my life to increase my sensitivity to the leading and guiding of your Holy Spirit in my life.

In Jesus's name. Amen.

Friday

accepting Jesus as a personal Saviour

For God so loved the world that He gave His only son,
so that everyone who believes in Him will
not perish but have eternal life.

John 3:16

This is probably the most memorized, printed, and quoted scripture verse in the Bible. If you have never memorized it, I urge you to do it now. It is the greatest promise and truth in the entire Bible. It tells us what God has done for us.

When God first created *man* He may have had great expectations but humans failed miserably by not being able to live up to the laws written.

For several thousand years, people had to make sacrifices to cover the sins committed. This was carried out with precise instructions. Blood had to be shed to cover the wrongdoing. The best animals were used. It was an onerous task.

Many years after creation, God made the way of salvation so plain and easy, anyone could receive it. He sent His only son Jesus, born of a woman, to give His life as the perfect sacrifice for our sins. The only requirement is for us to believe and accept this truth, ask forgiveness and invite Him into our life.

He fills us with the Holy Spirit and gives us a new life. The Bible says, all things become new, old things pass away, which means all our sins, are gone and we can go on into a new relationship with Christ Jesus. He leads and guides and gives us peace such as we have never known before.

If you have never invited Jesus into your life, praying the following prayer with commitment is one way you can experience a personal relationship with Jesus.

Heavenly Father, your Word says all have sinned and fall short of the glory of God. (Romans 3:23) I have never asked you to come into my life and lead me on the path you prepared for me. The Bible says all I have to do is come to you with a repentant heart and ask you to forgive me for going my own way. I want to be all you created me to be. I want you to come into my life, forgive my sins and fill me with your spirit so that I can experience a newness in a forgiven life with you as my guide and leader. I know you love me more than I know and you will never leave me or forsake me. Come into my life now, Jesus and help me to live for you.

In Jesus's name. Amen.

If you have accepted Christ for the first time, write your name and today's date below on the line as a record of your salvation.

Name.....................................Date................................

As a new Christian, I encourage you to find someone and tell him or her of your decision. Also I would urge you to find a Bible-believing friend and a church, so you can grow in your newfound faith and learn how to have a close relationship with Jesus Christ. Most importantly, find an easy to understand version of the Bible and read God's Word every day.

May God richly bless you as you endeavour to follow Him.

About the Author

Adena was born on a homestead farm in Northern Saskatchewan, moved to Calgary Alberta with her family at age five. Left high school and married her husband at a very young age 58 years ago. They raised five children and are grandparents of eleven. Returned to finish high school after most of her family was grown. Graduated from University of Calgary at a mature age and taught for Calgary Board of Education for 15 years. Several years after retiring from her teaching career, she served with RSVP ministries as Regional Director for Alberta and B.C, as well as Speaker Coordinator.

Adena has experienced many losses during her lifetime and several of these times inspired her to start writing insights from the scripture readings given to her for comfort, joy and peace. She writes about her loss of her beloved grampa, her mom, her sister, her son and her grandson and the loss of her beloved grampa. She credits her strong faith and relationship with God for the peace and joy accompanying her experiences and bringing her through unscathed, with a good measure of normalcy, sense of humor and still loving life.

Completing this manuscript was an amazing and enjoyable labor of love for Adena.

Printed in Canada